BEING RIGHT

A BEGINNER'S GUIDE TO LOGICAL FALLACIES
AND DEDUCTIVE REASONING

FOURTH EDITION

BY

STEPHEN PAPE

D1315383

Fourth edition

FOR E, H AND J

IN MEMORY OF JMP

"In questions of science, the authority of a thousand is not worth the humble reasoning of a single individual." — GALILEO GALILEI

Contents

FOREWORD TO THE FOURTH EDITION

In this version, I have updated some of the examples, rearranged the chapter numbering and included an index.

Following feedback, I have also updated the section on deductive reasoning in order to clarify one or two of the trickier aspects of formal fallacies. In particular, I added more detail to the undistributed middle problem with categorical syllogisms.

FORWARD TO THE THIRD EDITION

The obvious drawback of using recent examples is that references to yesterday's online news is today's 404 file-not-found error.

For this edition, I've again tried to ensure online references are still working. In a previous revision, I discovered the BBC had updated some language on its website and effectively spiked one of my favourite examples (see *false balance*) without noting the correction. I'm continuing to use the example because it's too wonderfully crass to lose.

Since this book was first published in January 2016, a lot of new examples have offered themselves – proof if any were needed that most people continue to talk bollocks most of the time. During the first six months of 2016 we in the UK have had EU referendum campaigns to provide examples of fallacy, non sequitur and just plain nonsense from both sides of the debate. I have refrained from drawing too much on that bonfire of arguments for examples. The logic of the UK's EU referendum campaigns deserves a book of its own.

In feedback, too, I have been thrilled to get complaints about using faith in examples of fallacies. People have suggested that I give religion a break, and let believers quietly mind their own business – they're not harming me. Let me think: after millennia of preaching, hectoring, proselytization, physical and mental torture, execution, fraud, theft, hypocrisy, child abuse, political abuse, societal manipulation, bodily mutilation, cultural annihilation, genocide, despot-gagging wealth accumulation; in all bringing untold suffering to millions whom faith is supposed to comfort; I don't think it's unfair for one book to point out the bad reasoning used along the way to justify the carnage. Besides, the flames of religion-based inhumanity rage around the world, so the claim that the faithful are quietly minding their own business is a bare assertion. Also, an appeal to faith is a fallacy in its own right, so it stays.

I hope *Being Right* helps you to make more sense of the world.

Introduction

Once, we had to remember things. Literacy was rare; books were scarce, even after writing was invented. Culture and entertainment meant hearing and re-telling epic stories (poems, history, legends)[1], revelling in dilemmas and re-living the reasoning that heroes used to resolve them. Fact and myth shared the page with equal status. It was a time when most of the elementary facts we take for granted were not only unknown, they were unknowable. Consequently, pretty much any assertion could be true if the listener believed it.

Even so, ancient philosophers understood that people could be manipulated, swayed by emotional arguments that ignored inconvenient facts. Aristotle, in the fourth century BC, identified logic, dialectic and rhetoric as the three cornerstones of philosophy. Logic was the way to reach scientific certainty. Dialectic provided a reasoned discourse between parties holding different points of view. It was a means for experienced listeners to probe and test uncertain facts and to learn. Rhetoric furnished the tools for practical debate – a way of persuading audiences in general, using probable facts in order to make decisions about day-to-day problems. Dialectic and rhetoric together, Aristotle argued, were a system of persuasion without manipulation or misrepresentation. One glance at today's newspapers will tell you how that worked out.

Millennia later, Schopenhauer published in 1831 *The Art of Being Right: 38 Ways to Win an Argument*. He referred to the "tricks, dodges and chicanery" that people resort to in order to win an argument, and collected these ploys as an ironic guide. Many of the techniques would have been familiar to the ancients, as they are today: personal attacks; generalising specific cases; appealing to authority not reason; among them.

Today, a lack of facts isn't the problem, and the internet offers almost universal knowledge as much as we know it – omniscience in a box. But that brings its own problems. In a world as complex as ours, there isn't a tidy basket of supporting facts that drive unambiguously

---

[1] They certainly knew how to have a banging time, those ancients. I firmly believe the creation of epic stories led directly to the invention of cushions. And perhaps earplugs.

toward a clear, indisputable conclusion. The world we know is way too intricate and nuanced. Teeming jungles of facts variously support or rebut every argument. In the steaming electronic biosphere, argument-killing evidence is extinct – there are too many specific facts for and against every point of view. Most online debaters will scour the world's servers for supporting data, no matter how tenuous or obscure, rather than weigh evidence that says they're wrong. All that happens is that more and more conflicting information gets trotted out, and debate circles the topic until the participants die of boredom, or their medication kicks in.

Online debate is a mosh pit, a pub brawl of wild assertion, exception, generalisation, incomprehensible analogy and irrelevance. An eye-swivelling excerpt from an internet forum:

> American football is the greatest game in the world. It requires strategy and planning.

> Then why wasn't chess invented in America, if you're so hot on strategy?

Although enthusiastically employed since time began, personal abuse was never considered a decisive debating technique until the internet age. Now a well-aimed zinger is applauded by the witless gallery – "we have a winner!" – while reasoning weeps in a corner.

Better reasoning won't stop fruitless internet debates, for two reasons:

1. Most people wouldn't recognise good reasoning if it gave them an Xbox and a hickey. They don't grasp that someone's running rings round them, and they neither know nor care they're making themselves look stupid. Anonymity rules.

2. People join online debates to put their tuppence in; to wheel out the one fact they believe they remember correctly; to make the point they imagine is a telling blow, germane or not. It makes them feel clever, it's free and it makes them happy. Bless.

When it matters

Social media arguments are like pub blarney. They don't count. The world doesn't revolve around the outcome of who's the better football player; who the best five drummers of the last fifty years are;

whether some inane celebrity thinks immigrants are to blame for something. Newspapers (and news websites) seem to think these matters are vital, but they are in the entertainment business. News, to them, is fresh material to attract and keep bigger audiences (and therefore advertising revenue); it's no longer the pot of gold itself. The relentless presentation of drivel as important news is probably the biggest fallacy we all face every day. "This is fact," we hear. "This is important," they say. No, really, they aren't.

For academic purposes, though, reasoning does matter. Reasoning directs all research. It underpins academic learning. It is the language used to persuade teachers, students, the world at large that you understand your subject, or even have something new to tell.

And at work decisions have consequences both for the business (let's pretend our hearts flutter if the company shares move up five pence) and for the only thing that, in the end, truly matters – us.

Business decisions determine whether Joshua, the gel-haired, marketing muppet in Madrid gets to spunk tens of millions of dollars on a campaign featuring a cartoon penguin with dandruff; whether Karen in Kalamazoo takes charge of the new logistics roll-out; whether Sean in San Diego heads a new customer research project or whether Lyra in London gets promoted for orchestrating a seamless disaster-recovery operation, or fired for burning down the data centre in the first place.

Being on the persuasive end of the business-policy see-saw will make a colossal difference to your career. Many organisations use reasoning tests as part of their recruitment process – you need to navigate these. Once on board, you will be able to fast-track from intern to president, via fist-pumping product launches and cost-cutting bloodbaths, festooned with garlands, merited and otherwise. People blithely assume that the only ladder to the top is to play politics. They're wrong. Politics is what you do as a substitute for the real thing. To be anywhere in the running as a corporate player you must be one thing above all else – right.

Being right means you:

- win arguments

- persuade your bosses

- convince colleagues who don't report to you

- justify your decisions succinctly to people who do, and

- something... something... stakeholders

Being right will unlock the opportunities you need to shine. It's up to you to be effective in what you do. But if people believe you, they will believe in you. Then they'll do their damndest to make sure your project or programme happens. And when you lead an army of supporters, pretty much anything is possible.

Being right falls into two parts: spotting erroneous conclusions of others; and putting together your own persuasive arguments. This book deals with the former – one step at a time.

To know what a good argument looks like, you need to understand what a bad one is, and Being Right explains all the common fallacies, formal and informal. Whether or not you can craft an irrefutable argument, you'll still be surrounded by people talking nonsense. But if you can point out how flimsy their reasoning is, you're half way to being right.

This book is not about the latest management fad

Reasoning and critical thinking aren't new ideas. They began when people started to think about thinking, perhaps long before the ancient Greeks. Management fads are dreamt up by people who don't manage. There are armies of management consultants sifting through unattended metaphors to see if there's one they can take, drape some simple, high-level, quasi-universal insight or best practice around its shoulders, and sell it. This book is about being right – its principles are as old as the hills.

Nor is this a creepy, hug-yourself, self-help book. If you want to listen to trippy music, align your chakras and meditate, knock yourself out. It won't help, but you'll feel better about losing out to stupid people. It's not a canny version of cosmic ordering. (Why do people feel entitled to get the rest of creation to supply what they're too feckless to work for?)

This book doesn't aim to be scholastic, nor will it be complete. It will omit a good many exotic, rare types of argument that few people will ever stumble across or recognise when they do. Most of the examples I have used I made up. They may be light-hearted by academic benchmarks, and you may feel there are better ways to illustrate the fallacy. Hey, mea culpa. I've spent a lifetime getting to grips with reasoning myself. That journey isn't over by any stretch of the imagination.

This book is about trying to make sense of the world, and putting a bit more sense back into it. I'd say that was a worthy aim.

1. TYPES OF REASONING

Fair warning

Once you understand reasoning and argument, you're going to notice nonsense everywhere.

You're going to spend a lot of time hearing other people talking through their hat. At home, in class, at the gym, at work, on TV, on the train, you're going to be surrounded by ostensibly smart people talking utter piffle a fair amount of the time. How you choose to deal with that is up to you. Try not to become insufferably smug – it didn't work for me.

The problem people have is putting together an argument. According to the Shorter Oxford English Dictionary[2], an argument is a connected series of statements intended to establish a position or a truth. It's a process of reasoning.

Yes, argument can also mean a good punch-up or, as we call it back in the land of my forefathers, a wedding. But in the world of reasoning, an argument is simply the case you put forward to explain why what you're saying is correct (or what the other person claims is wrong).

A fallacy is a fault that makes your argument wrong. It's an error in logic, reasoning or rhetoric that makes your conclusion unsound or invalid. There are many fallacies, but happily for us they live in family groups, which we'll look at later.

One phrase you should learn and repeat often, because it annoys people, is non sequitur. [non SECK-wit-ur] (Latin for *it does not follow*.) In general, a non sequitur can be any random statement that doesn't seem to belong to the ones before it:

> Cousin Bernard: "The booster rocket has placed the satellite into a geostationary orbit."
>
> Nephew Cuthbert: "Wallpaper paste tastes squidgy."

---

[2] Shorter is a comparative term. It's huge but, at two massive volumes, less frightening than the full Oxford English Dictionary, which kicks in at 20. The SOED is in my opinion is the best dictionary available. That is an unpaid-for recommendation – see *appeal to authority fallacy*.

Specifically, in reasoning a non sequitur is a duff conclusion, something that isn't proven by the statements in your argument. For instance:

> A company that makes computer games doubled its sales in three years, therefore twice as many people play computer games than three years ago.

The conclusion is a non sequitur. The statistic may happen to be true, but it's not supported by the evidence presented. Firstly, one company's sales probably doesn't reflect the whole market – it may have launched an especially successful game. Or perhaps customers are buying twice as many games as before. Or the firm doubled the price of its products. Or there may actually be three times as many players in the market and the firm is falling behind its competitors. In reality, some combination of those many reasons is likely.

Another word you'll see a lot in books about reasoning is *premise* (and its plural, unsurprisingly, premises). A premise is a statement, an assumption, that you use in your argument leading to your conclusion.

> Major premise: to be legal, car tyres must have tread 1.6mm deep across ¾ of the width of the tyre
>
> Minor premise: my car tyre is as smooth as Michelangelo's David's bum
>
> Conclusion: Therefore, my tyre is not legal.

Here, both premises are true, ergo the conclusion must be true. (*Ergo* is Latin for *therefore*.) The three-line argument:

> A general statement or truth
>
> Followed by specific statement or fact
>
> Leading to a conclusion that must be true.

… is called a categorical syllogism. Think of it as a limerick for logic. Categorical means the statements are unconditional, absolute, flat-out true assertions of fact. (Later we'll also see hypothetical syllogisms that contain conditions.) Syllogisms are the neatest, most succinct way of expressing formal or deductive reasoning. Deductive reasoning leads to conclusions that are absolutely true. To ensure that certainty, arguments must be logically valid and the premises used must be true.

The elephant in the room of deduction is Sherlock Holmes. It may be that the old boy's fondness for cocaine and opium confuses him, but most of his reasoning is not deductive, no matter how elementary he tells Watson it is. Holmes is an exponent of the other great form of reasoning – inductive reasoning.

You use inductive reasoning when you have no unquestionable, conclusive proof of something, just a bunch of evidence that points one way or another. Inductive reasoning cannot lead to true or false conclusions; it only produces arguments that are strong or weak. Strong arguments are persuasive if the premises they're based on are true and the reasoning avoids fallacies.

So here's the reality of everyday discussion. Your inductive argument's conclusion may be wrong (or weak) even when the premises are true. And your opponent's conclusion may happen to be sound even if the reasoning and premises could have been framed by a cuttlefish on LSD.

> My nephew Cuthbert emerges from the kitchen with jam and sugar smeared all around his chops. Going in, I see neat rows of doughnuts with one gap. I didn't see Cuthbert eating a doughnut, so I can't deduce he's the thief. But I observe one is missing. There's no-one else in the kitchen. There's evidence plastered all over Cuthbert's smug and ugly dial. I infer he's eaten something with jam and sugar. The evidence may circumstantial, but it's safe enough for me to decide beyond reasonable doubt that Cuthbert is a thieving little tyke. Were this a trial, his defence would probably claim that he bought the doughnut in good faith in the pub from a bloke he doesn't know the name of and hasn't seen since.

To form a reasonable conclusion, you need a number of pieces of evidence that support each other and all point to the same outcome. (Importantly, a bit of evidence that contradicts the rest must not be left out. It allows room for doubt.) Sherlock might claim: "I deduce the little monster is the thief." He does nothing of the sort. He infers it.

Since the words *infer* and *imply* crop up a lot, it's important to understand the difference.

Infer means to construe, deduce, conclude from information or premises. Infer is something the person receiving information does:

The teacher explains that some mammals are dogs, and some mammals are cats. The pupils infer that mammals are animals, not trees or spaceships.

On 7th February, a surprise parcel arrived for me. I inferred some kind soul had remembered my birthday.

Imply, by contrast, is what the giver of information does. It means literally to enfold; figuratively, to express indirectly, insinuate, hint, suggest:

Although the writer refrained from directly criticising politicians, his repeated use of the phrase *firing squad* implied a profound dislike of them.

The investigative journalist received a single bullet in the post. The implication was clear: desist or die.

Okay, back to talking about nonsense. Inductive reasoning is the kind of woolly, everyday thinking that leads us into trouble most of the time. When there's no unarguable fact, we use opinions, myths, common knowledge, bias, generalisations, prejudice, and so on, to validate what we claim to be true or real.

We like to pretend that our opinions are reasoned and based on firm ground. But usually we reach a conclusion (express an opinion, assert a fact) that we like, then use what we call reasoning to justify it. That muddled thinking is called confirmation bias and ex post facto rationalisation. It's probably why we get things so wrong most of the time.

The third significant form of reasoning is abductive reasoning. It's a hugely important approach in science and research, as well as in diagnostic systems and solving crime. Abductive reasoning begins with observation, then tries to find the most likely explanation in order to form a theory. In short, it asks: if this is the effect, what was the cause and how did it lead to this result? Abductive reasoning does not guarantee the conclusion, instead it seeks to find the best available, most probable answer.

By the way, a scientific theory is not the same as a good guess. It's a strongly corroborated explanation, arrived at by using scientific method, tested and confirmed in experiments and observations. Within abductive reasoning, you'll find inductive processes and deductions being made. But the overall approach goes from observation to a theory that best accounts for the observation.

Most of this book will be taken up exploring the vast labyrinth of wonky, informal, inductive thinking. Think of it as a gentle stretch and bend before we scale the implacable, sheer rock-face of deductive reasoning. By then you will be match-fit.

2. EVERYDAY REASONING AND FALLACIES

Every discussion invites scepticism

The main kind of reasoning we use day to day, and therefore the focus of this book, is informal, inductive reasoning. Most everyday discussions that try to prove a point, including:

> arguments, speeches, lessons, expressions of opinion for and against, recommendations, general chats, explaining things, complaints, and so on

...all, almost exclusively, take the form of inductive reasoning. It runs through almost every unstructured discussion. We present facts and make claims. They lead us to conclusions or judgements, sometimes strongly supported, other times weakly.

Compared to formal logic, informal reasoning is an argument wearing jeans, a rugby shirt and drinking beer from a can. We hear informal fallacies every single day from colleagues, teachers, TV, celebrities, family and friends. We're surrounded by entire conversations that are poorly reasoned, if at all. Most conversations are a stream of feelings, generalisations and baseless assertions. Usually, we just smile and add our tuppence worth.

Inductive reasoning is less formal than the deductive variety, which is where the problems start. Valid formal arguments provide complete proof of the conclusion. Informal arguments try to mount up the evidence in favour of what we believe. But often we rely on doubtful premises and our reasoning is riddled with fallacies. The best we can hope for is to be persuasive, rather than conclusive. Where deductive arguments are true or invalid, inductive reasoning is strong or weak – it begs for doubt.

Worse still, instead of narrowing the field of possibilities like deductive reasoning, inductive arguments generalise and multiply. They tend to reach general principals from sets of specific observations. Like circumstantial evidence presented to a jury, the more events the merrier. Relevant factors are brought together, and if they are consistent and convincing, you may be able to draw a conclusion. Inductive arguments, like prosecutions, are judged by a reasonable persuasiveness. Or to put it another way, do you buy it?

Where the planks of your argument don't support the point you're trying to prove, or fact you assert to be true, it's likely you used some form of fallacy – a faulty piece of reasoning. There are somewhere in the region of 150 to 300 informal fallacies, depending how you classify, group and distinguish between them. That's a lot of fallacies. Or, to put it coarsely, most people talk bollocks most of the time.

Consider:

> All dogs defecate. Uncle Billy's just spent a satisfying twenty minutes in the thunder-box, therefore he's a dog.

> Health warnings about smoking are rubbish. Great Aunt Ruby smoked 40 cigarettes a day and she lived to 90.

I trust you can spot the flaw in the first example. In the second, you can't dismiss health warnings because of anecdotal evidence about one person. To apply the pulmonary fortitude of Great Aunt Ruby to smokers in general is a faulty generalisation.

Informal fallacies are often grouped by scholars into types determined by the logical fracture involved. This is an excellent way for deep thinkers to show their command of abstract titles. Sadly, this also means the connection isn't apparent until you examine the problem in depth. That's not an easy way to understand what's happening.

Here, I'm choosing to assemble the fallacies in a way that makes sense to me (see *appendix 1 – a word on taxonomy*). My sole purpose is to help you remember the nature of the fallacy and understand the contexts in which you're likely to run into them. Purists will hate it.

3. COMMONEST FALLACIES

Among the hundreds of informal fallacies: some are obscure, occasional drop-ins; others are regular brawlers at the bar of reasoning. As an easy introduction, therefore, let's begin with the types you hear – quite literally – every day in conversation, on the news, at work, at school and leaving our own mouths. These are habitual offenders.

Note, though, that several of the commonest fallacies have a whole family of close relations: generalisation, personal attack, and emotional appeals, for instance. I've kept these families together, and for that reason those fallacies don't appear in this section, but in a chapter of their own.

Burden of proof – shifting the

In any debate, the burden of proving a point rests with the person making the claim, assertion, accusation or statement that another disputes or rejects. If I state a fact about something, and you don't accept what I say, it's my job to prove what I say is correct. It's a principle of reasoning that reaches back into antiquity.

If the burden of proof didn't lie this way, it would mean we must assume every claim might be true unless and until we disbelievers prove it wrong. That way madness lies. Imagine the entire world tied up furiously trying to disprove the fanciful ravings of a handful of provocateurs, idly dreaming up challenges for the brainiest of the world to disprove. Frankly, they have better things to do.

As far as the burden of proof is concerned, modern criminal cases are a good example. In adversarial systems, a prosecutor must prove that a defendant is guilty. A defendant doesn't need to prove his or her innocence. To us in comfortable Western democracies, it would seem a bizarre, Kafkaesque world if you were suddenly hauled off the street into court one day and charged with stealing £500 from a neighbour. You protest your innocence:

> "Prove it!" demands the prosecutor. "Yes, I've heard no evidence that she didn't steal the money," agrees the judge. "No smoke without fire," thinks the jury.

The only evidence that you did pinch the money from next-door is the absence of any proof that you didn't. (That in itself is a logical difficulty – see absence of evidence.) Proving innocence is to prove a negative. That can be tricky.

Thankfully, our legal system avoids the worst mistakes stemming from this fallacy. The party making a positive claim ("This person accuses you of stealing £500 from under his pillow.") has the burden of proving it. The jury is instructed to return a verdict of not guilty unless members are satisfied beyond reasonable doubt that the defendant did it based solely on the evidence they've been presented with, and not on what they might suppose or imagine. A defendant in court, in theory, doesn't have to say a word.

Detectives investigating a crime, on the other hand, should always be eager to explore a suspect's alibi. They're working under a different approach – abductive reasoning – which builds hypotheses from observed facts. Detectives need suspects to talk in the way research scientists need experimental data. So there's a conflict between the defendant's right to silence – ushered in by the burden of proof falling on prosecutors – and the need to investigate crime effectively using abductive methods.

Trying to shift the burden of proof is a common defensive tactic for supporters of political or religious dogma and whacky medical ideas – ideas based more in faith or belief than fact. If you challenge adherents to prove the unconfirmable notions they embrace, sooner or later they demand you prove them wrong. Well, you don't need to – they're not right until they prove themselves right, if they can.

> Cousin Vera swore that colonic irrigation was the best thing to detoxify the body. Cousin Bernard scoffed at her. "Well, prove it doesn't work!" Vera challenged. "I don't need to," he retorted. "I'm not even going to go through the motions."

When people try to shift the burden of proof, they often use an argument from ignorance – that is, when one party says their proposition has not been proven false, so it must be true; or that someone else's claim has not been proven true, so it must be false. This type of argument is a fallacy:

> "Well, you haven't proved the goddess Minerva doesn't exist, so she does."

> "You can't prove the goods you ordered haven't arrived, so your claim for a replacement is invalid."

Suppose your opponent actually does provide some evidence supporting their claim. It may be rubbish, but the burden is now on you to refute it. (It's the burden of rejoinder.) If it's weedy stuff, you should have no problem knocking it to the floor in the first round. Just point out faulty reasoning in your opponent's argument, identify any fallacies, examine the premises of the argument, give counter-examples, or show why a sound conclusion can't be reached from the reasons put forward. If the argument is over a belief or faith, you cannot logically lose. By definition, ideas that exist only in faith or belief have no tangible evidence. They don't exist in the real world, which is why you need faith to believe in them.

But suppose the claim you make is a negative one:

You: "The parcel I ordered from you hasn't been delivered."

Vendor: "Can you give us proof you didn't get it?"

How do you demonstrate convincingly that a parcel never arrived? There's only your word for it. The burden of proof requires you to make good on your claim. The only thing supporting you is that there's no proof that it actually was delivered. But this isn't convincing on its own. (See *absence of evidence*.) You could challenge the vendor to prove that they did deliver. But if they decline to play ball, you're in a fix.

It isn't generally possible to **prove a negative** decisively. (Ironically, that's a negative assertion.) In pure logic or mathematics you can prove that something is always false, but in everyday life it's less cut and dried. Sometimes, though, you have to try, using circumstantial evidence:

If I take a client to court for not paying my modest, well-deserved fees, the lying scumbag might claim he has paid me. As I'm bringing the claim, I have to prove my case: I have to prove a negative – non-payment. So I'd show my bank statements indicating no transfer of payment was received and seek the client's records to show no matching sum was sent. While not conclusive, these might show a judge, on the balance of probability, that I haven't been paid.

Another way of verifying a negative is to prove positively something that's inconsistent – **proof by contradiction**. An alibi is proof by contradiction. You could not have pinched £500 from your neighbour if you were abroad when the theft took place. Travel tickets, money movements and mobile phone records would inductively establish your alibi.

By now it should be obvious where the burden of proof lies, and why. Even so, smart people get it wrong. In the UK's pre-EU referendum skirmishes, former retail boss Stuart Rose, Chairman of the Stronger In campaign said in January 2016:

> "If we leave, those exports [to the EU] would be at risk, facing trade barriers and fees – hitting British businesses hard and increasing prices in the shops."

Had he left it there, we would only have the slippery slope fallacy to discuss (in short, hypothetical outcomes are not persuasive). However he went on to say:

> "Those proposing leaving the EU must show how this damage can be avoided."

Lord Rose tried to shift the burden of proof. It's his job, having made the assertion, to prove his claims are true now or certain to happen in the future. In fact, he ventured some hypothetical consequences following a Leave vote, then insisted opponents prove him wrong. His argument is akin to saying:

> If we broadcast TV and radio frequencies out into space, we leave ourselves at risk of invasion from warlike aliens. Those proposing to watch *Eastenders* must show how this annihilation can be avoided.

The burden of proof underpins all arguments. It compels people making claims to produce convincing support for their position. Without that, they're making a bare assertion, which carries no weight at all.

Red herring

We've all heard the phrase red herring. A red herring is a plausible but irrelevant distraction; a new element introduced which, intentionally or not, pulls the conversation or debate off course, in another direction.

There are a number of fallacies that operate by steering the discussion away from the main point. These are termed red herring fallacies as a general title. Here, though, we're concerned with the core weakness.

Red herrings abound. They litter every discussion. In fact, if you ever record an hour's conversation among your friends, you'll be amazed by the range of the territory you cover.[3] Often the impetus to move along between topics is a new idea introduced by one speaker, which becomes the topic of conversation for a brief spell, until another twist takes the discussion elsewhere.

You hear people asking, "Sorry, what were we talking about?" and "How did we get here?" It's the sign of a lively conversation.

Ponder:

> "We should legalise cannabis because it's much less harmful than alcohol."

> "No, the government would only tax it, and we pay enough tax as it is."

Someone advances the idea that cannabis is less harmful than booze. That's a fair opinion, and it opens up a range of thoughts. Can weed be a gateway drug to other substances that are more dangerous than half a pint of mild at the local pub? Is it universally harmless low-grade grass, or is there some seriously discombobulating skunk out there if you know who to talk to? Would the country need strategic stockpiles of munchies?

These thoughts would be relevant to the theme of legalising cannabis because it's less harmful than good old socially-acceptable booze. Taxation is a red herring. It's missing the point. The argument is harm compared to a legal substance. Besides, there's always a chance the government wouldn't tax legalised cannabis, admittedly a minuscule one.

As ever, we can rely on our children to raise the bar on red herrings:

> "Don't stay out too late tonight, you've got school tomorrow."

> "Come on, I've been revising all day."

Later on, we'll look at two fallacies – two wrongs and tu quoque – which provide rich feeding grounds for red herrings.

---

[3] Actually, don't do this. It's creepy.

"It's inhumane to torture terror suspects for information."

"Why? The 9/11 terrorists weren't that squeamish. They murdered thousands."

Torture, at best, is bad manners, never mind the legal and moral niceties. But the methods used by anyone else are irrelevant, no matter how tempting it is to use them to justify our own. Two wrongs don't make a right, not only for moral reasons, but for logical ones too.

A red herring is also a legitimate plot device in books to distract readers from too easily spotting who did for butler in the study with the frozen leg of lamb. It's a bogus clue that's intended to lead you down the wrong path. We like those red herrings.

Strawman argument

When your opponent mis-represents your argument to make it easier to shoot down, they've created a strawman argument. Strawman arguments happen in any discussion, but they crop up regularly in business meetings:

"Our business should invest more in staff training."

"So you'd be prepared to damage the firm's long-term prospects by cutting back on research and development? You're wrong, and I couldn't support that position."

Your colleague is being quarrelsome. She's put words in your mouth you never said. She's suggesting that support for training translates into hostility toward research and development (R&D) – it doesn't – and so you personally are against R&D, and have explicitly said as much.

It's much easier to shoot down the fake argument to cut R&D than the real one to increase training. The cut-R&D argument is a strawman. Be alert to the strawman argument when you hear responses that begin:

So what you're saying is…

But that's tantamount to…

So you'd rather…

In business, unrelated things are always linked by budget constraints. More spent on training can, but not necessarily must, mean less on any other area of investment.

It's important to nail the fallacy because your opponent has twisted your words and used them against you, and hijacked the debate from the merits of training to her hobby-horse. The strawman can easily become a red herring and develop a life of its own. Kill strawmen quickly:

> "I've not expressed any view on research, for or against. I'm talking about training and we shouldn't wander off the point."

In another example, when Switzerland held a referendum whether to pay an unconditional basic income to all adults and children[4], this pearl emerged in one online debate:

> "Just giving people money teaches them not to work, which takes away their purpose in life."

> "So you're saying the retired, unemployed and disabled have no purpose in life? Would you prefer to get rid of them altogether?"

The strawman yanks the debate away from the social value of work to prejudice against vulnerable groups who get state assistance, an easier argument to attack. But a strawman doesn't have to be overtly confrontational. It can arise through misunderstanding:

> "We should expand bicycle routes to ease pollution in the city centre."

> "Why do we want cyclists to have priority over cars? Isn't traffic slow enough?"

Traffic speed is not the argument being advanced, pollution is. (See *missing the point*.) The second speaker is mis-representing the proposal as one to prioritise bikes. In fact, a scheme to create dedicated cycle routes would take bicycles out of the traffic, which would probably allow motorised traffic to speed up.

As a deliberate ploy, people choose strawman arguments which they think are easier to win. Often they express the strawman as a truism or platitude along the lines of: nobody wants more crime, or more tax, and so on. (See also *argument-terminating cliché*.) The choice of strawman shows what's uppermost in your opponent's mind, and gives you a chance to bolster your case. For instance:

---

[4] In 2016. The proposal was roundly rejected.

> "The National Health Service is bursting at the seams with waiting times at A&E missing targets. This needs a radical overhaul."

> "No, it's an important principle that healthcare is free at point of delivery."[5]

Your argument is about performance, but your listener misrepresents it as something much easier to defend. No-one suggested charging for NHS treatment as a way to cut queues. That might be what your listener fears; it's not what you argued. But you can use it to help your proposal:

> "Thank you for making my next point. Of course we must keep healthcare free at the point of consumption, and to be able to continue to do that we need to reduce the most pressing problem that some people seize upon as an excuse to privatise the NHS."

Here's a personal guarantee: in any work meeting where there's a genuine range of opinions around the table, you will find at least one strawman argument being raised. That agitator, you will probably find, is the biggest source of debilitating, needless conflict in the team, sapping energy and enthusiasm from your colleagues. If you manage the team, you know what to do. And if the provocateur turns out to be you, so do you.

Bandwagon fallacy

Few people like to be the odd one out. We're all influenced by the people around us. We believe what friends, family and colleagues tell us, and we want to fit in with the majority, go with the flow. But what other people say, think or like doesn't make anything true. You commit the bandwagon fallacy when you're persuaded a statement is true (or false) because it's popular or widely believed.

It's one of the most common mistakes people have been making in reasoning since the concept of democracy. The bandwagon fallacy has many names: *appeal to popularity, appeal to common knowledge, argument by consensus*, the *authority of the many*, and so on.

---

[5] You still pay for health services as part of the national insurance deductions from your pay. It means you don't have to turn up at A&E with an insurance card or a cheque book. So it's free at the point of delivery / consumption.

But they all share the same flaw: while they prove the popularity of a belief; they don't prove it's true:

> "Lots of people avoid tax, so it's okay if I do it."

> "They say the MMR jab causes autism. I'm not taking my kid to the clinic."

> "She said she likes tattoos and got 100,000 likes on Facebook. Ink must be good."

> "The government got elected, therefore this policy is right."

> "Eighty per cent of people are in favour of the death penalty, so we should re-introduce it."

> "Let's ask the audience."

People confuse democracy with reasoning. Taking a vote is a fine way to choose between alternative courses of action, but it's not logical proof the result is correct or true.

> "Okay, people, we're taking a vote. Gravity, true or false?
> Everyone who thinks false, jump in the air now."

The reason popular opinion isn't a strong argument is this: if the belief of any individual can be wrong, then the belief of a collection of individuals can also be wrong. And if a majority view is deemed to be truth, what about the minority, people who voted the other way? Are they incorrect? Invalid? False?

Increasingly, people who disagree with the fashionable view are called *deniers*. They are portrayed as people at odds with some universal truth, in denial of reality or righteousness, and are met with open hostility.

> "I don't like your opinion. It hurts me. It triggers my pain. I need a safe space to physically protect me and to recover from hearing it."

To be clear: to deny a settled fact or actual occurrence is rightly labelled denial. In some European countries where the holocaust is still a touchy subject you can be imprisoned for denying the holocaust ever happened. The Flat Earth Society could fairly be labelled globe-deniers, given the rock-solid proof against them. Conspiracy theorists who deny that NASA ever landed on the moon could be called lunar landing deniers (although I prefer the term *idiot*).

But to hold a different political or social opinion is not denial. If confronted by a spittle-flecked loon who, for example, assails you:

"How can you deny there is a rape culture on campus?"

The answer is:

"I can't deny anything you prove exists. So, prove away."

Back to the bandwagon: how big a majority makes the truth? A simple majority – 51 per cent? A special majority – 66 per cent or 75 per cent? And what happens when the one or two people who disagree are the only experts in the field? (See *appeal to authority*)

Juries are asked to return a unanimous verdict (or a majority verdict under certain limited circumstances) to ensure the burden of proof is high. Convicting a person of a crime isn't a show of hands to choose which film to watch on TV. Even then, juries still get verdicts wrong, and this is the most cogent argument against bowing to the wishes of any majority favouring the death penalty.

The best skewering of the bandwagon tendency came in the TV series The West Wing. A political campaigner is told that 60 per cent of residents disagree with his position. He replies:

"Sixty per cent is six of ten in a focus group. You change one mind, it's a dead heat. Change two, it's a landslide."

Fitting snugly under the bandwagon blanket lies the appeal to common belief. Again, it goes by many names; some combination of *argument, appeal* or *authority*, linked with words like *mob, gallery, consensus, community, majority* or *masses*.

The appeal to common belief applies to the arguments in which "Everybody thinks..." crops up. A widely-held supposition does not make an opinion a fact. For instance:

"The millennium bug will cause aircraft to plummet from the skies when 1999 becomes 2000." [It didn't.]

"When a third of people believe in alien abduction, we have to seriously consider it happens." [They're wrong and we don't.]

"Everyone knows in the southern hemisphere, water drains out of the sink in the other direction." [It doesn't. I tried this.]

"It's a well known fact that a duck's quack can't echo." [Oh yes, it can.]

Phrases like:

"Common sense says; they say; I read that; it was on TV; we were taught that; everyone knows; it's a known fact that…"

… should be flags alerting you to a likely bandwagon argument. There is, though, a world of difference between popular misconception and a reasoned consensus.

"People say that if you eat food that's past the sell-by date, you'll die a slow and painful death."

"Scientists say that nothing can go faster than the speed of light."

The difference is that boffins have scientific proof on their side, while the sell-by-date faction just want you to buy more yoghurt.

Yes or no? – false dichotomy

It's entertaining to watch a skilled interviewer trying to force a reluctant witness to answer a specific question. (Skilled in this context may also mean dogged, monomaniacal, vindictive, boring or biased – you pay your money, you take your choice.)

In court, my Uncle Billy tried to explain that after being hit over the head ten times with a walking stick, and repeatedly shouting at his assailant to stop, he did lash out to protect himself. The prosecutor interrupted over and over again, demanding an answer to the same question: "Did you or did you not strike the victim? Yes or no? Yes or no? Yes or No?"

"Well, yes, but…"

"You admit you struck the elderly lady. No further questions."

Not exactly the whole truth, is it? A question framed to give only one of two possible answers is the fallacy of false dichotomy, also known as *false choice, false alternative,* the *excluded middle, black and white thinking,* and so on. The fallacy shuts out the chance of a third or any different option.

An energy company selling solar panels has an advert bearing the slogan: "Which would you prefer to see?" To the left is an industrial scene showing belching chimneys polluting a leaden sky; to the right a (frankly charmless) country cottage with a hideous array of solar panels obscuring what might have been a pretty tiled roof.

The company's attempt to portray the choice as one or the other is infantile. The only sensible answer is neither. Sometimes, though, the simple choice must be used to compel someone to decide fast:

"The enemy's at the gate. Are you with us or against us?"

It's a rare situation where necessity kicks reasoning in the backside, but an emergency act or don't act would be a true and fair dichotomy.

On occasion, you are forced to vote for one of just two candidates, neither of whom represent your views. Do you vote for one of them? Do you stay at home that day? Or do you spoil your ballot paper to show you did bother to turn up to vote, but support neither candidate? It rather depends on the message you want to communicate.

Many issues seem to be polarised between two opposites. For or against. Agree or disagree. Climate change, yes or no? In American politics, abortion, yes or no? War. Immigration. The EU. The Euro. All, it seems, can be reduced to one side versus another, like a boxing match. But, really, they can't.

The world is far too complex to distil down to one-word answers, or to sound-bites so loved by political spin-doctors. Very occasionally – once in a blue moon – there comes a matter with an absolute right and an absolute wrong; a decision that only demands a one-word answer; literally life and death decisions:

A baby abandoned in a shop doorway.

An animal trapped and in unimaginable pain.

Civilians being picked off by snipers.

Other than a few egregious examples, there are precious few un-nuanced moments in modern life. The problem with black and white thinking is that it excludes the spectrum of possibility that lies between.

Residents argue that a pub should be shut down because of noise late at night. The Keep It Open campaign versus the Shut It Down polarises the village. They ignore other options for the pub to close earlier; to lower music levels; to set a stricter policy for clientele; and other measures.

Whenever you hear statements like you can either... it's usually forcing you into a false choice. It's time, then, to ask yourself what do I actually want to happen?

Slippery slope fallacy

A slippery slope argument crops up when someone argues against a proposal on the grounds that it will lead onto further, less desirable, hypothetical consequences. The fallacy is also known as the thin end of the wedge.

> "Same-sex marriage should not be allowed. It's just the start. Next people will want to marry their pets or garden furniture."

> "If the council grants this planning application, it won't be able to refuse the next and the next. Soon the village green will be a car park, the pub yet another unlovely supermarket and our wildflower-strewn hedgerows will all be uneven pavements and double-yellow lines."

> "It's ridiculous to ask passengers to pay for us to print out their boarding pass. What's next? Will we charge them to use the toilet, and make them pay a supplement if the oxygen masks drop? Do we plan to make them pay to get off the plane?"

Don't imagine the low-cost airlines haven't considered that one. Slippery slope arguments are weak because it's not inevitable that the imagined consequences will happen. Note that the slippery slope reasoning doesn't address the proposal itself or its merits. It merely points to a hypothetical consequence which would be unwelcome. (See *appeal to consequences*.)

A slippery slope argument is easy to spot. The phrases, before you know it and who knows where it'll all end? often bookend the outburst. For dramatic effect, people like to make their slippery slope vertiginous – using ludicrously extreme consequences to underscore their concern. (See *reductio ad absurdum*.)

One of the more egregious claims before the UK's EU referendum in 2016 was that of the then prime minister, David Cameron. He said a vote to leave the EU would allow French politicians to tear up an agreement with the UK, which would mean that the so-called Jungle migrant camp in Calais could move across the Channel to England. Mr Cameron rejected the claim he was scaremongering.[6]

While arguing the slippery slope is logically fallacious, people do tend to warm to it, because the slippery slope is exactly how progression occurs naturally. Change rarely happens in big jumps, rather in a series of small steps.

> UK income tax, for example, was introduced in 1799 at less than 1 per cent to pay for wars against Napoleon and is still responsible two centuries later for that gaping chasm in your pay slip. And that big lump of value added tax (VAT – currently 20 per cent) you pay on most things?

> VAT in the UK began at 10 per cent in 1973, in effect close to the then prevailing value of purchase tax which was applied and collected at the point of manufacture and distribution (at 25 per cent). It was heralded in by the UK joining the then EEC. Ten per cent of the price at each stage along the distribution line, they argued, was low, convenient to remember and easy to calculate. Over time it has bounced around between 8 per cent and 25 per cent for different classes of goods. But the headline rate has risen from 10 per cent through 15 per cent to 17.5 per cent to 20 per cent now. People got used to the idea. While 20 per cent is still easy enough to remember and calculate, any resemblance to purchase tax levels is a misty dream.

For an immediate and visceral appreciation of the slippery slope, ask a UK university student about the history of tuition fees. The natural bedfellow of the slippery slope is "mission-creep". While commercial companies grow through enterprise, organisations in the public sector (usually with regulatory powers) justify their existence over time by spreading their responsibilities further, and quietly securing greater powers and responsibilities, and the budgets to pay for them.

> The EU began life in 1951 as the post-war European Coal and Steel Community with Belgium, Germany, France, Italy, Luxembourg and the Netherlands participating. In 1957 the

---

[6] The 2003 bilateral Le Touquet Treaty between the UK and France covering reciprocal cross-channel security arrangements is separate from EU treaties and legislation.

Treaty of Rome was signed to create closer co-operation on a range of economic and trade matters, including agriculture, overseas aid, commerce and taxation. Today the EU has regulations in 32 areas of activity from fishing to media that reach into every crevice of national and international public and private law, welfare, employment, human rights, safety and the environment, which are enforced in 28 member states.[7]

With a few notable exceptions, it's a rare event when a public body, one free from the burden of creating and selling products or services that people want to buy, in order to pay for itself[8], ever decided it had completed its job; that there was enough regulation or policy or departmental activity; that it was time to reduce itself to a skeleton staff to monitor existing regulations; that it had accomplished its mission. If you keep broadening the remit, the mission is never accomplished. Thanks a lot, Bonaparte. Ironically, one of the few state roll-backs that has occurred since WWII is a big cut in armed forces. Did it reduce your taxes? No. Some other essential government cause emerged to absorb your money through a process called... mission-creep.

Organisations (and governments) know that small incremental adjustments are easier to sell than single big jumps, which is why they develop strategies for long-term change that are rolled out over time.

Even so, the slippery scope argument is not persuasive. While direct and immediate consequences are relevant, a claim as to what might happen next is hypothetical. As such, it has no bearing on the matter in hand.

Missing the point – irrelevant conclusion

You encounter this problem regularly in day-to-day conversations with friends, colleagues and family. It's called *ignoring the issue* or missing the point. Someone makes a good argument that's not relevant because it's different to the matter in hand. For example, in a debate

---

[7] Including the UK, for the time being.

[8] The public sector does not create needs – it manufactures duress. The charges for licenses, taxes, fees are easy to levy when you have the power of legal compulsion.

about the need for course of action A, a person persuasively puts the case for the course of action B.

It's not as clear-cut a situation as a complete non sequitur, nor a deliberate distraction like a red herring. Some commentators describe irrelevant conclusion as a bit of a catch-all fallacy of irrelevance. In fact, it's often an instance of people doing their best to deal with the matter in a way that makes sense to them, there and then. To explain why we agree or support a particular opinion, we marshal our uppermost thoughts and current concerns. We may make a perfectly valid argument, but often not one that tackles the problem at hand.

> Cousin Bernard: "The steps to the front door are dangerous. The stones are loose and the moss is slippy."
>
> Uncle Billy: "We'll get someone in to look at it and get an estimate. It'll be expensive, but we could do a remortgage and have the roof done at the same time. What about a new patio?"
>
> Cousin Bernard: "You're missing the point – if it rains tomorrow, the postman is going to fall to his death."

Uncle Billy makes an excellent case for doing some strategic maintenance on the house, but he's overlooking the fact that dangerous steps must be taken care of quickly. The point he's missing is urgency. Another instance:

> In an online forum, a member complained that a browser add-on was showing his products for sale cheaper elsewhere. The member asked for advice on how to stop the add-on doing that. The first reply was: "It's not the add-on's fault your products are priced higher than your competitors, you'll have to become more competitive."

Missing the point is a problem for people who find themselves having to argue in favour of a particular outcome, but they aren't up to speed with the supporting facts. Politicians, for example, ever ready to make an appeal for popularity, resort to general blandishments of unassailable worthiness to bolster the case for a conclusion.

> "There is a shortage of affordable housing. Young people can't get onto the ladder of home ownership. Not enough new houses are being built. Therefore, the council should approve this planning application."

The speaker makes a fair case for more house-building in general, but the matter in question is a specific planning application. While not a complete non sequitur, the point about housing isn't relevant.

In business, too, managers do the same using management-speak. They parrot scarcely connected business truisms – the only way they know to think through a problem that requires a greater familiarity than they possess:

> "New customers are vital to this business. We have to make sure our account handling is seamless, fully-integrated, with all contact points singing from the same hymn book. We need to make a paradigm shift in customer satisfaction, reflecting our highest values, positioning us as the fastest-growing thought-leader in our chosen markets and sectors. That's why it's completely right to increase investment in customer service. So, yes, we need this account management system."

Somewhere in that sloganeering mess, the speaker makes a fair, if airy-fairy, point about investing in new customers, but there's no relevant reasoning to support buying a specific account management software system. For that, you'd want to see observations on the specification of the system, user needs, reliability, cost effectiveness, scalability, usability, and so on.

My personal experience is that up to 50 per cent of all contributions to business meetings miss the point. (See *appeal to authority*.) In your next meeting, keep a score.

Bare assertion – the non-argument

A bare assertion is a claim without back-up. Your friend makes a statement as if it's a definite fact. He puts forward no proof to validate it. An overwhelming proportion of "facts" we hear everyday are nothing of the kind. They are beliefs or opinions, like children dressed up in overalls and hi-vis jackets sent out to do a grown-up's job.

> Great Aunt Ruby says foreign drivers on UK roads are dangerous.

> Cousin Bernard says his firm had to buy the school playing field to build a warehouse because all companies must grow or die.

> My nephew Cuthbert says no-one studies Latin any more.

Uncle Billy says mongrels are better behaved than pedigree dogs.

Cousin Vera says redheads feel pain more than other people.

My niece Trixie says it's a fact that menthol cigarettes aren't as bad for you.

If Great Aunt Ruby had any supporting evidence about non-UK drivers having more accidents than residents, she would have the basis of an argument. Cousin Bernard conveniently forgets that businesses can consolidate and thrive. And so on.

If a claim begins:

Believe me...

Speaking as a...

... you might classify the bare assertion as a limp appeal to authority. It can also prove to be a red herring when it takes the discussion in an irrelevant direction. And when you take away the sting of a stereotype, you have something of a bare assertion.

Bare assertions can be a conventional wisdom, a common myth, or a simple piece of wishful thinking. The political landscape offers a rich habitat for bare assertion:

A quarter of the children born today are living in poverty.

People are healthier and better off today than at any time in history.

Only our nuclear deterrent keeps us safe.

Membership of the EU gives the UK a voice on the world stage.

Leaving the EU lets the UK speak to the world in its own voice.

Without limits on carbon emissions, sea levels will rise by 200 metres.

Global warming isn't real. It's a way to make us pay more taxes.

Socialism is the bridge to communism.

If people had known how the election was going to turn out, they would have voted differently.

The action by the trade union is wholly futile.

The right to strike is the cornerstone of industrial democracy.

Ad infinitum. A bare assertion isn't necessarily wrong. With a supporting argument it may even become persuasive. But it's an expression of the speaker's belief. If there's no broad acknowledgement that the assertion is true – at least between speaker and listener – and no supporting argument, a bare assertion is worthless as an argument.

4. GENERALISATION

Everybody generalises. Everybody. All the time. Especially writers, they're the worst.

We generalise because we try to make sense of the world using our own knowledge and experience. We apply what we see or know or believe to the world at large. We anoint the wider population with characteristics we observe in the one or two examples we know, or imagine we know. For us the conclusion is obvious. In reasoning, though, generalisations are not especially persuasive.

Faulty / hasty generalisation

Faulty or hasty generalisation is an informal fallacy in which we reach a conclusion without strong enough evidence. It's a defective induction, which means the premise we use might be fair and true, but it only supports a conclusion or judgement very weakly. Some authorities call it hasty generalisation, others faulty. In practice it doesn't matter. I mention both for completeness, not as an endorsement for either term.

> Uncle Billy drank a gallon of beer every day all his life. It didn't do him any harm at all. It's not too much.

It may well be true that Uncle Billy drank that much and thrived on it, but the yarn doesn't mention if the pickled uncle survived past his teens. Even if Uncle Billy lived to a ripe old age and was as spry as a sparrow (that is, the premise is true), you can't reasonably extrapolate Uncle Billy's hepatic endurance to a wider population. One anecdote isn't a properly conducted medical study, no matter how much we admire Uncle Billy's lifestyle and, presumably, his ability to pay for it. And even if the medical profession was over-cautious in its pronouncements about booze, that doesn't make the medics necessarily wrong on any other topic.

When we apply our assumptions to types of people often enough, we create stereotypes:

> All blondes are ditzy; redheads are fiery; unemployed people are feckless and workshy; Americans are all loud; Germans have no sense of humour; Scots are mean; the Irish like drink and fighting, including some of the men.

Just as those images are unfair and untrue, so the broad generalisations we make every day are equally unreliable. Just because the car tailgating you on the motorway, flashing its lights to get past, is a BMW, it does not follow that everyone who wants to drive like an idiot must choose that make of car – though many do. Nor does every owner of that fine marque necessarily have to drive badly, it just appears to be a default setting.

Nor does it follow that every white van contains a malodorous, knuckle-dragging, burger-addict with a mobile phone clamped to its ear – just the one that a minute ago tore along the road I live on as a short cut. But it's a common way for us to express our frustrations:

> Great Aunt Ruby can't work her tablet computer, therefore all retired people are computer illiterate.
>
> The lad staggered out of the bar and urinated in the street, therefore all young men are drunken yobs.
>
> A young woman crashed her car, therefore all young women are terrible drivers.
>
> A Moldovan man helped the old lady and sent her home in a taxi, therefore all Moldovan men are Good Samaritans.
>
> An Islamist extremist murdered ten people, therefore all Muslims are terrorists.

When you come across generalisations like these, it's charitable to interpret them as fallacies rather than prejudice. It doesn't follow that any other member of the class of people concerned is as virtuous or objectionable as those one-off cases that colour our views. (See *fallacy of composition*.)

In business, you would think business decisions are well-informed and rational. But in many discussions I've taken part in, over several decades as a manager, someone – and I'm not saying it wasn't me – has turned to fanciful generalisations to bolster or (more often) shoot down an idea.

Here's a huge generalisation of my own. While people proposing ideas at work bring evidence to support them: research, surveys, analyses, and so on, those against tend to drag out the personal anecdotes and faulty generalisations. In business cases, individuals confidently assert that the things they don't like the sound of are toxic to important groups, like customers or shareholders, management or unions. In desperation, they may even resort to *it'll never get past the lawyers* which always makes me want to reach for a taser. Some examples from my spotty youth in business:

> "Donors prefer the same familiar format for our newsletter every quarter." [Donations were steadily falling.]

> "Dealers never stock more than two models of the same range." [Hence the new stock financing plan. The district manager didn't understand it.]

> "Customers don't like the park-and-ride scheme. I know I don't." [A regional manager wanted to keep his reserved car parking space for twice-yearly visits.]

> "People don't buy if there's a charge for using credit cards." [Some don't; many do.]

Snarky comments aside, it's straightforward to deal with if you feel that popularity is no substitute for sound reasoning. Simply ask the speaker to produce meaningful evidence:

> "When did you survey those groups? How did you do it? Was the survey fair and balanced? Can I see the analysis?"

At that point, people get flustered. Then you'll hear personal credentials (see *appeal to authority*) to back up their personal view:

> "Over several decades as a manager…"

> "I've been in this business for thirty years."

> "Speaking as an engineer, nobody likes this idea."

> "I meet my customers every month, and they think…"

Frankly, you need something more concrete to base business decisions on. Self-importance and personal preference are a crummy way to run a business, and yet you'd be appalled to know how often they prevail.

Anecdotal fallacy

Sometimes we use a one-off example or a personal experience to make a point instead of convincing evidence. When we tell a story to illustrate a point, and the yarn itself becomes both demonstration and proof of our argument, that's an anecdotal fallacy.

We all draw on our own experience to put the rest of the world into context. Things that have occurred to us, or to people we know, shape our opinions. Importantly, it makes us more aware of the topic in question which, in turn, leads us to assume it's more prevalent than the perhaps isolated case we know about. And from that one instance, we feel like experts.

> "Uncle Billy got mugged in Rio de Janeiro once. South America is completely unsafe."

> "Fly from Gatwick? No chance. One of the check-in people dropped my sister's passport under the desk, then claimed she'd given it back. The staff at Gatwick are incompetent."[9]

> "Cousin Bernard had an automatic car once. The gearbox packed in after fifty-thousand miles. Automatics are rubbish."

Anecdotal evidence lures us into making hasty generalisations. One example of a bad gearbox means, for us, all automatics are bad, or that duff gearboxes are a widespread problem, but it makes for a weak argument. Anecdotal fallacy sometimes has the quality of misleading vividness.

> "Give up drinking? No chance. Uncle Billy's friend Cyril went to the pub every day, until his doctor told him to pack it in. So he went for a walk in the park instead and a tree fell over and killed him. It's dangerous giving up drinking."

If your story is entertaining, it can carry your listeners, not because your reasoning is good, but because they like the story and can repeat it themselves, thereby adopting your point of view as their own.

Scholars claim that the vividness of the anecdote is the thing that suckers us into making hasty generalisations. That may be true when we have more than one point of view to pick from; we choose the case that has the biggest impact. But if the topic is one we're unfamiliar with, a single example, however humdrum, can lead us to accept it as evidence solid enough to make our mind up.

---

[9] Actually, this really happened. But the conclusion is still weak. Only one check-in employee was inexcusably incompetent (although her supervisor wasn't a great deal of help either).

Hearsay evidence – from friends, colleagues, the bloke in the pub – can be just as powerful if it's our sole source of intelligence on the matter. If the source of the anecdote is someone in a position of influence, then the example can have the power of law. (See *appeal to authority.*)

"Teacher says…"

What parent has not been brutally overruled by those two mighty words?

Argument-terminating cliché

If you're a parent, just plead guilty now.

All children are annoying, especially our own. We don't have the grit or stamina for a protracted metaphysical debate on bedtime, sleeping, biscuits or puppies, so we try to terminate the tantrum with:

"Because I say so. That's why."

"You can't have everything you want."

"I've told you before, no."

"You're not a baby any more."

"Father Christmas is watching."

"Good children don't do that."

"Well, life's not fair."

"You're adopted."

It won't end the argument – it'll start another one, usually about why we should give the kid back to its real mummy and daddy who "will really love me." But if we give them an inch, they'll take a mile, unless you nip it in the bud – so to speak.

Clichés are generalisations. They are oft-repeated statements that have acquired some patina of truth by dint of repetition. We trot them out as the final word on some matter, and their familiarity brings a welcome close – end of discussion:

"Time will tell – there's no accounting for taste – all's fair in love and war – every cloud has a silver lining – what goes round comes around – let's not get our knickers in a twist – the grass is always greener – you can't please everyone – all's well that ends well – no time like the present – better safe than sorry..."

Debate-quelling gambits carry on into the worlds of business and politics in equally patronising clichés. Here are some personal favourites, as well as my reaction to hearing them:

"We'll have to agree to disagree."	Not when I'm right and you're wrong.
"Not what we expect from a team player."	Ah, dissent verboten. Got it.
"No, because our policy is…"	Flexibility or fairness aren't important here.
"Que sera, sera."	That sounds like defeatist claptrap.
"Whatever."	I accept your surrender.
"Only the gods can judge me."	No, I can too. You're still fired.
"Thanks for your input. Leave it with me."	Translation: go away.
"It's no use crying over spilt milk."	You screwed up, didn't you?
"We can't change the past."	You screwed up, didn't you?
"Money spent is money gone."	You screwed up, didn't you?

I recently observed an online debate about religion. Logic-pushers pointed out that the burden of proof lay with those asserting the existence of their deities. The friends of the divine claimed faith was exempt from reasoning. Finally, one of the ardent believers flounced out of the debate with:

"Nothing can be proven to a fool."

As an argument-terminating cliché, it's among the best. Essentially, it says:

"Because I can't prove my claim to a verifiable standard, it means you're too stupid to understand my evidence."

The smart-alec retort would have been:

"Any nonsense is proof to the gullible."

If you have to have the last word in any discussion, an argument-terminating cliché might be the way to go. It's satisfying, if not persuasive.

The phrase:

"I'm entitled to my opinion"

... crops up when one party has been proved wrong. It's intended to mean:

"My opinion is just as true and valid as yours."

Opinions may be equally worthy, and equally honestly held. But neither of those qualities makes them true or sound.[10]

The aim of an argument-terminating cliché is to end further discussion using a familiar saying as if it's a final truth, a conclusion in itself. It isn't. No cliché draws a line under fair reasoning. In business, more often than not, it means you're making your point to someone who feels uncomfortable being in the wrong, or is just bored with the topic. If the point is important, my advice is to stick with it, but find another avenue for getting your way.

---

[10] Author Isaac Asimov famously noted there was a 'false notion that democracy means that *"my ignorance is just as good as your knowledge."*'

5. Appeals

When a truffle hunter and his pig are out scouting for that most valuable fungus, the hunter takes a pocketful of acorns. If the keen-nosed porker scents some of the magic essence, the hunter can't let it grub the thing up and scoff it like some cheap, bosky turnip. So he throws some acorns on the ground to distract the pig, while he gets quick and lively with a trowel.

Appeals are the acorns of the argument world. They are distractions, sometimes deliberate, often unintentional, that others hope will persuade you. But usually they're not relevant to the argument. Appeals come in many flavours. Some call on to your emotions, others to common prejudices. Sometimes people just don't have a stronger argument. Other times opponents think you're a sucker, and they try to manipulate you.

Emotion – appeal to

Everyone reacts emotionally. It's impossible not to – we are, after all, human. When sentiment reinforces a persuasive, factual argument, you have a winning combination. However, without solid reasoning, the argument becomes an exercise in manipulating sentiment:

> "Eat your broccoli – there are people starving in Africa."

> "My kids go to a local school. I'm an ordinary person like you. Vote for me."

> "Terrorists do anything to murder innocent people. We can save lives by giving security people all the powers they ask for."

> "You should carry a national identity card to stop foreigners ripping off your National Health Service, getting the free treatment you've paid for, and making you wait."

> "If you really loved me, you'd tell the police it was you driving."

As an argument, it's a kind of red herring. People say things to evoke fear, pity or spite so that you're won over by your emotions rather than by reasoning.

Politicians love appeals to emotion. Politics is about belief and persuasion. Aristotle said that hitting the right emotional note is the fastest way to make a convert. Philosophers down the ages have noted that people are apt to believe things they find attractive. Recent history shows that leaders who rouse strong emotions, rather than convince through proof, can attract passionate followers. Nazis and Islamist extremists have that in common: a murderous belief in the righteousness of their cause.

Which brings us to propaganda. Propaganda targets the emotions of fear and hatred to demonise enemies, opponents and their causes. Governments, in time of war, make sure their message is clear and unambiguous. The enemy is evil. They want to harm your family. Our enemy's enemy is now our friend.[11] In war, necessity trumps reasoning.

Tyrants and despots tell citizens that a strong state will keep them safe from enemies abroad – appealing to their fear of enemies and relief at finding a saviour.

But even when we're presented with rational proof, reason loses to emotion a lot of the time. Most of the decisions we make are subjective, based on preference or gut feeling, which we rationalise afterwards – cognitive bias. Sometimes we even use information we got after the decision to explain why we decided a particular way.

Political neophytes offer factual information to support claims, but they pick up only as much public backing as their argument merits. They quickly learn to use rhetoric to whip up voters' feelings. Experienced politicians skip the factual stage, and jump straight into emotional appeals. The emotions that politicians play on can be positive or negative.

Negative emotions include fear and hate,[12] as well as guilt, anger, sadness, compassion (*think of the children!*), and revulsion. Conversely politicians can appeal to our pride, relief and especially hope (*for a better future*; *stronger Britain*; *fairer society*; usually followed by the words *vote for me*.

---

[11] In WWII, the British Ministry of Information issued propaganda that the dangers of Soviet Bolshevism were merely part of Germany's propaganda. This moved George Orwell to write *Animal Farm* – which was suppressed until after the war.

[12] Much of the debate in the UK's 2016 EU referendum – from both sides – consisted of relentless and bogus scaremongering of the most puerile kind. Reasoning's finest hour, it was not.

Anger / hatred / loathing / outrage / spite – appeal to

A claim makes you so angry, you immediately react:

"Good, I'm glad. Serves them right."

"I don't believe that. It's a lie."

"That's terrible. Head must roll!"

If your opponent's statements stir you into a froth of bile and loathing, it doesn't disprove their argument. Nor, obviously, does it prove them right if the claims they make have you punching the air in delight. (See *confirmation bias*.)

Anger, hatred, and so on, are powerful emotions. It's easy to get swept up and forget that no persuasive case has been made to support some proposed action.

"Terrorists murder innocent people without hesitation. We should torture suspects to save children's lives."

"Why should we pay for school buses for kids? I had to walk to school. Kids these days should walk as well. Right?"

"Benefits for nothing? Let's get the unemployed to pick up litter and do shopping for pensioners."

"If I gambled all my money and went bust, the government wouldn't bail me out. Bankers should all forfeit their bonuses until every taxpayer's penny is paid back."

"Typical British government. A US president invades a small, weak country and we follow them in like the bully's toadying friend. How can we vote for them?"

"Are you sick of foreigners getting higher on the housing list than you because they bring all their relatives' kids with them? Well, I'm standing for the council. Vote for me."

"People who experiment on animals are scum. They should be forced to donate bone marrow and a kidney. Maybe then they'll feel what it's like."

Appeals to anger pinpoint a situation and play it up like a pantomime villain. They lure us to the dark side and let us relish the power of strong emotion. As arguments go, they're deficient. Whenever you hear or read something that evokes strong sentiment, it's worth asking yourself if you've been persuaded, or you've persuaded yourself.

Fear – appeal to

Propaganda fits in here. When someone tries to curry support for a cause, belief or argument by scaring you away from an alternative, they're trying to appeal to your fear. Note the hypothetical premise:

> "If we don't invade Iraq, they could deploy chemical weapons in forty minutes."

> "If you keep drinking, you'll end up in an early grave like your Uncle Billy."

> "If we don't introduce identity cards, we are all at risk from identity theft, terrorism and immigrants bleeding our National Health Service dry."

In the last example, a UK government genuinely employed all three reasons to justify introducing 'voluntary' national identity cards. The scheme eventually disappeared into thin air (presumably stolen by heavily-armed fraudsters in burqas with freshly replaced hip joints – see **appeal to** ridicule).

Politicians love this one, as do marketing people. Insurance is an obvious product category to use fear in its sales argument. Others include personal hygiene, health and beauty, and anti-smoking and anti-drinking campaigns.

> "You should pack in smoking. If you smoke your lungs look like this…"

> "Don't risk the public humiliation of rancid body odour by using other, ineffective personal hygiene products. New Wolf-Sweat Fragrance for Men is the only answer."

> "Embarrassed by your poor grammar? You need…"

> "Got a date but you're afraid of spots?"

You get the picture. Sadly, fear is too often part of a bullying culture at work. It's amazing how often organisations imagine they are being fair and persuasive when they push forward policies such as these:

> "Staff can either accept the new procedures or the company

might be forced to require staff to make good any stock shrinkage on their shift out of their own pocket."

"New security measures mean that employees must allow 45 minutes from arrival on site to reaching the shop floor to clock on. Employees late on station will lose pay in 15 minute increments."

"Staff are reminded that some flexibility over working hours is required to meet last-minute orders. Overtime is a duty, not a privilege or a right Overtime is paid at standard hourly rates."

You can scare most employees to jump through hoops when they're afraid of losing their job. Yes, as a final resort, it might be justifiable to dangle dire consequences before an employee prone to misconduct. But if you have a wider problem with recalcitrant staff, you might want to take a look at your recruitment standards and staff supervision. As an observation, using fear at work is contemptible.

Flattery – appeal to

Another everyday conversation, another fallacy. While everyone likes a compliment, some blandishments are too obvious and too smarmy to fall for.

"You're an educated person, wouldn't you agree this beer's flat?"

"Surely someone as smart as you can see all religion is rubbish."

"We need our most skilful, courageous pilot to volunteer for this hopeless mission."

Flattery is meant to weaken our steely resolve and make us Just Do The Right Thing. The suggestion is that if we don't do the speaker's bidding, we're not smart or skilful.

Obviously, your smartness or skill has no bearing on the merits of the argument. No-one as intelligent as you is ever going to fall for such weak and transparent cajolery as that. Back to advertising:

"Because you're worth it."

"The magazine for people who understand style."

"Reassuringly expensive."

"Pamper yourself – you deserve it."

"Because you know a bargain when you see one."

None of these are persuasive arguments why a customer should buy the product. They pander to our vanity. And if they didn't work, advertisers would do something different. Yes, we're all shallow. (See *hasty generalisation*.)

Pity – appeal to

Everyone in the history of humanity has tried to use pity (or guilt) to get their own way at some point. No exceptions.

> "Harry served six years in the Royal Navy. He took part in the Arctic Convoys. Now he has no family or friends left to attend his funeral this Thursday. If you can spare an hour…"

> "This baby gorilla's mother was killed by poachers. Now she needs our help. Please donate…"

> "Please, you can't fail my car's MOT[13] I'm a student. I can't afford repairs."

There's a place for pity – compassion is one of our finest human qualities. Pity or guilt aside, there may be good reasons to fall in with the request. But a flagrant attempt to get sympathy isn't a reasoned argument. Would this work?

> "M'lud, the prosecution alleges my client punched the witness on the nose. I refute this, and would like to show the jury a picture of my client's puppy."

An exception (there has to be one!) might be if the object of pity is itself the argument:

> "We should re-grade this student's paper because her mother died two weeks before the exam."

Pity forms the basis of most charitable appeals. They specifically aim to stir an emotional response and loosen our purse strings with melancholy images and pitiable stories:

> "Without your help, Sarah will spend another night sleeping on

---

13 MOT – a compulsory annual inspection of safety and emissions for vehicles over a certain age.

the streets."

"John served his country during its hour of need. Now he needs his country's help."

This orphaned baby elephant lost his mother to poachers.

The fact that so many of us donate to charity proves that an appeal to pity can be effective, even if it's not strong on reasoning. There are times when rationality is overrated.

Ridicule – appeal to

Some ideas and some people, frankly, deserve it. Actually, many. Ridicule is the finest form of criticism devised. It takes tyrants down a peg or two. It pricks pomposity. It mocks authority both fair and foul. Politicians' crass populism; celebrities' witless lives; the cant of multi-millionaire musicians exhorting us to empty our threadbare pockets to give to poorer people; all deserve public derision. No-one and nothing is exempt from disparagement by laughter.

We invite people to agree with us by mocking our opponents and their opinions. It's just another emotion we're trying to tap into and, as such, it's not especially cogent. An example from George Carlin:

"Religion has actually convinced people that there's an invisible man living in the sky who watches everything you do, every minute of every day. And the invisible man has a special list of ten things he does not want you to do. And if you do any of these ten things, he has a special place, full of fire and smoke and burning and torture and anguish, where he will send you to live and suffer and burn and choke and scream and cry forever and ever 'til the end of time!

But He loves you. He loves you, and He needs money! He always needs money! He's all-powerful, all-perfect, all-knowing, and all-wise, somehow just can't handle money."

A couple more:

"Ah, yes. Those music awards. Are they important? I hear there's a new category for the Best Use Of Auto-Tune. Apparently, there are over a thousand nominations including two chain-saws and an ambulance. So, no."

"The musician said the 17 million people who voted the wrong way were ignorant and stupid. He's right – don't they know he's had a hit single? If only they'd known that before they voted."

Statements that don't address a specific argument are no more than fun. Appealing to an audience's sense of humour plays well, but isn't persuasive. (See *ad hominem* and *reductio ad absurdum*.)

Probability – appeal to

Appeal to probability is the fallacy of assuming that something definitely will happen because it might possibly happen.

"Sod's law. If it can go wrong, it will do."

"It'll probably never happen."

"I doubt those snipers could hit a barn door from…"

"The weather forecast says fine, but you know what they're like. Take an umbrella just in case."

Its sister is called appeal to possibility, a spurious argument carrying a strong whiff of blind optimism in some remotely possible occurrence.

"Now, cheer up. You're going to be with us for a long time. There are researchers all over the world looking for a cure."

"His execution might not happen – the president can grant a reprieve at any point before the deadline. Oh, did I just say 'dead'"?

"I've chosen the yacht I'm going to buy. I just need this lottery ticket to win us the money. What shall we call it?"

As with all fallacies, the conclusion isn't supported by the facts. In this case, you can't rely on something solely because it's technically possible, or at least not impossible.

Consequences – appeal to

Often we're swayed one way or another by the consequences of a dilemma, rather than the material facts. What happens next seems more important than what came before. If the outcome is beneficial, we favour that point of view, and steer away from endings we don't want.

"Sex offenders should never be let out of prison. They might offend again."

"Rising house prices are a good thing. We home-owners love feeling rich."

"If I vote not guilty, I'll be saying the police lied and made up evidence. I really don't want that. I choose guilty."

It's not a weak argument if the proposition is some kind of plan or course of action. Pointing out the benefits of following a particular option is a fair argument, even if the consequences aren't in the public good:

"We can write our engine management software to give lower emissions in tests. That way, our cars will seem to be more efficient and attract lower tax rates."

The fallacy crops up when a proposition can be decided one way or another, and we're swayed by the good or bad consequences of choosing one over the other.

"There's nothing wrong with downloading films for free. It saves us money that we can spend on beer and cigarettes."

Amid the fretting that followed the UK's referendum vote to leave the EU, a court ruled that Parliament itself had to trigger the departure, not the government. There were some public protests. Naturally, the loser appealed the decision. As the case came up before the UK Supreme Court, one former judge declared:[14]

"Let's say for the sake of argument the Supreme Court decides the High Court was wrong, it will undoubtedly be conveyed as a victory for the demonstrators. It won't be but that's what will be conveyed. And if that is conveyed, you've undermined the administration of justice."

His argument is an appeal to the consequences. A decision allowing the appeal would look like appeasing protesters, which would be a bad thing for justice. The Supreme Court is extremely unlikely to be swayed either way by this argument.

That's basically it. Appeal to consequences. Persuasion not by an argument but by what might happen as a result. Not very convincing.

---

[14] The felicitously named Lord Judge, Lord Chief Justice of England and Wales 2008 to 2013.

Wishful thinking

Ah, so tempting. Sometimes the line between fact or reality and what we wish to be true gets a bit too thin. When that happens, the only supporting evidence that the world is as we pronounce it is our desire for it to be so. It's an argument based on emotion – our own desire for something to be true.

> "Newcastle United will win the FA Cup this year. I've supported them man and boy for forty years."

> "My cousin's new single deserves to be number one."

> "I just need to lose fifty kilos or so, then I'll give Usain Bolt a run for his money."

An extreme example of wishful thinking might be a stalker who believes that he or she is the partner of, or married to, the object of their affection. True fanatics weave wishful delusions into reality:

> "When the end of the world comes, the aliens will come in space ships to save believers wearing purple. I'll be saved."

> "If I die murdering non-believers, I will spend all eternity in bliss with thirteen immortal puppies and unlimited Netflix. What does this switch do?"

It's not a fallacy to express a fond hope, or argue in favour of something you've dreamed of. But if that wish becomes the reasoning of an argument, it's unsound.

> "As we're going to win the lottery tonight, we should give our car away to the neighbours."

Religions insist that followers believe without verifiable evidence the promises and strictures of their deity. In Christianity, belief without evidence is even held up to be a sign of greater faith. It's normal, therefore, for followers to claim as a fact that which they earnestly hope and pray (read: *wish*) for. But consider this inverted reasoning from a Christian website:

> "Atheists engage in wishful thinking when they disbelieve in God because they do not want Him to exist, rather than because they have any direct evidence for the nonexistence of God."

The reasons given in favour of the simplistic dismissal of atheism is itself an instance of wishful thinking. It's also a strawman argument.

Atheists don't believe in gods because they don't believe gods exist, not because they don't *want* them to exist for some selfish motive. Also note: "direct evidence for the nonexistence..." See the burden of proof. And also note that believers have no direct evidence for the existence of their deity. If they did, they wouldn't need faith.

Sometimes we just wish things hadn't happened. Supporters of the losing candidate in the 2016 US Presidential Election held placards saying: "Not in my name" or "Not my president". This is both denial and wishful thinking. Disliking the outcome of an election doesn't alter the reality that someone did win it. But it's not just individuals who stick fingers in their ears and sing la-la-la:

> In December 2015, the German government publically rebuked its own intelligence service for writing and publishing a report critical of Saudi Arabia's leadership, describing the kingdom's destabilising role in the Middle East. The German government found the comments problematic because of its economic ties to the Saudi government, including arms sales. The briefing was flatly repudiated by the government as "not the position of the federal government". The embarrassed German government evidently wished the intelligence service's analysis were not true, or not written, or not made public. That, however, did not make the facts described by the intelligence service any less true, or its analysis any less accurate. (Nor did it diminish Germany's EU partners' schadenfreude.)

Wishful thinking can be a form of denial, expression of personal incredulity, and a sort of appeal to consequences.

Nature – appeal to

We commit a naturalistic fallacy, or appeal to nature, when we argue that some property, behaviour or quality is natural, and therefore whatever has the quality is superior, right, morally acceptable, and a strong argument in favour of the outcome we want. Conversely, any property, behaviour or quality that is not natural must be wrong or unacceptable.

The naturalistic argument allows you to pass judgements on things you strongly approve or disapprove of. For some, the line between *nature* and *divine purpose* is wafer thin. You can also see people taking the naturalistic view to portray themselves as holier-than-thou, or occupying the moral high ground.

> "Of course certain plants should be banned, they have unnatural effects on people."

> "The natural purpose of sex is making babies, so homosexuality is wrong."

> "Fossil fuels are natural. The chemicals that go into electric car batteries, on the other hand, are toxic. Fire that engine up!"

The word *natural* turns up in many advertising claims and statements. It's supposed to mean the proposal or product is right, or good for you, or at least better than unnatural things like competitors, opponents and anything you can't grow in an allotment. It's fallacious to conclude that natural things must always top others, whatever natural means anyway.

> "No natural plant should be illegal – it's like saying nature commits a crime."

> "Vegetarians and vegans are wrong; we evolved as omnivores and meat is a natural part of our diet."

> "We provide alternative, natural remedies, in tune with your body."

> "Made from naturally-sourced ingredients."

> "At our farm shop, we sell only natural produce."

This, presumably, means the supermarket's vegetables were assembled from inorganic parts in a factory on an industrial estate. An appeal to nature is a weak argument if it has nothing beefier to back it up.

By this argument, cannabis and cocaine are top drawer, as are wasps, cannibalism, meteor strikes and Ebola. If nature is the guiding light to what's good and right, how come it keeps trying to kill us all the time? Nature's gentle beneficence also includes earthquakes, tidal waves, volcanoes and ice ages. Besides, unnatural things can be good, too. Cars are handy, electric guitars are cool, smartphones are essential, and surgery's a life-saver.

Be wary when you hear the equivocal use of *natural* in statements such as:

It's natural to be nervous before an exam.

Where it means understandable or forgivable, fair enough. But if someone argues that a course of action is approved or normal, or somehow in tune with the laws of nature, pay attention.

"It's only natural to want revenge."

"It's only natural for a teacher to be attracted to a good-looking teenage pupil."

"It's only natural for teenage boys to gang up and try to show off how tough and brave they are."

Note the word *only* which serves to plead the case. The activities in these examples may be common, but that can't mean they're wholly tolerable.

When we use the word *natural* (meaning belonging to nature – a benign thing) in another context (meaning *pardonable*, or *to be expected*, for example) with the aim of giving less noble actions a veneer of acceptability, we're stumbling into the fallacy of equivocation.

Wealth – appeal to

This kind of weak reasoning assumes an opinion or statement is right solely because the speaker is wealthy, and, conversely, that an argument put forward by someone poor is wrong.

"A rich businessman gave a million pounds to the Scottish independence campaign. That must be the right way to vote."

"If you're right about this, how come you're not a millionaire?"

"The owner's husband hates the Labour Party, so we mustn't use any red in our corporate design."

Note, though, if the argument from the rich person is directly connected to getting or being rich, the argument is not necessarily unsound. For instance:

"Invest in property to become a billionaire", says the Duke of Westminster.

Sir James Dyson states that studying engineering can lead to a successful and rewarding career.

In these cases, rich people give an opinion on matters you would expect them to have a fair understanding of. The reverse fallacy also applies, where a pauper is seen as a conclusive authority of non-material virtues:

> "That hermit's spent ten years living in a cave and eating boiled soil. He knows the true meaning of life. Therefore, let's start with a soil-boiling pan and give the Range Rover away. Hang onto the Aga."

This last example is an appeal to enlightened poverty. The wealth fallacy operates both ways. Rich and poor people can be correct or wrong, but not because of their bank balance. It is, however, especially enjoyable when a rich person puts their foot in their mouth more stupidly than the rest of us:

> Hotel tycoon Leona Helmsley famously said, "Only little people pay taxes" shortly before getting sentenced to 16 years in prison for tax offences.

Authority – appeal to

From our earliest days, we learn from others. Without being influenced by parent or teacher, we would be incapable of speech, reading or writing, let alone reasoned argument. Perhaps we're pre-programmed to place great store by the lessons we get from figures of authority. Accordingly, in conversation, we often use the authority of someone else to bolster our position, or to justify us supporting some purported expert.

It rather depends on what we're relying on our authority figure to substantiate:

> "Fred Dibnah said the factory chimney was Victorian. Fred was an expert on chimneys, so it's probably Victorian."

Fred, a steeplejack, knew his stuff and was in a far better position than most to give an opinion on the provenance of chimneys. Now the big *however*: because Fred said something it doesn't have to be true. He might have been having an off day, misleading you for a bet, or just plain wrong. Nevertheless, we seek the opinion of experts to guide us:

> Eric Clapton is an authority on blues music. Eric says that Robert Johnson was an important blues songwriter and player. Therefore, Robert Johnson is an important musician.

That's his view, a judgment. Take it or leave it. However:

Eric ventures that a song he made famous, *Cocaine*, was written by J.J. Cale. It must be true if Eric says so. Right?

This is a question of fact. It's highly likely that Mr Clapton knows who wrote a song that features so often in his stage repertoire, but because he says so does not mean it must be true. We can all make mistakes. Here Mr Clapton is spot on. However, if he commented on the formation of the universe:

Penzias and Wilson discovered evidence of the Big Bang[15]

Eric Clapton says the Big Bang is wrong

Therefore, Penzias' and Wilson's discovery is false.

Eric is not an authority on cosmic microwave background radiation so, much like citing celebrities on topics as off-piste as world poverty, climate change and political engagement, he has no persuasive authority on the matter. As for celebrities, much as we may admire the comedian / singer / topless model for the talents they display, it's wrong to think the stuff that comes out of their mouth has any bottom, so to speak.

Authority figures are all around us – scientist, doctor, teacher, politician – spouting on all kinds of topics. In effect, we're being told that this person has studied the problem and has expertise in a particular field. If they say that such and such is the correct position, let's just accept that. If our doctor's opinion has serious implications, we might ask for a second opinion from another authority figure, in the hope the diagnosis is wrong.

Expert opinion can be a persuasive form of guidance. Courts use expert witnesses to give factual guidance on topics not concerned with law itself. An unlucky jury may be faced with an expert for the prosecution and another for the defence, each contradicting the other. So the opinions of experts are useful, but not conclusive.

Citing authorities is standard practice in academic papers. We refer to them so that we can incorporate their information and findings

---

[15] They discovered in 1964 cosmic microwave background radiation left over from the Big Bang, for which they shared the Nobel Prize for Physics in 1978.

as part of our own argument. Respected academics publish papers in peer-reviewed journals. They're not invariably correct, but the onus lies with subsequent academics to show that accepted knowledge is wrong, and present better information.

Don't mistake expertise in one field for proficiency in another. A top heart surgeon knows a lot about the squelchy parts of a person's chest, that does not make him or her an authority on how to run a hospital. A celebrity naturalist is not necessarily an expert on long-term climate trends, even though they have a passionate concern for the effects. A comedian is not an authority on voter apathy, and is never likely to be.

Lately we've seen a gaggle of professors of maths, physics, history, archaeology, and so on, making TV documentaries, actually educating us in an entertaining way. These teachers (and their series-accompanying books, of course) are authority figures. Unless they're dealing with pure science, however, somewhere in the story they'll repeat the orthodox view of teachers in their field. Teachers' authority figures for their interpretation of events are their own teachers, who wrote the earlier text books, but who relied on their own teachers (See *homunculus fallacy*), all the way back to some sandal-shod, querulous monk who got drunk one day and wrote:

> "I blame those Angles and Saxons, coming over here and talking Germanic, driving us Gaelic-speaking people into the western extremes and pushing up hut prices."

Thus, accumulated authority becomes received wisdom. Unfounded, but unchallenged down the aeons, stories and myth become the accepted view. But legends remain legends, no matter how many generations of professors have earned a living teaching it as solid fact. In the absence of original sources, much of our understanding of the past is no more robust than supposition. Archaeology and history are as prone to confirmation bias as any other field of study.

When it comes to authority, a great many people of a religious bent like to claim they are on their gods' side or, more vaingloriously, that the gods are on theirs. Accordingly, followers are able to spontaneously quote the gods' thoughts and intentions almost as if they were their very own. There can't be any higher authority than the founder and sole stockholder of the universe, observing the minutiae of daily ritual in thousands of billions of galaxies, each with hundreds of billions of stars, each possibly with dozens of planets, and potentially dozens of competing faiths on each inhabited planet.[16] Luckily, here, those omnipotent, preoccupied deities have Earthly followers and priests to publish and enforce their views on:

> Meat products, food preparation and storage, cartoons, foreskins, working on a designated rest days, contraception, driving licences, marriage, astronomy, masturbation, divorce, alcohol, religious brand-switching, murder, seasonal celebrations, coming of age, admission into the eternal celestial hereafter, corpse disposal, shaving, homosexuality, television, architecture, footwear, monarchs, loans and interest rates, castration, political parties, honour, virginity, wealth, slavery, shellfish, appropriate forms of execution, cross dressing, buying forgiveness for sins, popular music… and so many more things.

And that's just the Abrahamic[17] traditions on one planet around one star. With 4×10^{23} stars in the observable universe, no wonder the gods have to ordain local voyeurs to keep us from assured perdition. (See *reductio ad absurdum*.)

Depending on which flavour of religion you pick, here are some examples of what the creator has taught us:[18]

> Everyone was symmetrical until a meteorite landed and made human hearts move to the left and stopped us from being ambidextrous.

> Sacred underpants will save you from sin and speeding bullets.

> The essential pillars of the church are abortion, cannibalism, sodomy and suicide.

The authority just rings through, doesn't it? If I were a prophet, I'd say my deity wants everyone to do whatever they like that hurts no-one else. There. That makes me an authority figure.

---

[16] The estimated number of galaxies is now one to two trillion.

[17] Monotheistic, West Asian religions, primarily Judaism, Christianity and Islam.

[18] Fire up your favourite search engine. None of these is fictional.

Common sense – appeal to

One of the most frequent arguments used is that something makes common sense. It's usually a belief that's plausible on the surface, but with no guarantee to be more robust than a proverb or old wives' tale.

It's a first cousin to the bandwagon fallacy, but without the connotation of popularity. Common sense alludes to the vague idea of blinding obviousness. It seems to strike a chord with our personal experience. We instinctively *know* common sense things without needing to study or learn.

> "'Wiring a plug is just common sense," said Uncle Billy.
> Fortunately, the fire brigade arrived quickly.'

Common sense isn't necessarily backed up with fact or reason, which makes it an unreliable basis for arguments and conclusions. Common sense is an important supplier of confirmation bias, in which we prefer to credit what we believe already.

Common sense also disguises bald assertions, making them seem naturally correct and logical.

> "'Dozens of pubs are closing every week," said the brewery chairman, "It's common sense that the government's policy of excessively taxing beer and wine is shutting down a precious way of life in the UK. Obviously, people buy their favourite drinks at the supermarket."'

Taxation doesn't help, but supermarket booze is taxed at the same eye-watering level as pubs'. The chairman is careful to avoid mentioning the less obvious 'pub tie', which sees pub landlords paying a full commercial rent for their premises, plus a contractual obligation to buy beer, wine and spirits at two to three times the price paid by free houses. It's a deliberate policy of 'sweating the channel' to ensure the maximum return to pub owners and brewers.

The rate of pub closures confirms that the business model for tenanted pubs is unsustainable. The UK's licensed trade is kept afloat by a steady supply of inexperienced, first-time landlords 'investing' their redundancy pay-off or their pension lump-sum in the hope of a continuing income after retirement.

The common sense fallacy is usually sprinkled with phrases like *obviously, we all know, everyone accepts,* and so on. While common sense may be adequate for everyday situations, it's not a good basis for sound reasoning, and not useful for complex problems.

Faith – appeal to

Politicians of the world are masters at getting people to do or accept what they want, sometimes without the inconvenience of elections and voting. They know that people get swept up in rhetorical slogans and emotional appeals. Totalitarian political systems insist on unswerving allegiance to a political ideology. To debate the correctness of the founding despot is to invite a death sentence. Political dogma and the threat of oblivion seem to go hand in hand – a sort of appeal to involuntary faith, if you like.

Organised religions are scarcely better. Reasoning is not only redundant, it is discouraged – quite strongly, if you consider ritual murder a powerful statement of disapproval. Any belief, no matter how spurious, trumps solid fact where faith is concerned. There's nothing quite as persuasive as being able to call in your chosen deity in support of your argument, like some kind of celestial bodyguard (see *appeal to authority*):

> "Earth orbits the Sun, Signor Galileo? God disagrees. You can make observations with your little telescope and reason as much as you like, so long as you don't mind being burned to death, then burning in hell for all eternity. Your choice."

Faith means taking someone's word for it, believing them, trusting them. You don't ask for verification of any claim or statement – teaching or doctrine. According to the Catholic catechism:

> Faith is a supernatural gift of God, which enables us to believe without doubting whatever God has revealed.

Faith, no matter which deity is cracking the whip, is the denial of evidence, reason and proof. *Without doubting* means no challenging, questioning, demanding data, testing for reason or logic, and no being insubordinate to the deity's representatives on Earth. You can't help but feel the representatives slipped that one in themselves without troubling their deity for its thoughts on the matter. After all, what's the point in being an acolyte for the most powerful being in the universe if you can't command a bit of respect among the masses. Plus, you get to reveal what the deity thinks. As the sole mouthpiece of divine thinking, you're in a comfy position to support or undermine the attitude, morals or behaviour of your fellow mortals, fully sanctioned by the creator of the universe. Mostly, it seems, the deity wants mortals to give money and status to its Earthly representatives. This saves the omnipotent creator the irksome chore of setting up its own payroll system and pension plan. (See *appeal to ridicule*.)

An appeal to faith is a poor argument, one that claims that certain facts are true simply because some people believe it. These facts might be political ideology or religious doctrine, from the loftiest theological concept to the trivia of daily life, but no supporting evidence, they count no more strongly than an opinion or anecdote.

Because reasoning is off-limits, all appeals to faith are literally unreasonable. Which is a pity, because some of the buildings are nice.

6. PERSONAL ATTACK — AD HOMINEM

More Latin: ad hominem means against the person. Instead of countering your argument, an opponent launches a personal attack on you. The idea is to undermine you as a person, and thereby your argument. It's not persuasive, and therefore not a successful argument in itself.

But the intention is to put you on the back foot, to make you defensive, and if possible to make you lose your composure. It's a facet of rhetoric since before the mists of time itself. The fact that it endures means it's both part of human nature to throw barbs at opponents, and that it works. Personal attacks come in a range of flavours, some less subtle than others.

Personal attack

Mostly, personal attacks do nothing to help or rebut an argument. They take the form of derogatory remarks about the person arguing against them. For example:

> "It's all very well for an Eton-educated, multi-millionaire prime minister to say food banks aren't needed. He's a toff – what would he know about ordinary people?"

> "That comedian's political ideas might be more worthy of consideration if he weren't so ignorant, offensive or unfunny."

> "There's an article here that says... Never mind, it's the Daily Fail."

However satisfying, pointing out the double-standards, personal history and duplicity of an opponent doesn't deal with their argument itself. It's not poor reasoning – it's an absence of reasoning. Despite the manifest failings of our prime ministers, comedians and popular press, the points they make may be good and valid. After all:

> Not only out of the mouths of babes and sucklings, but out of the mouths of fools and cheats, we may often get our truest lessons.[19]

---

[19] *The Professor at the Breakfast Table,* 1859 – Oliver Wendell Holmes.

People launch personal attacks when they don't have a good counter-argument to hand. If they had a more cogent argument, they'd use it. Tactically, personal attacks can work. They put you off your stride and make you look like an idiot when you lose your temper.

However tempting, avoid joining in. If you do, both of you look petty, and listeners will put you and your opponent both in the same box and a plague on both your houses. Instead, focus back on the nub of the argument:

> "Let's put the personal attacks to one side. Food banks: yes, no or maybe, and why?"

> "I'll ignore the personal insults, because you still haven't explained why we have to stop doing…"

Of course, personal abuse that doesn't try to undermine someone's argument is just personal abuse. Some commentators refer to this as an ad personam attack, although ad hominem and ad personam mean more or less the same thing. Even if satisfying, it's not effective as far as the argument goes. Compare and contrast:

> "This proposal from the person who gave us last year's less-than-triumphant chocolate-covered spinach." [ad hominem]

> "Are you serious? Wait, are you drunk again? Come here let me smell your breath!" [personal abuse]

> "You're a porridge-brained cockwomble!" [personal abuse]

> "How can you even think that stupidly? Do you have an extra chromosome or something?" [personal abuse]

In these examples, we see ad hominem attacks blended with personal abuse, personal incredulity and colourful language. Debate doesn't have to be dull, after all.

Circumstantial attack

Sometimes people just want to find reasons not to believe or trust you. In this type of fallacy, they pick on your personal circumstances. Your opponent accuses you of being biased, of enjoying a position that favours you, and conclude that because of this, your statement, advice, recommendation, proposal, conclusion or argument must be wrong.

> Tyre fitter: This brand is the most reliable and hardest-wearing."

Customer: "That's hard to believe. You just want to sell me the most expensive tyres you've got. Find me the really most reliable and hard-wearing."

While it's true that every sales person has some skin in the game – we all know how sales commission works – that doesn't necessarily invalidate their recommendation. You can't assume everyone selling you things is lying through their teeth. It's just as likely they know their products and can make a fair recommendation for what you need.

"Of course, the town councillor is arguing in favour of the development, she owns property on that site."

Again, people who stand to gain financially from a particular stance are likely to back their personal interest. But if they put forward a reasoned argument why a proposal should be accepted, it's not unsound simply because of their interest. Of course, it would be better if people who were thus involved were to declare an interest and stand down from any decision. But that might be to expect too high a level of honour in local politics. (See *judgemental language*.)

"Of course the HR director is pitching for a bigger training budget. She's not above a bit of empire building."

In business, people put their department forward for more resources all the time. Decisions are (usually) based on whether that investment advances the business better than another. A department head can't be ruled out automatically on the grounds of conflict of interest since they are responsible for promoting the interests of their department.

Motive – appeal to

Any time you see a product in a film or in a television programme, the chances are someone paid to have it appear. Whenever a politician speaks in favour of some policy, it probably supports the party line – the politician wants to appear loyal. If a newspaper column takes the time to single out an individual for lavish praise, it's likely that the beneficiary has a connection to the editor or owner. Without wishing to sound overly cynical, the world is a venal place, and everyone and everything has a price.

Consequently, it's always tempting to dismiss an opponent's argument because of their motives:

"The judge is biased; she studied law at the same college as the defence counsel."

"There's a glowing review of the new musical right beside a half-page advert for, guess what? That must have been an easy piece to write. I bet the show is rubbish."

"This book reviewer gives five stars to the new novel by... oh, look, it's his girlfriend."

You can never assume bias is certain, because some individuals are fiercely honest and independent. But fair-minded people think the slightest chance of motive might be sufficient to sully the honesty or openness of a situation. For that reason, neutral referees are used in sports, even though officials are quite capable of refereeing without preference. The assumption of bias is so ingrained (especially by fans), that sports' governing bodies try to remove any possibility of partiality, real or imagined.

In presenting an argument or supporting a position, it's good practice for people to declare any interest, notifying the other participants of any possible conflict, and stepping aside from an active part in the decision itself. In legal cases this is called recusing oneself. In most other situations, honour is a rare commodity.

Bulverism

This quaintly-termed fallacy was described by C. S. Lewis in the 1940s.[20] It also goes under the distinctly charmless moniker: the psychogenetic fallacy.

It's similar to a circumstantial attack or an appeal to motive. Here, though, you claim an argument is wrong for irrelevant personal reasons of your opponent, rather than explain why it's unsound. For instance:

"You say people with red hair have two copies of a recessive gene on chromosome 16? You're only saying that because you're Scottish."

"No way there are over 400 castles in Wales. Doesn't your wife work for the tourist authority?"

---

[20] CS Lewis invented its inventor, Bulver, much as an Oscar Wilde character created a imaginary friend, Bunbury in *The Importance of Being Ernest.*

"Of course he wants our votes, he's got a huge mortgage to pay."

"No, he's not just marrying her for her money. You're only saying that because you're broke yourself."

"Of course he's in favour of more immigration, his grandfather was Venezuelan."

The argument tries to establish that something is true or false for some unrelated personal reason. It makes conversation a little surreal.

It's a fun little fallacy, if a little obscure, with a lot of potential entertainment value. In theory, any statement can be challenged, regardless of factual accuracy, with an aspersion about the speaker's deep-seated thinking. It's fair to say it reveals more about what's uppermost on the speaker's mind than about the argument in play. As you'd imagine, Bulverism lends itself to some spectacularly left-field red herrings. (See *appeal to motive*.)

Tarred with the same brush

Guilt by association is another name for this fallacy. Here, you reject a fact or argument put forward by someone simply because they belong to a group or political party (or shares some of the views of such an organisation) which is itself already poorly thought of.

"Frank believes that the island of Ireland should be one, united, free country. That's the same aim pursued by the IRA. We can't take Frank's political views on housing seriously."

"Charlie swears blind he didn't steal your golf clubs. But how can you believe someone whose father's in prison?"

"Father Michael advocates tolerance of other faiths. Well, that's nonsense. You can't leave his type alone with your children."

Personal prejudice creeps into many everyday areas. We agree with statements we like from people we admire, and dismiss whatever is said by anyone who irritates us. (See *confirmation bias*.) It's all too human, but arguments based on prejudice carry little weight. As the expression goes:

Prejudice is the reasoning of fools.

Which in itself may be an ad hominem attack on a group we all belong to.

Tu quoque

Tu quoque (more Latin, pronounced too kwo kway) means "you too". Picture someone in a dispute, hands on hips, saying, "Well, you're a fine one to talk..." It's a feature of angry exchanges the world over. For instance:

> 'The doctor told Cousin Bernard that he was overweight; he should eat less and exercise more. Bernard snapped back, "You don't look like you skipped too many puddings yourself." Cousin Bernard has a new doctor now.'

We get cross. We lose our temper. The cheek of some people accusing us of... Instead of dealing with the substance of their charge, we accuse them of hypocrisy.

Of course, it's not a persuasive way to make your case. Just because a doctor is fond of a pie or two, and perhaps a ladle of creamy custard, it doesn't invalidate the advice she gives a patient. If you ever find yourself in the position of having to lecture anyone on the perils of something you're personally fond of doing, it's probably best to kick off with: "Do as I say, not do as I do." At least that gets their comeback out of the way.

Organisations that should know better fall into the tu quoque frame of mind.

> The USSR was repeatedly accused of violating human rights. Its government responded to the USA: You execute mentally-ill people. To the UK: Your history is an encyclopaedia of imperial aggression and invasion.

These remarks may have been true, but irrelevant to the state of human rights in the Soviet Union. The English phrase: "pot calling the kettle black." has many equivalents in other languages, because the tu quoque tactic seems to be universal, as does its first cousin, two wrongs.

The tu quoque fallacy is an appeal to hypocrisy. There are situations when an accuser is indeed being hypocritical, in which case it doesn't harm your rebuttal to point it out.

In 2015, Apple CEO Tim Cook accused the people involved in

making a film about the corporation's late boss, Steve Jobs, of being "opportunistic". The film's writer, Aaron Sorkin, responded: "If you've got a factory full of children in China assembling phones for 17 cents an hour, you've got a lot of nerve calling someone else opportunistic."

Touché! Sorkin's remark doesn't refute the opportunism charge, but his point about hypocrisy was a telling blow, and proof – if any were needed – that people in Apple Glass houses shouldn't throw stones. (See *appeal to ridicule*.)

A subset of the tu quoque (where it collides with the appeal to bigger problems) is the fallacy of compulsory contextualisation. This wordy trendsetter arises when the topic – usually a person or event – is taken out of its immediate context and portrayed in the most extreme light. For instance:

"We can't commemorate the holocaust in Germany because the state of Israel came about through terrorist acts."

"People shouldn't enjoy the music of Eric Clapton because in 1976 when he was onstage and visibly intoxicated, he made controversial remarks about immigration."

"It's wrong to commemorate British Army deaths given the events of Bloody Sunday."

"We shouldn't pick that player for the England team because he once scored an own-goal."

"I don't want to hear their music because they supported the Republicans."

Sometimes the faults linked to are instances of false equivalence. The fallacy operates by taking any subject under discussion, broadening the context until it encompasses something adverse, declaring this to be of equal or superior importance, and sufficient reason to reject the argument.

Poisoning the well

Sometimes we just can't wait to get the boot into our opponent. Why hang around to hear the argument put forward when we can scupper their chances before the debate or hearing?

"You're lucky to get Kate to speak to your conference,

considering she's been on anxiety medication for months."

"Yes, let's put Angus in charge of this vital project. After all, he's been in the organisation for five minutes now and must know his way through Reception."

"It's very understanding of you to give Gary a place in the team. I believe he's good friends with your wife."

"This could be an informative meeting; I bet Maureen learned a lot in prison."

"Artemis is driving you to the airport? He's a wonderfully safe driver. Obviously we keep the sherry under lock and key."

Poisoning the well is a specific form of ad hominem attack. You pass unfavourable – true or false, it doesn't matter – comments about a person before they get started on some activity. You imply is that the person can't be relied upon or their opinion trusted.

Poisoning the well is a popular tactic with religious zealots:

I've told you what our holy book says. Anyone who disagrees with the word of the prophets is a sinner, an apostate, and will burn for all eternity in hell. Wait, I can smell smoke already! Would you give a second's thought to the lies of a sinner? Well, let's listen to this godless atheist.

Next speaker, please, and good luck.

Accomplishment – appeal to

We all do it. You're listening to some big-head spouting off, bashing you with their opinion, telling you how to do things better. You snap:

"I was fascinated to read your review of my play as you've had so many Broadway hits yourself... Oh, wait. You've never written a play?"

"Let me know when you've built your own business up from scratch, then you can talk to me about salesmanship."

"You can tell me about education, Minister, when you've actually taught a class of year-4 children for ten years. Of course, you'd have to qualify as a teacher first And pass a police background check to work with children. I can wait."

"You say our striker is rubbish. I don't see you wearing an England shirt."

"What do you know about bringing up kids? You don't have any."

"Welcome to your first day at the Ministry of Defence, Minister. We'll be delighted to hear your opinion on all the things we're doing wrong, just as soon as you learn which way to point a gun."

Alas, it's a weak argument. Whatever opinion or recommendation you opponent makes can be perfectly sound, even if they lack some personal qualification that you see as important.

An appeal to (lack of) accomplishment is an ad hominem and sits alongside appeal to authority. It's a claim to some superior authority by dint of accomplishing something your opponent has not.

The unavoidable fact is, however, that sooner or later many of us find ourselves at work answering to an individual with little or no experience in the practical operations of our part of the organisation. Yes, it's important to manage your manager, and sometimes you just have to remind him or her not to assume their brief insight is a diamond-encrusted missile of logic just because they find themselves one rung further up the corporate ladder. However, riffing on their shortcomings may not be a endearing way to make your point. In the longer term. Just saying.

7. THE WHOLE TRUTH (NOT)

Facts are inconvenient. They get in the way of our finely honed arguments, our neat arrays of evidence, our strongly held opinions. Sometimes it helps our case if we forget about some of the facts, and just use the ones that fit our not-so-carefully-arrived-at conclusion.

The problem is that evidence must be seen in the round, weighed, evaluated, sifted. To form a fair conclusion, or at least a cogent one, all the relevant information should be included in the process, for and against.

Prosecutors only present evidence that supports their case against a defendant – it's up to the defence to point out weaknesses in it and present contradictory points. But it's wrong for prosecutors to actively conceal evidence from the defence. In fact, in many jurisdictions it's grounds for appeal against conviction.

In the same way, being selective about the facts might help our argument, but it invalidates the result. But still we do it. In this section, we'll look at the main ways people avoid telling the whole truth.

Cherry picking

We have to be selective about the information we put forward. Life is too short, the world too complex for all the exhaustive detail that even minor events stir up. So reports should contain all the material facts and omit small points that don't affect the conclusion.

We form an opinion from things we witness or learn. But using identical facts, other people can easily reach a different conclusion. Facts can support several points of view. So we tend to select the details that support our case and ignore the rest, no matter how important or germane to our conclusion. We are cherry picking.

We all do it. The average curriculum vitae (CV, or résumé) is a concerto of cherry picking. Great job titles, prestigious employers, and sterling achievements all shine through. But no mention of poor punctuality, long liquid lunches or the somewhat pricey incident with the catering lorry and the aircraft fuselage.

We like to pretend our conclusions are based on facts, carefully sifted, weighed, considered. More than not, we choose what we want the truth to be, then we marshal the supporting arguments. It's called ex post facto rationalisation – finding the reason after the decision.

It's part of the rough and tumble of fair debate to cherry pick facts and examples to support your argument. If they're smart enough, your opponents will find other information and use it to try and prove you wrong. But from time to time you'll stumble over people intentionally fiddling some fact-gathering process to generate only information that supports their pre-ordained conclusion.

Faking scientific or medical results by using selective data is wrong, but it happens. One industry in particular is notorious for sweeping inconvenient research under the carpet – the pharmaceutical industry. Up to half of all clinical trials of drugs are not reported at all.[21]

Equally, advocates of alternative medicine (including acupuncture, aromatherapy, chiropractice, crystal healing, faith healing, homeopathy, osteopathy, and so on) resolutely ignore the 99 per cent of research reports by qualified researchers which confirm that alternative therapy is harmless nonsense at best, or downright dangerous at worst. Well, they're doing their best to earn a living.

Exposing bad science and its effects on the public is a vital task – too important to ignore, but too detailed for this book. I urge you to read further and to take up cudgels alongside campaigners for scientific integrity.[22]

Back to picking cherries. You can cherry pick results, or you can cherry pick the sampling. Both lead to the outcome you prefer:

> Once upon a time, a manager complained about cigarette smoke permeating a moveable partition wall from the firm's smoking room into his department next door. (Yes, smoking indoors, in a

---

[21] The Alltrials Campaign is fighting to have all clinical trials registered and all results reported. Many hundreds of credible organisations support these efforts. The only notable opponents are the bodies representing European and American Pharmaceutical companies.

[22] See www.badscience.net for hair-curling examples of scurrilous science. And if you want to be appalled by the shenanigans of boffins who really should live up to their qualifications, read the books *Bad Science* and *Bad Pharma*, both by Ben Goldacre.

cosy, fug-filled room –all day long!) Throughout the working week the pollution built up, making clothes, hair, belongings – everything in the department – reek. The firm grudgingly agreed to have a health inspector take measurements. And so at 8.00 am on a Monday morning following a weekend during which the building had been utterly devoid of staff, smoking or otherwise, the inspector took his readings, and pronounced the office unpolluted.[23] And yet it was.

Organisations and people concentrate on the data that confirms what they want to see. Confirmation bias is prevalent and expected in public debates, where speakers shape their arguments by choosing the evidence that supports their case. In the modern world, there is always evidence somewhere to support every case. (See *Texas sharpshooter.*)

Suppressing legal evidence is cherry picking of the most grievous kind:

In January 2015 the foreman of a jury that convicted a nurse of serial killing[24] recanted, saying had he known all the evidence, he would have acquitted the defendant. One crucial piece of inconvenient evidence that detectives failed to act on was that an additional victim died in an identical way, but at a time when the defendant had an alibi. Police failed to investigate and prosecutors failed to present all the evidence, a highly relevant part of which would have been helpful to the defence.

Using anecdotal evidence is a form of cherry picking, because you ignore all the research that says, for example, smoking is bad for you and defer to the ancestor who puffed away until 90, or your cousin who never dragged on a cigarette in his life but died of lung cancer at 30.

We remember remarkable examples, not typical ones because of a phenomenon called *misleading vividness*.) Almost every yarn about one individual bucking the trend, evading science, defying medicine or some other extraordinary outlier behaviour is at best an exaggeration, and probably part fiction. But even if true to the very letter, personal

---

[23] Yes, I was that manager, and the firm was an HR management consultancy that should have known much, much better.

[24] Colin Norris was convicted of four patient murders in 2008.

anecdotes are never typical or representative unless they are paired with reliable statistical support. People are good at spotting patterns and forming analogies, but poor at assessing probability and prevalence.

Presenting someone with a false dichotomy ("yes or no") is a form of cherry picking. So is offering proof by example.

Sampling bias

The fun and carefree world of market research[25] is built on statistical generalisation. If you want to know what people think about a new product, you'd ask them all. That is, you'd carry out a census of the full population. Practicality being what it is, though, you pick a representative sample of the type of people you're interested in, ask them, and extrapolate the results. The answers you get will be accurate plus or minus a few percentage points (depending on the size of the sample and number of possible answers), and should give you a fair reading of how your product will fare in the wider market.

The key word is "representative":

> We asked a dozen voters in Henley-on-Thames, Tunbridge Wells and Chelsea how they intend to vote in the general election. We're predicting an absolute landslide for the Middle-Class With Nice Homes Party.

If an opinion poll sample isn't representative, the forecast won't be sound (even though it might coincidentally predict the eventual outcome). These days, opinion polls use pretty robust sampling, but forecasts can still be spectacularly wrong.[26] It seems we lie through our teeth to opinion pollsters.

Even when you go to the trouble of carrying out a formal survey, you can still come unstuck with the results. Your sample might be biased because it doesn't include enough (or too many) of some characteristics that are part of the population you're examining. This

---

[25] These days it's often called "Customer Insights", which sounds like some specialists in the marketing department want a pay rise.

[26] The UK's EU Referendum and the US Presidential Election results in 2016 were not the pollsters' finest hours.

skews your results, and makes them unreliable. You can't then generalise the findings to the whole population.

If you want information about beer preferences, a survey in a country village micro-pub will be heavy with real ale drinkers and light on lager fans. In town centre bars, the reverse will apply. True story:

> A market research operative once went into a rough-looking pub on an estate to ask what kinds of wine they sold. "Both," came the reply.

You can skew results of surveys by asking leading questions that point people in the 'right' direction:

> How delighted were you with our service?

Loaded language, too, is emotionally charged or leans on people to choose socially desirable answers:

> Do you condone the murder of whales?

> Should we buy foreign goods that take away British jobs?

In the UK 2016 referendum on EU membership, the prime minister agreed to change the wording of the ballot. At first, the question was:

> Should the United Kingdom remain a member of the European Union?

> The answers open to voters were *yes* or *no*.

The Electoral Commission thought there might be a perception of bias in a yes / no answer, and suggested more neutral wording:

> Should the United Kingdom remain a member of the European Union or leave the European Union?

> The answers on the ballot were changed to: Remain a member of the European Union or Leave the European Union.

Market research agencies are pros at building samples and, if needed, applying weightings to ramp up or tone down under- or over-represented classes. They can draft questions that will elicit the most accurate information from your chosen population. If you're staking millions of pounds or piastres on some new endeavour, get experts to help. Don't dump it on Zach, the unpaid marketing intern with a degree in art history.

When you're presented with the findings of a survey, find out who did it, then find out who they are. A pukka market research report should have the agency's credentials somewhere in it or online. There are, however, many academic-sounding bodies that are think-tanks for charitable ideologists, political parties or industry lobbyists. The UK alone has over a hundred Centres, Institutes, Foundations, Trusts, Societies, Research Groups, Forums, Networks and Exchanges – all with a mission and a purpose, and all funded by someone. It would be a fallacy to suggest all their research conclusions are at fault. (See *the fallacy fallacy.*) But when were the last findings published that ran counter to the sponsor's aims? Never, that's when.

A huge problem with sampling bias is self-selection, when the people you're studying choose whether to take part or not. Through social media, smart phones, tablets and laptops bring surveys to millions of potential respondents wherever they are. Online, phone-in and text polls are, by definition, self-selecting. But, as they're cheap and easy to set up, you'll see them everywhere.

Some people never touch them; others can't stop themselves. Individuals with a bee in their bonnet on a subject, or have a deeper knowledge, are apt to take part. They spend longer filling in answers and offer more verbatim opinions ("if yes, please explain..."). The apathetic just hit delete. Findings, consequently, lean towards strong or extreme points of view, which may be genuinely held, but not representative of a population.

So there's a lot of polling going on, but you wouldn't want to plan anything important on back of it. When a colleague tells you customer feedback says this or that, be sceptical, and satisfy yourself the findings are valid and robust. Remember that the burden of proof lies with the party asserting a claim. So you're not being a pain the neck for asking for verification; your colleague is being deficient for not offering it. You might want to keep that in mind for when a colleague complains about your attitude to your manager. Sooner or later, one will.

Special pleading

Rules are rules, right? They should apply to everyone without exception, yes?

Sometimes people try to overcome the inconvenience of a general principle or rule. They point out that this or that case is different or special, but they can't justify the claim convincingly. It's a bit like trying to move the goalposts, but that's another fallacy in its own right.

We all like a bit of self-interest:

> "Emergency vehicles are subject to the same laws as all other drivers. Quite right too. They should stick to speed limits at all times, unless it's my house on fire."

In our own mind, it's not a double standard; we're all that special little snowflake. We like to carve out exceptions for our circumstances, interests and beliefs. Special pleading can be the basis for a range of fallacies under the appeals to heading. Some folks feel they are important enough for the world to arrange itself obligingly in their favour. Then again, the rest of us like to bring "some folks" down a peg or two:

> "What do you mean the flight is over-booked? I must be on this flight. Don't you know who I am?"

Often special pleading is a spontaneous emotional outburst:

> "Why are you arresting my son? He's a good boy. He didn't do anything. He wouldn't harm a fly. He was led on by his friends. Arrest them."

Who wouldn't want to protect their child from serious consequences? But the bare assertion of a non-witness parent cuts no ice. In general, though, special pleading takes the form of a poorly thought-through or incomplete argument:

> Drugs should be illegal, but not cannabis. It's a natural plant.

Nice try, Lebowski, but so are opium poppies and coca bushes. A better argument for exception might be that cannabis helps a number of medical conditions when conventional medicine isn't working. That takes the discussion away from recreational use and in the direction of treatment and clinical trials and, you know, facts.

In statistics, massaging data and explaining away awkward and contrary results can be instances of special pleading:

> "You can see from the graph that in keeping with our employer-of-choice brand promise, we pay our staff well into the third quartile of industry remuneration."

> "What about that big cluster at the bottom?"

"They're zero-hour contracts. They don't count."

Being blandly dismissive scarcely qualifies as a justification for making the exception. Special pleading is a way of being selective about what should be included or excluded from a selection, in other words, a big, in-your-face piece of cherry picking.

Proof by example

My smoking room story in the section on cherry picking gives an example of suspiciously selective data collection, but it also serves as an example of inappropriate generalisation. My personal grudge cannot be taken as proof that management consultants are always self-interested, devious and manipulative. They have to sleep sometime.

Furnishing proof by example is also called inappropriate generalisation. One example, or several, cannot be used to invent a rule for all situations. It's one of the most common errors in reasoning in everyday conversation:

> "You can't trust dentists. There was an American one who killed a wild lion with a crossbow."

> "Next door's 18-year-old was convicted of dangerous driving. All young drivers drive too fast."

> "Foreign farm workers take all our houses. Uncle Billy's friend, Robert, had to move out of his house because the farmer who owns it wanted to let it to his Polish workers."

> 'My niece Trixie claimed the economy was going down the pan: "The tanning salon on the High Street's gone bust."'

However, in some circumstances, proof by example can be valid. A single instance can validate something that is generally accepted to be false. For instance, it was believed that a commercial airliner could never ditch safely on water. It had never been achieved despite several doomed attempts over the history of aviation. Then the so-called *Miracle on the Hudson* happened in 2009 when Flight 1549 made a perfect, unpowered emergency landing on a New York river, with no lives lost.

One example proves it can be done – even if it demands exceptional skill. This is a singular premise to an existential conclusion. In short, if one instance exists, the entire class exists:

"Flight 1549 landed safely on water. Therefore, it is possible for a commercial airliner to land safely on water."

"Valentina Tereshkova was the first woman in space. She proved women could become cosmonauts."

"England won the World Cup in 1966. Therefore, it is not impossible for England to win the World Cup."

It only seems that way.

8. Time Bombs

The passage of time seems to confuse us a little. It separates cause and effect. Time creates nostalgia for old traditions and ancient meanings. But we also enjoy the novelty of new things. Time brings order to our lives and activates our preferences. Accordingly, there are a number of logical fallacies in which time plays a starring role.

For instance, nowhere is sound reasoning more essential than in finding out why something went wrong. By uncovering the cause of a plane crash, factory collapse, skyscraper in flames, serious road accident, catastrophes large and small, we can find out who did what wrong, and try to make sure the disaster doesn't happen again.

In simple events, cause and effect are easy to identify. A ball hits a window; the window breaks. Using deductive reasoning, we'd be looking for a general rule to explain the events – mass of the ball, speed, direction, force, means of propulsion, breaking strain of the glass – giving us a guaranteed conclusion. Some combination of Newton's Laws of Motion and a double-glazing catalogue should cover it.

In abductive reasoning, premises don't provide a sure outcome. We'd observe the broken window and a ball among the shards, then form some hypothesis about what went on without necessarily establishing a relationship between cause and effect. It's a good way to speculate about many possible causes, both likely and remote.

What exactly has my nephew Cuthbert been up to, and where is the little tyke hiding, would be among my earliest speculations.

In the field of inductive reasoning, we make inferences. These aren't certain, so even if the inferences are strong and our argument is persuasive, we're not guaranteed to reach the right conclusion. We're wired to make inferences. We take cues from the time sequences that earlier events cause later effects. We look at movement and proximity to infer some relationship between objects and events.

But we get it wrong. We don't always understand the mechanisms working behind cause and effect, so we make the wrong inferences. We assume some things determine or are influenced by others. We allow what we want to blame to control our conclusions. No wonder, then, that time bomb non sequiturs lead to some of our worst decisions.

False or questionable cause – post hoc fallacy

Life has never been as simple as it looks. Most events are a complex interplay of mechanisms. Unfolding matters may take many paths, and all the actions we take influence them, sometimes greatly, other times hardly at all.

Causation (or cause and effect or causality) is the connection – some linkage or agency – between one thing (cause) and another (effect) where the first is at least partly responsible for the second event, and where the later is dependent on the earlier.

When man-made disasters strike, it's usually a cascade of things going wrong. Rather than point to single causes, it's frequently more accurate to talk of causal factors that contribute to ensuing events. But what causes what? Determining cause and effect challenges the finest minds, provoking controversy in fields as diverse as climate change, air accidents, the decriminalisation of drugs, obesity, cancer, war and religion.

Mention the word *cause* to most people and along come *blame*, *liability* and *compensation*, riding bareback on promises of untold riches from no-win no-fee lawyers. Cause and blame are not the same thing at all. Causes, like natural events, can just happen. Blame is about apportioning responsibility and establishing liability. If on television you see a representative of a victim's family saying:

"We need to find out what caused this tragedy."

... the subtitles should read:

"We're trying to work out who we can blame for the accident and sue them."

Faced with complexity, it's tempting to seek quick and simple answers, short cuts to save us wading through contradictory evidence. One of the first things we latch onto is that if event B happens after event A, then A must have caused B. You'll come across this Latin phrase (or a close variant):

Post hoc ergo propter hoc – after this, therefore because of it

A post hoc fallacy is to assume that an event that happens before another, causes it.

It snowed. Great Aunt Ruby suffered a power-cut. She claims the snowfall caused the power-cut.

Sounds fair, yes? Not really. You can't safely conclude that snow caused the power-cut. We need more detail about how a surge in demand might have led to a burn-out, or how weight of snow brought down overground cables. We need some agency or link between snowfall and the outage. Otherwise it might just be her main fuse that blew.

> Suppose a snowplough careered off the road into the power sub-station...

Did snow cause the skid? If so, now can we blame it for her power-cut?

> We learn the tyres on the snowplough were in a bad condition and one of them blew out.

So human negligence caused the accident. But wait, would the snowplough have been on the road passing the sub-station were it not for the snow?

> In the power-cut Great Aunt Ruby's freezer stopped and a lot of food spoiled.

Can she get compensation from someone? The driver of the snowplough? The tyre maintenance supervisor? The electricity company? Chione, the Greek goddess of snow? Law tries to establish liability, which is a thornier issue than factual cause and effect. Liability means being answerable or financially responsible for some loss or damage, a sort of blame plus money. Legal discussion would bring in questions including:

> Is there a direct chain of causation between some fault and the loss to Great Aunt Ruby? Was some duty of care owed to her specifically or as a member of the public in general? Did someone fail in that duty? Was the spoiled food foreseeable as a result? What should she have done to minimise her losses – like storing the frozen food in a snowdrift or in the boot of a car parked outside?

I bet there are lawyers who'd try for compensation for the anguish of losing her frozen Yorkshire puddings.

Let's talk about causation and booze:

> Arguing for stiffer penalties and a zero level of alcohol for drink driving, a campaigner quotes government figures that alcohol was a factor in 14 per cent of road deaths in Britain. "Drink driving causes deaths" is the campaign slogan.[27]

Here, we are plainly intended to rage about drink driving. To be honest, it has few advocates. The statistic studiously avoids stating that drunk drivers were the cause of 14 per cent of deaths. But we are being stampeded towards that inference by the slogan.

The actual UK Government statistic is that in 14 per cent of road accident deaths (around 240 fatalities a year) at least one of the drivers was over the legal limit. That's not quite the same as saying drunk drivers caused 14 per cent of road deaths. Given the premise, we must admit the possibility that the driver at fault for an accident could have been sober, while the victim driver was the one over the limit.

Nevertheless, we are being invited to conclude that an amount of alcohol in one of the drivers led to the deaths. However, it is equally true that 86 per cent of road deaths happened without unlawful amounts of booze involved.[28] For the purpose of causal dependence[29], we can only attribute to drink driving those deaths that would not happen but for the driver at fault being over the limit. This requires some counter-factual thinking:[30]

What if we wound back time, extracted the booze from the drivers, then set them off on their journey again. Would the fatality still occur?

---

[27] Department of Transport – Reported Road Casualties Great Britain 2014 Annual Report.

[28] The factors most commonly reported by police are *failing to look properly* – 44 per cent of all accidents – and *loss of control* – 32 per cent

[29] *Causation* – David Lewis (1973): an event E *causally depends* on a cause C if, and only if, (i) if C had occurred, then E would have occurred, and (ii) if C had not occurred, then E would not have occurred.

[30] Counterfactual thinking is to re-imagine different outcomes of events that have already taken place. Counterfactual means *counter to the facts. What if?* and *If only…* musings and regrets are examples.

We can never know the answer, which means we can only infer alcohol was a factor, not the sole cause. (See *single cause fallacy*.) So road death is not a necessary consequence of drink driving (because not every instance of drink driving causes a death – please don't try to prove me right!). Nor is drink driving a necessary cause (because 86 per cent of road deaths don't involve drink). In reasoning, necessity is a condition that one thing must be true for another to be true. For instance:

> In the UK a driver must be at least 17 years old to hold a licence.
> It follows that if you have a licence, you are at least 17 years old.

We can also conclude that drink driving is not a sufficient cause of road death as we can't conclude that because a driver was over the limit a death inevitably occurred. In reasoning, sufficiency is the case when one thing guarantees another thing to be true. For example:

> The phrase "Jane is an actress" implies that Jane is female.
> Knowing Jane is an actress is enough to conclude Jane is female.

So we have to conclude that drink driving is a contributory cause, of road deaths alongside other factors such as failing to look properly and loss of control, which are reported by police as the main overall factors in accidents.

Back to our campaigner. The slogan is technically incorrect. "Drink driving contributes to road deaths" would be more accurate, if a little less snappy. It is enough for criminal prosecution that a driver be over the limit and in possession of a set of car keys (and, presumably, a car?). But from a reasoning standpoint, until he uses the keys to start the car, a drinker is only a danger to his liver.

So, whenever you see headlines screaming that one thing caused another, ask yourself: did it cause or contribute? It shouldn't be that hard for our informers to get it right. After all, proving causation itself should be a straightforward matter of fact and reasoning. But it gets murky when you have an emotive topic, and causation needs expert research in a field most of us couldn't begin to fathom. Which leads us to the notorious MMR jab-causes-autism myth:

> In 1998 a single doctor published a paper in a medical journal claiming the MMR vaccination caused autism. It later emerged that lawyers had paid over £400,000 for the "expert opinion" to

help them sue vaccine makers. The lawyers had clients who claimed their child had been diagnosed with autism after getting the MMR jab. It took 12 years for the medical journal to fully retract the story. Meanwhile anti-vaccine campaigns sprang up around the world, law suits kicked off and, predictably, measles epidemics blossomed. A massive amount of research concluded that while vaccines can produce side effects, autism isn't one of them. The original medic was barred from practising medicine. The lawyers who paid for the fraud in the first place? Who knows.

Incredibly, the anti-vaccine farce still rumbles on. It must be tempting for parents to blame any unsettling symptoms on earlier events in their children's lives rather than accept a naturally-occurring condition. But it's illogical to assume that an earlier treatment must necessarily cause the later problem. Reasoning is further muddied when lawyers, doctors and vaccine makers come together in some finger-pointing alchemy designed to turn parents' anxiety into money.

Correlation does not imply causation – cum hoc fallacy

The second big time-based mistake we make in reasoning is to assume that two things happening together must inevitably be linked. More Latin:

Cum hoc ergo propter hoc – with this, therefore because of it

On a practical day-to-day level, it sounds intuitive.

"I find some half-eaten onions in the kitchen and pet barf all over the rug. I conclude that Towser attacked the onions, and the onions took their revenge."

Well, I wouldn't smell Towser's breath to check, but you might reasonably infer that the hound has been supplementing its diet. The two facts may be connected. But let's not jump to conclusions – they don't have to be. In the wider world, we humans have tried to find meaningful connections between things since the dawn of reason:

"The ground shakes. There's a rumbling noise. The house falls down. Next time I'm getting out of the house quick."

We want to connect things both to understand them better and to predict when events will happen. The process of testing the relationship is correlation. Correlation is a relationship between two variables in which one thing depends on another.

Let's repeat that for emphasis: correlation is about establishing if one thing depends on another, not whether something caused another.

In winter, ice cream sales fall. (Demand and temperature.)

Low-cost air tickets greatly increase passenger numbers. (Demand and price.)

Auction values of vintage motor cars shoot up. (Price and rarity.)

Correlation is extremely useful in predicting likely future variables. If you're planning to sell swimming costumes or generate electricity, a look at the calendar and weather forecast will help. To see if there is a dependency, we compare information to see if there is a linear relationship between variables. But even a mathematical relationship is no guarantee of dependency:

A rise in knife crime in the UK correlates strongly with the growth in banana imports. To end the violence, the Home Office clamps down on banana wholesalers.

A rise in knife crime in the UK correlates strongly with the growth in banana imports. To encourage sales, banana shippers scatter daggers on street corners.

Neither makes sense. Here are some real examples where events have a strong mathematical correlation.[31] You'd have to be clinically insane to conclude that either actually caused or depended on the other:

The number of UK citizens who emigrated to America correlates strongly with US uranium exports.

In the USA, per capita consumption of mozzarella cheese correlates to the number of civil engineering doctorates awarded.

The number of films starring Nicholas Cage per year correlates strongly with the number of female editors of the Harvard Law Review.

Look hard and you can find matching data for anything. Are they dependently linked? Only if your medication is strong enough. You must

---

[31] These examples feature on the wonderful *tylervigen.com*.

always challenge the coincidence of numbers. (See *Texas sharpshooter fallacy*.) Yes, it's a slothful induction to argue coincidence in the face of persuasive evidence, but we need to see some credible link to give the numbers persuasive force.

There doesn't have to be a causal link between the two because – spoiler alert! – correlation does not imply causation. Yes, causal relations can exist between two things, but the causes underlying the correlation may be unknown, indirect or fanciful.

We might find a causal relationship between personal wealth and an individual's carbon footprint. But is there a correlation between wealth and happiness? Does one cause the other? Are rich people happy? Are happy people rich? Or are poor people just as cheerful? If so, could it be that good health and happiness correlate, rich or poor?

A strong mathematical correlation between wealth, happiness or health might offer some evidence of causation, but it can't establish causality conclusively.

Remember our drink driving campaigner from earlier who wants two changes? We agreed there's a causal link between unlawful drink driving and road fatalities. But which of the two demands – stiffer penalties or lower limits – works?

Since 2000, UK road deaths overall have fallen by half, but alcohol remains a factor in roughly the same percentage of cases, despite increasingly severe penalties for drink driving offences. Tougher penalties don't seem to have worked. We see no correlation. So the claim that more stringent drink driving penalties alone would lead to a fall in road deaths is not persuasive. There's an argument that stiffer penalties aren't needed for those who obey the law, and they won't deter those who don't.

A stronger factor appears to be a fall in overall accident numbers. If drink driving fatalities are constant at 14 per cent, cutting total fatalities might filter through. Better driver training, safer vehicles, safer road design, more traffic calming (more traffic jams!) have all contributed to a general fall in road deaths. This, coupled with more socially responsible attitudes towards drink driving, may have warmed the public to accept stricter laws, which encouraged opportunist politicians to pass them. Thus it might even be a wrong direction fallacy to argue that stiffer penalties cut drink driving road deaths.

However, the introduction of Blood Alcohol Concentration limits and roadside breath testing in the late 1960s saw an immediate fall in fatal accidents where alcohol was a factor – from 25 per cent to 15 per cent in the first year. That's a strong correlation between the introduction of drink driving limits and their vigorous enforcement with the incidence of drink-related road deaths.

Our conclusion to the anti-drink driving campaigner's claims should be that stiffer penalties are not the answer, but lowering the alcohol limits and conspicuously enforcing them would cut the incidence of drink driving fatalities.

Juxtaposition

How does this read to you?

Unemployment is rising, so is infant mortality.

Does unemployment cause infant mortality? Does infant mortality lead to job losses? Does something else cause them both as a common effect? Juxtaposition is an interesting card in the questionable cause deck. Two statements dealt alongside each other; seemingly one implies or is related to the other. The juxtaposition begs you to reach that conclusion. But you need much more evidence, including information about what else could be involved. Can we assume the premises are robust in the first place? Show me growing numbers of unemployed people and I'll find a statistician who'll prove to you that unemployment is falling. Then the vexed question of correlation and dependency. Consider this more familiar juxtaposition:

More high street shops are closing. Home deliveries are on the rise.

Are they two idle thoughts out for a walk? Are we to infer one depends on the other? If so, which way round? Perhaps both trends arose separately, or they are symptoms of a third factor which caused both? Perhaps internet growth and online shopping explains both. Perhaps there is a sequence of part causes:

Internet activity leads to... more online shopping leads to... more home deliveries leads to... high street shops closing leads to... internet activity...

We know intuitively that the internet has spawned a great many changes. Home delivery activity depends on online shopping. The card recycling industry depends on home delivery. It looks like some sort of correlation. But there's rarely a clear-cut model of correlation and dependency because the world is too complex. If you find yourself juggling arguments about closely-related phenomena, be careful to stay away from circular reasoning. (See *causal homeostasis*.)

> More high street shops are closing, so home deliveries are on the rise, causing high street shops to close...

So there are two important points about juxtaposition. First, it's a stretch to draw any logical connection between the components from the information provided. Any cause and effect or correlation between them is hypothetical. They are two ideas placed side by side.

The second point is about intent. Sometimes, people simply state what they observe, making an innocent juxtaposition. Other times they are trying to influence you by yoking two unrelated bare assertions, hoping the combination obscures their lack of mutual relevance.

Wrong direction fallacy

Even when we're happy that two simultaneous events are linked, time still plays tricks on us. Sometimes an argument is too close for comfort and we adjust – consciously or otherwise – cause and effect to better suit how we prefer to view the situation.

> "Cousin Vera could stand to lose a few pounds; she says being fat makes her eat too many chocolates."

Poor self-image won't help, but it's more likely that a fondness for chocolate started the ball rolling. But assumptions can be deceptive:

> Headline: new, experimental, driverless cars involved in several accidents during trials on the open roads.

How on Earth can you expect a computer program to navigate a car through the chaos that roads, traffic, weather and other users create? Read on:

> Most accidents were caused by human drivers colliding with experimental cars which were responding too accurately to road situations around them.

You might easily jump to a wrong-direction conclusion that driverless cars were inherently less safe than regular ones. But the evidence is that they were driving more carefully than humans were used to, and were not the cause of accidents.

The wrong direction fallacy beckons to us from all sides:

> As TV commentators, top ex-football players can instantly sum up the tactical situation at any moment of the game. Therefore, people with good visualisation and analytical skills become top footballers.

> London hackney cab drivers have an enlarged hippocampus, part of the brain associated with memory development. Therefore, people with excellent memories tend to become London cab drivers.

The other way round, in fact, in both cases. Studies suggest that the memory-building process involved in gaining The Knowledge[32] actually enlarges the memory part of the student's brain.

The worst examples of a wrong direction conclusion are when victims are blamed for something others did to them. The victims of so-called "honour killings" are accused of bringing shame on their family and "deserve" to be murdered. Victims of sexual assault and rape are sometimes blamed for being drunk or immodestly dressed, as if either of those translates into consent or permission. It's not only criminals who blunder into the wrong direction fallacy:

> In Toronto in 2011, a police officer advised women to "avoid dressing like sluts" to prevent sexual assaults. The reaction saw protests known as "slutwalks".

> After a New Year migrant gang attack on women in Cologne in 2016, the mayor suggested that women should adopt a code of conduct to prevent future assaults.

> The Imam of a Cologne mosque said: "The events of New Year's Eve were the girls' own fault, because they were half naked and wearing perfume."

> Muslimstern on Facebook said: "Germany needs to ban alcohol

---

[32] *The knowledge* requires London's black cab drivers to learn about 25,000 streets within a six-mile radius of Charing Cross, and hundreds of places of interest along the routes.

if it wants to prevent further sexual violence and to help North African migrants integrate into society."

At best, wrong direction reasoning is a farce, with people getting comically muddled. At worst, it's not just a travesty of analysis, it's a grotesque perversion of justice.

Single cause fallacy

Even if we get cause and effect in the correct order, we can still head down the wrong path for answers. In a complex, interconnected world, few things have simple, single causes.

The cat knocks a glass off the table and it breaks. Simple, no? Clumsy cat. Or can I blame my nephew Cuthbert for leaving the glass on the edge of the table?

Life would be helpful if problems had a single cause. Alas, many things can be brought about by a number of equally sufficient causes. And sometimes it's just one thing after another:

An air crash, for example, can have a cascade of failures from the disaster smorgasbord: pilot error, inadequate procedures, poor training, bad maintenance, weather, air traffic control mistakes and random bird strike.

To explain the fallacy of single cause, it's worth knowing the main models of cause. When you think about it, very few things happen in isolation:

Common cause – a single cause leads to several effects. That is, cause X leads to events Y and Z. For example: drinking too much alcohol leads to headache, nausea, memory-loss, regret and the occasional tattoo.

Common effect – several causes come together to cause one result. Here A and B together cause C. Identity fraud, threat of terrorism and benefit tourism by immigrants encourage a government to try to force identity cards on its citizens.

Causal chains – where one event triggers another, which in turn causes another. D leads to E leads to F. For instance: an air crash happens because bird strike damages one engine, but pilots then mistakenly shut down the wrong engine.

Causal homeostasis – where several factors work together in a virtuous (or vicious) circle to form a reinforcing mechanism. That is, J leads to K which leads to L which leads to J. For example, in the sub-prime mortgage crisis: falling house prices led to negative equity[33] which encouraged owners to abandon the house and default on mortgage payments; more foreclosures led to emergency property sales which hammered house prices.

Any one of the models might lead us to mistakenly look for a single cause if we seize on just one narrow slice of the action. Sometimes we just need to see the bigger picture. The single cause fallacy is also called oversimplification of cause, which more or less spells it out.

When catastrophes and tragedies happen we look for the cause because, in part, we're checking to see if someone is accountable. If we can lay blame squarely at the door of one factor or failure, it makes for a neat answer. That said, it's human nature to point the finger in every direction we see a contributing factor, and blame them all:

> Global warming is not caused solely by Uncle Billy's patio heater, Cousin Vera's poor insulation, Great Aunt Ruby's ancient fridge, Cousin Bernard's computer on stand-by overnight, or even cow farts. But these all help.

To complicate matters, some things are routinely attributed to many causes with little or no verifiable evidence or causal proof. It's now a running joke that virtually everything imaginable has been linked to cancer:

> According to epidemiologists, things that cause cancer include: wallpaper, weed killer, welding fumes, well water, weight gain, winter, wood dust, and work. That's only the things that start with W.

Be wary of people attributing equal, unweighted blame to every possible contributing factor, or of picking one contributory factor for a starring role because it suits their political agenda:

> In 2005, the London bus and underground attacks were carried

---

[33] Where the mortgage outstanding on a house is more than the house is worth. The equity the home owners have from paying some of the purchase price with their own money has disappeared. In America, the situation is called "going underwater".

out by British-born Islamist bombers. The then London mayor (among others) laid "ultimate responsibility" for the atrocity on the British government for its military action in Iraq.

The bombers may have been outraged by Middle East events, but so were millions of others not drawn into mass murder. The killers were undoubtedly influenced, trained, equipped or encouraged by others. These factors contributed. But the one necessary element was building and detonating bombs. So laying "ultimate responsibility" with anybody other than the perpetrators is weak reasoning and crass sloganeering. "Ultimate responsibility" seems to mean:

> "One thing I dislike intensely and can connect with this catastrophe."

When a small child is killed by the cruelty of a parent, the failure of social workers, police, doctors and teachers to prevent the murder is thrown into the spotlight. Calls to sack people scream from the headlines; there are debates in parliament. In one case, the head of social services in a London borough was fired by a government minister.

Self-evidently, some people didn't do their job well enough. Hindsight being wisdom, it's easy to point to the things they did or didn't do. But nobody intended for a child to die except those who actually killed it, either deliberately or by neglect. Learn lessons, admonish poor performers, by all means. But the principal blame – ultimate responsibility – must lie with those who commit acts, not those who are judged to have failed to prevent them. This is not over-simplification of cause, it is over-complication of blame.

Away from determining cause, some simplification can be useful to establish the main area to work on, because corrective action works best when effort is focussed on a small number of priorities, rather than a scattergun reaction.

Nevertheless, putting blame on a single cause is a weak argument unless there really is demonstrably one cause only. The state of our life / country / world is not the exclusive fault of any family member, MP, terrorist, company, immigrant, banker, minority, celebrity, president or unemployed person. It takes a collective effort across a broad front to screw things up the way they are. Well done, team.

Historian's fallacy

One of the reasons we find it hard to definitively nail down historical causes is because we view past events through the lens of the present. We forget that people in history did not have the same information we do now, and we unconsciously assume they made decisions using the same perspective and knowledge we have. This erroneous thinking is the historian's fallacy.

> It is said the attack on Pearl Harbour should not have been a complete surprise to the USA, as there were warning signs. But the signs were contradictory. In retrospect, historians can piece together the evidence pointing inevitably to the attack. At the time, though, the full facts were not known; those that were known were not clear.

A similar fallacy is presentism, in which modern values and ideas are projected onto historical events and decisions. For example:

> It's clear that Genghis Khan's attitude toward feminist issues was deficient, and a rape culture permeated his invading hordes with little or no instinctive awareness or mandatory training. His habit of building pyramids of skulls is a phallo-centric demonstration of indifference to gender micro-aggressions and the inalienable rights of prisoners. Victim safe zones were neither established nor respected.

In 2016 Facebook censored the iconic Vietnam War photo referred to as "napalm girl".[34] The shocking picture of a naked child running away from a US bombing raid, was judged to be pornographic. Facebook judges both current and historical pictures through the eyes and attitudes of a present-day algorithm. It has the presentism fallacy encoded into its product. As well as a powerful statement about the Vietnam War itself, the picture speaks loudly to the freedom of the press who published it at the time, and the willingness of the media to shock in order to make a point.

In academic fields, the historian's fallacy is well understood. Academics work hard to figure out what information could have been

---

[34] Facebook subsequently backed down, saying: "In this case, we recognize the history and global importance of this image in documenting a particular moment in time."

available to people in the past and to evaluate the influence of that knowledge on historical events. In business, not so much. For all the apparent certainty of market research (sorry – customer insights), business modelling and the "science" of management and planning, the unexpected happens. If the outcome is beneficial, the managers involved are credited as "hot" – as in the hot-hand fallacy. Glory and riches ensue. If the outcome is bad, there follows an exercise euphemistically known as "learning the lessons", but in reality takes the form of:

- a search for the guilty

- punishment of the innocent

- promotion and bonuses for all those who took no part

When it comes to retrospective fault-finding, the main problem for the blameless is that information they didn't know at the time becomes highly important later on:

A local authority invests in triple-A rated bonds, not knowing the first-class rating was paid for by the bank selling the bonds, nor that the assets backing those bonds consist of sub-prime mortgages – that is, junk – which have been worthless from the outset. The bank has known this all along, which is why it paid for a triple-A rating. The local authority officials are blamed for losing money.

The long-planned launch of a new ice-cream range coincides with the coldest, wettest summer since records began.

The sales force continues to take orders for the new range of smart phones up to a week after the sweatshop in Asia making it burns to the ground.

The market planner whose launch sales exceed everyone's wildest dreams is reprimanded for underestimating sales and consequently under-stocking the retailers.

The most difficult person to convince of the historian's fallacy is the chief executive whose multi-million pound bonus just went pop. I have actually heard this exchange:

Boss: "I know you didn't know about it, but you should have stopped this screw up."

Employee: "Alas, my company Ouija board was on a team-building course that day."

Boss: "That's not too helpful."

Employee: "You started it." (See *tu quoque*.)

The second most resistant entities are the popular press. Apart from the small number of investigative journalists, the press lives for the here-and-now, today's headlines, driven by the fact that being strongly critical of anything sells better than enthusiastic support.

Accordingly, teachers, police, social services, probation officers, judges, immigration panels and parole boards should all have foreseen the cruelty, murder, re-offending, absconding, incitement, and so on, subsequently committed by a person earlier in their purview.

"They could have prevented it," scream the headlines.

Yes, in some cases. But not in all. A meticulous review of what information was actually available at the time takes too long for the press's deadlines, or indeed interest levels. Whenever you see the phrases: they should have known, they failed to prevent or they could have acted, consider the historian's fallacy.

Retrospective determinism

Hindsight, they say, is wisdom. Hindsight can also be wrong.

"It was bound to happen…"

…people say, with a sigh, pondering the blinding inevitability of an event no-one foresaw. Retrospective determinism is what happens when you look back at events and assume they were completely predictable, because they subsequently occurred.

The surprise attack on Pearl Harbour in 1941 by Japan made the US atomic bombings of Hiroshima and Nagasaki in 1945 inevitable.

Arguably, the attack made war inevitable. It precipitated a chain of events and technical developments that culminated in the atomic bombings. But there were many possible outcomes that could have followed Pearl Harbour. Building the atom bombs and using them was one of those outcomes, but it was by no means unavoidable.

Watch out for the moral slant. Is the speaker trying to justify the bombings on the basis of the surprise attack? Using *inevitable* to mean *a warranted response*? If so, it's not persuasive – there are far stronger justifications. Consider this:

> When Saddam Hussein launched the invasion of Kuwait in 1990, it was an action that was bound to lead to the gallows, such is the fate of all tyrants.

Here, retrospective determinism is followed up with a hasty generalisation about justice. It clearly shows a moralist, just-world perspective rather than a historical argument. The certainty of the noose is just plain wrong; the claim that all tyrants swing for their crimes is wishful thinking.

> When the incomparable David Bowie died in 2016, the media was quick to claim that his final album *Blackstar* was a deliberate parting gift to fans, made when he knew he was dying.

The assertion is retrospective determinism (and wishful thinking), because that's how events unfolded. Close collaborators, in fact, report that Bowie's attitude towards his illness and multiple concurrent projects was more ambiguous than the simple, sentimental idea.

Which takes us finally onto destiny. The voiceover on the documentary about a star performer's life may burble something like:

> "From an early age, Clothilde knew she was always destined to be a star of the lion-taming world."

Clothilde's future looks assured – in retrospect – because that's what happened later. But if we assume a kid with a dream is a cast-iron bet to achieve it, we must ignore the millions among us who aren't astronauts, ballet dancers, champion jockeys, fire-fighters, princesses, blues guitarists or *Big Brother* contestants. Looking back and showing how things turned out, then claiming the result was bound to happen, is retrospective determinism. As reasoning, it's nonsensical.

Novelty – appeal to

An appeal to novelty comes about when you argue that something new is necessarily better than older options. You claim that a newer thing should be preferred simply because it's newer. *New* just sounds better, doesn't it?

Note, though, that some of the accompanying, new-related factors can make a valid argument:

> "The new version of our software will be supported further into the future than the old version."

> "We're aiming to improve our reliability and brand new parts have better failure rates than refurbished ones."

> "We know it's superficial, but shiny, new premises are more consistent with our brand image."

> "New politicians won't be tarred with the old brush of corruption."

> "A new government will immediately overturn the policies that have led to this crisis."

The best description of the power of new came in the series Mad Men[35] when the character Don Draper began his sales pitch to a client:

> "My first job, I was in-house at a fur company, with this old-pro copywriter, a Greek named Teddy. Teddy told me the most important idea in advertising is *new*. It creates an itch. You simply put your product in there as a kind of calamine lotion."

Advertisers keep using the word because it works. We consumers are suckers for *new*. Some industries are entirely dependent on novelty: Hollywood, TV channels, book publishers all must churn out new products to maintain consumer interest. It's tough. Look at how many re-makes and sequels are churned out to capitalise on the success of original creations. Popular books become films become TV series. Film sequels burgeon into franchises.

New not only launches products onto the market, it introduces old ones. Updated old formulations are *new* and *improved*, upgrades to hard- and software are new releases.

It's not just products. The novelty fallacy is everywhere. New is used to persuade us that:

> The latest, must-follow diet is bound to work this time.

> Newly-hired football team managers will always get better results.

---

[35] Written by Matthew Weiner.

A new broom sweeps clean.

The new corporate structure will lead to bigger amounts of whatever it is the company wants, mostly bonuses for the CEO.

Some buyers react with chronological snobbery – they must have the latest version of a game console, tablet or smartphone. Some people queue outside shops for days before a launch of the latest gizmo. That's taking early-adopter status to an obsession. Somehow, it never happens for a new, improved gravy powder.

But novelties are not in and of themselves better. Plenty of new products have proved to be stinkers:

New Coke, anyone?; Windows Vista, Windows 8; Cosmopolitan Yoghurt; DeLorean Cars; Sinclair C5; Harley Davidson Perfume…

Depending on your source, between 80 and 95 per cent of new products fail. Even new products rated as successful are not necessarily better than previous offerings. Manufacturers find themselves supporting old versions often for decades after they supposedly replaced them in the market. Sometimes the only way to chivvy consumers along is to end support for the old model. So when large corporations are reluctant to upgrade tens of thousands of computers running bespoke software attached to a legacy operating system, they find it cheaper to pay the manufacturer to directly support their computers than to upgrade the entire corporation. From the manufacturer's point of view, it's money for old rope.

Old hands often turn to an appeal to tradition – arguing that older, more established ideas or products are always superior, just because. It's an equally fallacious argument. Look at how many businesses tell us they were established in 1853 or 1957. We're invited to conclude that long-established businesses survive because they offer old-fashioned personal service, craftsmanship, generations of expertise, and so on.

Ceremonial traditions have value. They may look archaic, but they provide a spectacle that encourages people to remember why they are being held. Real tradition preserves something the way it was – something that doesn't improve. Preservation of the original (or something as close to it as possible) is the whole point. However, tradition, per se, is no guarantee of better performance, quality or service.

Innovation and connecting to the past both appeal to us, but it's a fallacy that new or old must be better for its own sake.

Chronological preference fallacy

Another contribution to the fallacy canon by C. S. Lewis is something he termed chronological snobbery. This is a belief that something from an earlier period is automatically inferior to that of today; that *modern* is superior.

> "Yes, the ancient Greeks had a lot to say about philosophy, but then they thought you could fly by sticking feathers on your arms with wax. So all that philosophy is a crock."

> "Romans roads, viaducts and aqueducts were pretty good for their time. But they also worshipped some barmy old gods, so their engineering has to be a bit suspect too."

> "It's hard to admire medieval architecture knowing they were burning witches at the time they built this cathedral."

The form of the fallacy is simple enough: a premise dates back to when people also embraced something we now know to be wrong, therefore the premise is false.

It's a widespread attitude. We describe things we strenuously disapprove of as *medieval* (often followed by *torture* or *punishment*). Attitudes can be Victorian, antediluvian and primitive. Acts can be barbaric – showing we all suffer unconsciously from chronological snobbery. (See also *appeal to novelty* and *genetic fallacy*.)

Genetic fallacy

This fallacy happens when someone reaches a conclusion based only on the origin of something (or someone) rather than its present significance. The premise is not considered on its own merit, only on the positive or negative association with the past or present.

It's a kind of chronological snobbery that works both ways. In this flawed reasoning, either new things are good because they're new (and therefore old stuff is rubbish), or tried-and-tested is best.

It's a pervasive argument. Think how many products are labelled or described as:

> New, brand new, new formula, new look, latest, state-of-the-art,

groundbreaking, trailblazing, up-to-the-minute, next generation, contemporary, fully revised, now with more, enriched, expanded, and so on

And if modernity doesn't convey the right brand values, advertisers can always appeal to tradition:

Established, tried-and-tested, proven, a reputation for, faithful to, stood the test of time, the way grandma used to make it, the original, old family recipe, no nonsense, dependable, satisfied customers, the quality you expect, and so on

Many people – indeed, organisations – avoid change because new is unfamiliar and traditional is safe. So you hear statements like:

"We've always done it this way."

"Our customers are used to…"

"If it ain't broke don't fix it."

"It's our annual promotion / sale / family day / staff party."

"They don't make them like they used to."

These are all manifestations of the genetic fallacy. And if you don't have a tradition to call on, invent one. Get the bright-eyed young things in marketing to apply their brief but wily experience and create a new and shiny tradition from scratch.

Bailey's Irish Cream brand was launched in 1974, echoing the brand elements of many older, established alcohol products, including the venerable signature of a fictional creator. The brand offers instant tradition, authenticity, assured quality, and family integrity.

The UK is excellent at importing ready-made traditions from elsewhere. Valentine's Day has become a Holy Day of Obligation in the Romance Industry. Borrowed from America, we have established in a couple of short years the traditional Black Friday shopping bonanza.[36] Guy Fawkes now plays second fiddle to Halloween, although Halloween

---

[36] It's a pre-Christmas dumping of surplus inventory of household goods, attracting money that would otherwise be wasted on gifts for people you love. *"Look! Santa Claus brought you a new vacuum cleaner…"*

is an old British custom that survived better in America than here, and was ripe for re-introduction. The annual St Patrick's Day drink-athon reached the UK from neighbouring Ireland via America.

Burns' Night is widely honoured beyond Scotland's borders, mainly as an chance for men to wear skirts, put daggers in their socks, quote regional poetry, and to soak up excessive quantities of ardent spirits using the profoundly unappetising entrails of a sheep. The liquor is absolutely vital: the only way a human frame can endure the noise of bagpipes is to get blind drunk, in the hope that the blessing of merciful deafness will follow. But that's another fallacy – it never does.

Etymological fallacy

This genetic-type fallacy is one for word-lovers and pedants everywhere. Etymology studies the evolution of words and their meaning. In committing an etymological fallacy you insist that a word should still mean today what it meant in the past. When a word is used in a modern sense, you claim it is wrong.

The entry ticket to this fallacy is a word that's changed over time in one of a few ways:

- meaning

- scope – the word has a broader or narrower application

- connotation – becoming more or less pejorative

Meaning changes all the time. Teenagers, in particular, are a powerhouse of re-definition. Recently, slang words like *sick* and *wicked* now acquired meanings opposite to what they once signified. We're literally witnessing change as the word *literally* is now more often used to mean *figuratively*.

Slightly further back, *gay* and *queer* had no connotation of sexual preference. *Nice* meant foolish or stupid – now its meaning is much, er, nicer. *Wench* once meant children, boys or girls, then just girl, then female servant, then woman of loose morals. *Fun* is a noun that was once a verb meaning to cheat or hoax. *Awful* once meant inspiring awe, rather than very bad. *Naughty* now means badly behaved, but once meant evil. *Egregious* – meaning outstanding – once meant remarkably good, excellent. Now it means conspicuously bad. *Meat* meant any foodstuff that wasn't drink. Broadcasting was a way of sowing seeds until radio prompted a figurative usage in the 1920s. *Prestigious* originally meant deceptive – which it still does in the word prestidigitation.

We'd be *foolish* (or *nice*) to insist that distant meanings should be preserved. If nothing else, we'd confuse a lot of people, mostly ourselves. And if we try to maintain that modern statements should be interpreted in their long-forgotten senses we'd be succumbing to an etymological fallacy.

> "I came back from holiday and found a huge backlog on my desk."
>
> "You found a fire burning in your office? You're saying we have an arsonist?"
>
> "What? No, I didn't."
>
> "I'm afraid you did. So who is it? Or is there something you want to get off your chest?"

The etymological fallacy lies behind the seesaw of opinion whether a dictionary should prescribe what words mean, or describe how words are currently used, right and wrong. In practice, though, if you know the difference in meaning of words, you'll use the right one. If you don't, you'll use whatever sounds right, and hang the critics.[37]

The important thing is clear, unambiguous communication. When you blur usage, you lose the subtly-shaded distinctions words often

---

[37] Please note: people who correct your choice of words or punctuation are not *Grammar Nazis*. Taking the trouble to learn the word that best fits, or how to punctuate your writing, in no way equates to murdering six million people in the holocaust. Moreover, those six million were not merely ticked off by someone with a red Biro tut-tutting over their possessives.

If being corrected is irksome, keep a sense of proportion. Review your English language lessons from school. It will help your grammar. Buy a dictionary, which will take care of spelling and word usage at the same time. And when you're confident you know what good or acceptable practice is, you can break the rules to your heart's content. Like starting sentences with *and* and *like*, and using prepositions to finish sentences off with.

have. Also, your listener might not be au fait with the latest vernacular. So, at work, if you pepper your statements with the latest argot used among your peers, don't be surprised if you're misunderstood. Don't accuse colleagues of committing some etymological fallacy if you decide you're too *fleek* to talk like adults. They complete your appraisal.

And there's no excuse for starting an email to a colleague, supplier or customer with: *"Yeah, blud!"*

Hashtag facepalm.

9. DENIAL

Denial, as Mark Twain observed, ain't just a river in Egypt. Many people would rather deny a proven fact than admit they are wrong. Others find it easier to solve an inconvenient problem by denying it exists.

Denial is that most human of failings. It's the flipside of persistence and hope and doggedness, qualities we regard as virtues when they pay off. But when they lead to failure we describe them as delusion, stubbornness and intransigence.

Denial takes a number of forms – claiming exception to a general rule; blanking out anything that shocks or offends; or simply refusing to believe proof when it's shown to you. To deny something flat and imagine that's a fair rebuttal is the weakest form of argument.

Ignorance – argument from, appeal to

Come with me to Scotland. Loch Ness and neighbouring Highlands are well worth a visit. There's bags of geology in those mournful hills and deep, peaty waters. But the chances are that Nessie is not going to favour you with The Selfie Of A Lifetime.

Despite the vanishingly small probability that an ancient monster really does lurk in those dark waters, there have been numerous, thorough, scientific expeditions to track down the beast. Apart from a doubtful image on a grainy monochrome photograph and some spectacularly unconvincing footage of a rippling wave, no-one has ever confirmed Nessie's existence.

Even more crucial to the enduring myth and the Scottish tourism industry, no-one has categorically disproved its existence either. The juggernaut of Loch Ness fans is fuelled by the fact that Nessie has not been proven false, therefore it is true.

This reasoning is called argument from ignorance – contending that something must be true because it has not yet been proven false. It works the other way too: concluding that something must be false because no-one has proved it to be true. (See *burden of proof*.)

Note that, here, ignorance doesn't mean *stupid*, it means lacking information. And in that void, all manner of theories and imaginings spring to life:

"Scientists can't explain how gravity transmits force to other objects to attract them, therefore gravity doesn't attract."

"No-one's proved my gods don't exist, therefore they do."

"No-one has proved conclusively that ghosts exist, therefore they don't."

Bear in mind that the burden of proof lies with the party making the assertion. When the world lacks evidence one way or another, you're often being presented with a false dichotomy. You're invited to reach a hard and fast, true or false conclusion, without some further logical possibilities for any given problem, namely that:

Some true things may never be categorically proven.

Some false things may never be disproved with certainty.

The truth or falsity of some things may be unknowable.

We may not know which of the three above applies.

The frustrating fact is that reality goes its own sweet way unencumbered by our imperfect knowledge and understanding.

Suppose we're hunting for aliens from another world. Despite the sterling efforts of UFO investigators worldwide, no-one has proved that beings from another planet either exist, or visit us, and abduct people as souvenirs of Earth. The argument from ignorance says:

No-one has proven aliens don't exist. Their existence is not false. Therefore, aliens are true.

We have no concrete proof of aliens biffing around in flying saucers. Their existence is not true. Therefore, aliens are false.

In reality, we just don't know whether there's intelligent life on other worlds or not. If there is, we don't know if they choose to visit Earth to play hide-and-seek. The size of the universe, and the vast numbers of stars and planets tell us it is hugely probable that E.T. is out there somewhere. We only know of one planet where life has definitely evolved and we live on it, so evolution of intelligent life works 100 per cent of the time for us. But it might be that the conditions needed were so hideously complex and rare that we are unique. We would be, indeed, special little snowflakes. In short, though, we just don't have enough information – yet.

It may be that we never know the answer because it is unknowable. The vast scale of the universe, with information limited to the speed of light, may mean intelligent civilisations have been (or will be) born, thrive and extinguish separated from us by billions of light years of time and distance. There may be millions of civilisations out there, but our human race may pass the whole of its existence – until the Sun eventually devours the Earth – utterly alone.

The principle that we may never disprove some false things with certainty is often over-simplified to:

> You can't prove a negative.

Which only encourages people to say things like:

> I can prove a Blue Whale can't fly if you lend me a helicopter and a Blue Whale.

Impossibility is a good way to refute a negative. But in the hazy world of day-to-day debate, it may be beyond us to nail some myths conclusively. To do so, we'd have to scour every square inch of Planet Earth to be able to rule them out, or in the case of aliens, every planet in the entire universe, which would take a while.

Consequently, invisible and intangible things like: fairies, aliens, leprechauns, magic potions, faster than light travel, Father Christmas, assorted deities, afterlife, wizards, souls, sins, Bigfoot, heaven and hell are all capable of existing, albeit speculatively. While the burden of proof always lies with those who claim invisible and magical things do exist, rationalists can't always disprove them categorically. This disposition of reasoning allows every believer to draw on the argument from ignorance, and continue their life with the object of their faith a glowing truth for them, but a frozen non sequitur for the rest of us.

Equally, we may never satisfactorily prove some true things. But everything that counts as true or real does so because it is proven. We are entitled to treat unproven things not as false, but as speculation.

So when someone comes to you with a claim or argument that rests on an a priori assumption that something exists or is true, it should be provable. You're perfectly entitled to ask for that proof. For instance:

> "Crime never pays. Even if a criminal gets away with it, they are punished in hell after they die."

Hmm, just run that proof of an afterlife past me again.

If they can't, or are unwilling to try, or the best they can come up with is no more than a personal belief, hope or wishful thinking, you've found a person more devoted to conviction than to reason. You can stop the debate right there.

Back down to earth, the argument from ignorance is the basis of suspicion about new inventions and developments.

"Mr Stephenson, there's isn't enough proof that trains are safe. The speeds might harm passengers. Trains must have speed limits."

"We can't foresee all the possible outcomes of genetically-modified crops. They should all be banned forever."

"If you use earphones, you might go deaf. No-one's tested these over a lifetime."

"No-one's used mobile phones for long enough. They could cause brain damage."

The argument that we should know everything about new technology in all circumstances is weak. Sensible precaution and testing is one thing; putting the brakes on new developments for fear of some unspecified or unknowable problem is excessively timid.

Slothful induction

You give an argument your best shot. Your facts are solid; your reasoning is cogent; your rhetoric positively charming. Then your listener says:

"It sounds a bit of a coincidence to me."

"No, it isn't, you porridge-brained poltroon!"

... is an unsuitable response. As it turned out.

This is a slothful induction. Rather than think through the argument, we dismiss it in the handiest way possible. It's a coincidence. Just an accident. Random. We're denying that there is a causal link between two events. Sometimes there really is no causal link between events:

A newspaper claims that Gilbert, a pet gerbil, can correctly predict the outcome of World Cup football matches by choosing one of two feeding stations. Gilbert chooses the station labelled with the team that subsequently won. The newspaper claims: "It's Gilbert What Won It!"

No, Gilbert didn't determine or predict the winner. To point out the coincidence here would not be a slothful induction.

We use this bad reasoning often in our personal lives, partly to exonerate ourselves from blame; partly to shift the category of conversation from fault to bad luck. For instance, some anguished people say they're star-crossed in love:

"My boyfriends are always too clingy. I'm doomed to anxious relationships."

"My girlfriends always cheat on me. I'm unlucky."

It's not coincidence or bad luck. We are attracted to, and therefore repeatedly choose, the sort of partner who has characteristics we like, the bad with the good. We unconsciously set up our own coincidences, then slothful induction lets us off the hook.

Others blame their frequent job changes on recurring bad luck with bosses, or the economy. They don't think it has anything to do with their personal performance, or getting on badly with colleagues or customers. And of course we're all excellent drivers:

"I always have rotten luck with cars. Another car stopped right in front of me. You wouldn't think a hearse would be so reckless."

'Unlucky' drivers pay higher car insurance. If a pattern begins to emerge with the same thing happening to you time and again, the chances are the problem lies with you.

Overwhelming exception

Sometimes, you reach your resounding conclusion, then realise there's a whopping exception, one that torpedoes your argument below the water-line. The effect is to entirely detroy your finely wrought explanation. Denial is unintended, and takes the form of you snatching defeat from the jaws of triumph.

This is an overwhelming exception – the name explains itself – which lends itself nicely to comedy.

"In our new business we're positioning ourselves as the one-stop shop for pub supplies. Except beer."

"The car is a reliable runner, apart from the engine."

"You can always count on Americans to do the right thing, after they have exhausted every other possibility."[38]

And because no book is complete without a quotation from Monty Python:

"Apart from the sanitation, medicine, education, wine, public order, irrigation, roads, a fresh water system and public health, what have the Romans ever done for us?"[39]

The overwhelming exception is a classic fallacious argument, one that shoots itself in the foot. It's a pretty good indication that whoever uttered it was speaking on the hoof and hadn't thought their case all the way through.

Bigger problems – appeal to

When you're caught up in the middle of a problem, it's easy to lose your sense of proportion. At some point, you've almost certainly heard something like this:

"Why are we even talking about this when there's so much suffering / starvation / disease / war / in the world?"

"Okay, I screwed up but, come on, nobody died."

"This government's patting itself on the back over a minor change in the crime statistics, but they're totally ignoring the two million unemployed in this country."

"All this EU stuff is missing the point. The real issue has to be global warming."

"It's all very well corporations making good profits, but what about the workers?"

"Thousands of migrants drown trying to make a better life and no-one lifts a finger. One gorilla in a zoo gets shot and everyone

---

[38] Attributed, probably incorrectly, to Winston Churchill.

[39] The peerless *Life of Brian*.

goes insane!"

It's a fallacy to insist that whatever the problem or argument is, it's unimportant and can be ignored because there are bigger problems to worry about. It's also called the fallacy of relative privation, or to put it another way, there's always someone worse off than you.

The appeal to bigger problems is a special kind of red herring argument. Without trying to minimise the seriousness of the bigger issue, it's not relevant to the debate in hand. It misses the point. Often people are earnest in their concern for what they see as a greater crisis. A few, though, seem to be interested in scoring extra brownie points for having loftier, weightier and somehow nobler worries than the rest of us, and waste no opportunity in letting us know. Virtue-signalling seems to be the agreed label for this self-aggrandisement.

The examples above may be caricatures of teenage angst, but this fallacy crops up frequently in political exchanges, that other rich seam of petulance and immaturity:

> "While we welcome the news that the economy is booming, the prime minister has utterly failed to solve global warming."

> "The news about greater investment in our national infrastructure might be good news for the construction industry, but it goes no way at all to address everyone's pressing concerns about the environment."

Opponents across the political divide cannot bring themselves to praise the successes of adversaries without disparaging the effort as valueless compared to some greater concern. (This overly-critical judgement is called floccinaucinihilipilification – the act of estimating something as worthless. That's a tip-top word, if a smidge tricky to squeeze into a game of Scrabble.)

Probably the best known example in the UK is that evergreen yuletide favourite, the *Band Aid* song, *Do They Know It's Christmas*. The gist is something along the lines of:

> "Great, it's Christmas! Oh, wait... Africa's still screwed."[40]

---

[40] It's churlish to belittle efforts to support needy people. So although the lyrics of the song assert that in Africa "nothing ever grows and no rain or rivers flow", we should mentally add the proviso, *"at least in the arid parts of that vast,*

Those who regularly refer to bigger problems seem to be life's glass-half-empty people, pessimists who spread their joylessness with an ironic gusto.

Personal incredulity

Some things in the world are too straightforward to argue with. Day-to-day items like pencils, pet rocks, buttons and cheese sandwiches are easy to get your head around. Plenty aren't. Most of the time we trust smarter people to deal with the tough stuff. I can't fathom quantum physics but I'm happy to believe boffins who describe what they observe, and explain it in small words.

But sometimes the truth is something we just don't want to believe. We reject it for no better reason than that.

> "The Big Bang can't be right. How can the whole universe be smaller than a pinhead? I'm not having that."

> "No way. My ancestors were never monkeys. Evolution is plain wrong."

> "My son is a good boy. He would never commit that crime. He's innocent."

> "No-one would be that cruel; the defendant can't be guilty."

> "Show me all the CCTV footage you want, I don't believe in ghosts."

> "No-one would keep their daughter locked up in the cellar for 24 years. I don't believe that report."

Simple disbelief is a fallacy because something can be hard to accept yet true, or totally credible but false. The big metaphysical questions slot nicely in here. Faith, creation, the destiny of man or the nature of reality are way too deep and meaningful for most of us who get flummoxed by football scores and takeaway menus.

So personal incredulity is the go-to fallacy for rejecting any argument that's too much to take in, or runs counter to our wishful

---

tropical continent, but excluding the bits we used to call the 'jungle' and now call the 'rain forest'". (See also *Appeal to Pity*.)

thinking. In business, you may hear the fallacy of personal incredulity cloaked in silk-lined managerial reasonableness:

"I don't share that opinion."

"I don't like this course of action."

"This takes us down a rocky path."

It means the speaker doesn't want to follow the recommended course of action for some reason: dislike or disbelief are both poor reasons for rejecting a sound argument or solid fact.

Self-censorship in the face of schooled offence

I'd like to claim I just invented that title, but the important words are those of philosopher Roger Scruton. I'm also toying with fallacy of argument-killing fulmination, which may be more descriptive of the situation.

It has become, in the last few decades, a potent rhetorical tool for special interest groups to react to fair criticism and debate by detonating in a calculated, excessive display of outrage, rounding on their opponent with accusations of whatever ~ism will cause the most grievous wounds.

Where there's a will, people detect offence where none exists, and none was intended. And some groups have become expert in feeling hurt, because each instance they manufacture becomes an opportunity to broadcast their views, and reinforce their victimhood. At its most extreme, teachers and professors are hounded out of their job by self-appointed pressure groups who deem words and phrases, opinions, even elements of the taught syllabus, to be outrageously offensive, leading to *trigger*[41] moments.

In the 1960s and 1970s university campuses were crucibles of ideas, where all points of view could be heard, debated and judged. Now pressure groups want campuses to be safety zones, where students can't hear any views the group doesn't approve of. Groups insist that speakers with unauthorised views be turned away on the grounds they

---

[41] The trigger phenomenon has been hi-jacked from post-traumatic stress disorder, wherein sufferers suddenly re-experience the horror of war triggered by innocent noises or events.

will cause offence and actual harm. Organisers are asked to provide safe rooms (presumably stocked with fainting couches) for students to be comforted in if they get an attack of the vapours from inadvertent exposure to incorrect points of view. Individuals or organisations that resist such demands for censorship are then attacked and accused of embodying any hateful thing the group wants to censor. The mentality seems to be: if you aren't with us, then you personify anything we say should be despised.

Spurious accusations of sexism, racism, homophobia, anti-Semitism or Islamophobia are so toxic, and orchestrated social media campaigns are so overwhelming, that many people refrain from public debate or pursuing valid arguments. If fair comment is off-limits, when can we ridicule extremists? When can we challenge ideas? What happened to free speech? Philosopher Roger Scruton[42] summed it up:

> "You cannot legislate against offence. No legislation, no invention of new crimes and punishments, can possibly introduce irony, forgiveness and good will into minds schooled in the art of being offended. This is as true of radical feminists as of sectarians and radical Islamists. While we have a moral duty to laugh at them, they have also made it dangerous to do so. But we should never lose sight of the fact that it is they, not we, who are the transgressors. Those who suspect mockery at every turn, and who react with implacable anger when they think they have discovered it, are the real offenders."

Those of us who fight for argument and reasoning may be in the right, but the sad fact remains that we have to:

> "... tiptoe through a minefield, and to avoid all the areas where the bomb of outrage might go off in your face."

As a result, public servants hesitate to teach what they know to be accurate, and dither over stopping blatant wrongdoing where the perpetrators (or their supporters) are known to calculatedly over-react.

Where is the fallacy is all this? Calculated offence is a pure and potent form of denial. If one party is bullied into silence because of the

---

[42] These remarks were made in a BBC *Point of View* programme in November 2015.

outrage – actual or expected – of an infuriated opponent, then the purple-faced fulminators cannot win a debate, because none takes place. To allow such a conclusion to stand would be to accept bullying and intimidation, the enemies of reason, as legitimate argument.

Orchestrated accusations of something-ism; calls for the resignation or dismissal of academics; social media campaigns targeting individuals guilty of nothing more than expressing a view the group doesn't like – these are the arguments of a lynch mob.

No true Scotsman

In its purest form, this situation arises when someone doesn't like being embarrassed by a group they belong to. That person is proved wrong about a member and is forced to eat his own words. It's a last-ditch argument of denial. It's like a child saying:

"This one doesn't count."

To explain the Scotsman title, people cite various examples that stereotype Scots' customs: they don't put sugar on porridge, or put dry ginger in whisky, for instance:

Struan states that no Scotsman would ever wear anything under his kilt. His pal Hamish says, "I'm a Scot and check out these Calvin Kleins!" Whereupon Struan declares, "No true Scotsman would wear anything under his kilt."

Used generally, it can be amusingly snooty. You'll spot it in all sorts of places:

"No-one with good taste likes rap music."

"Proper football players don't use a round ball."

"Real professionals work through a hangover."

Back to egregious denial. A recent example:

In January 2015 Islamist fanatics machine-gunned an office of cartoonists in Paris killing 12 people and injuring 11, and screaming "Alahu Akbar" ("God is Greatest") as they did so. "But," exclaimed the Muslim brother of a murdered policeman, "these killers were not true Muslims."

In more distant times, no true German was a member of the Nazi party, in the SS or an informant for the Stasi. No true Catholic planted

IRA bombs. No true Frenchman eats in McDonalds. No true Old Etonian ever molested a pig's head.[43] No true Geordie supports Sunderland Football Club. The list could be endless.

You can find examples of individuals in every walk of life who fail to live up to the lofty ideals of their fellows, who then label them an exception, a special case, not included, doesn't count. People who resort to this fallacy are naïve at best, at worst they are pig-headedly defiant. (No pun intended.)

---

[43] Into your favourite search engine, type David Cameron + pork.

10. TWIST AND SHOUT

Among the hundreds of fallacies, some are irrelevant arguments, others are dim thinking, while some fall into the category of wilful deception.

Let's look at some of the tricks, dodges and chicanery[44] that are used to bypass debate, and to slip one past you. Some twist words, others pretend the situation is a different one, a few simply try to browbeat you into submission. These are the arguments used by people who think they're being clever, and believe their victims are fools to be hoodwinked in pursuit of money, glory, or advancement.

The worst examples of deliberate deception involve arguments with colossal financial implications for entire industries. At the other extreme, a lone, vainglorious individual can hold the whole scientific community to ransom. There are cases where a boffin somewhere in the world makes fair and provable public criticism of a charlatan's scientific claims, and that phony sues for defamation in the UK. It's a lamentable fact that libel tourists have found Britain's climate especially congenial.

Welcome to the world of intellectual sleight of hand.

Inflation of conflict fallacy

Experts don't always agree. That very contention helps spur research for better evidence and stronger proofs. But it's a mistake to assume that because scientists disagree, there can be no right or wrong answer at all and, therefore, the entire discussion is void.

> "One doctor said I could safely drink ten pints of beer a week, but another said I could have 15. Since they can't agree on it, I don't think they know what they're talking about. Seventy feels about right to me."

It's a fallacy to suggest that we ought to know an exact answer or none at all – a yes or no proposition (our old friend, the false dichotomy). Or you might erroneously decide that some third answer or compromise is correct. (See *argument from moderation*.)

---

[44] Schopenhauer's phrase for the wiles of rhetoric.

The climate change debate, for instance, has many interested parties who disagree about almost every aspect of the problem, therefore many feel able to ignore the broad scientific consensus.

> "One climate change expert says in 20 years we'll be up to our knees in seawater. Another's saying we'll be up to our chins.
> They can't agree on rising sea-levels so they are probably both completely wrong. Climate change is a fiction."

Whether it's climate change, genetically-modified crops, the Big Bang or evolution, scientists have overwhelmingly formed a consensus about what's happening around us. But the general public tends to be much more sceptical. Why?

Well, some people are just contrary. Others equate real science with government and big corporations, and they're not fans of either. Don't forget, there are a lot of people earning a very good living in the quasi-science arena who hate real science for dismissing their craft and exposing their bogus claims to the public. In return, quasi-science pretenders accuse real science of being elitist and arrogant, presumably for hogging the lion's share of taxpayers' money, kudos and attractive sex partners.

Consequently, unable to aspire to the authority and rigour of real science, pretenders adopt anti-science tactics to drag down real science to their level. The media help because they present topics with false balance, equating the real science consensus with the lesser proofs of a glib talker. Torn between two camps, the public is browbeaten or bamboozled into confusion: real science or pretender? – they're all the same. A plague on both their houses.

So what are anti-science tactics? The first way pretenders challenge a scientific consensus is to inflate the conflict in the field. They play up ambiguity, play down agreement. The insinuation is that a lack of unanimity means the scientific community is unsure of its facts and at odds with itself. In that way, their quasi-science presents itself as just another approach, fully equal to mainstream scientific theory, partners in the search for scientific truth.

Next, scientific theories are dismissed as mere guesses (see *equivocation*):

> "Scientists don't have facts, only theories. So you can't trust their criticism of my quasi-science when they don't know anything for

128

sure."

A scientific theory is not a mere guess. It's a confirmed explanation, one that accounts for observed facts and is accepted as settled by scientific consensus. Gravity, germs, atomic physics and living cells are all still 'only' theories, even though we trust our lives to them.

Then quasi-science pretenders over-exaggerate relatively unimportant differences in data or its interpretation:

> Two experts test the bones of a human ancestor. They reach different estimates as to the age: one says 2.1 million years plus or minus X; another says 2.2 million plus or minus Y. Aha, says the pretender, palaeontologists cannot age bones with any accuracy. It's guesswork. The framework behind human evolution is suspect. Therefore, there's no solid proof that the world wasn't created fully formed five thousand years ago.

This non-argument is a quibble over measurement techniques, not grounds for rejecting the theory of evolution. A big bonus for pretenders is a boffin who breaks ranks and speaks out against the scientific consensus. While the rest of the community regards him or her as an outlier in their field, pretenders can play up the dissent among scientists.

Failing that, pretenders find a tame expert to say what they want. Most properly qualified scientists know the limits of reasonable disagreement, so pretenders find another boffin with a doctorate in, say, medieval history and put him or her forward as an expert in climate change, hoping no-one spots they don't have the right credentials to support the views they repeat (see *false authority*).

With disagreement in the air, pretenders today use social media to create the illusion of mass support for their position.

> "Gravity is a crock. If we can get one million likes we can force the government to take our opposition seriously."

The ultimate technique is to use the law to silence critics. A scientist of excellent standing publishes a fair and objective critique of a pretender's false scientific claims in a journal of repute. At this point, the brazen pretender cries, "Gotcha!" and his lawyers reach for the yacht catalogues.

A pretender selling majick dog-poop as a cure for cancer is

excoriated by a leading oncologist in a medical journal. The pretender decides to sue for libel, claiming his reputation has been damaged. Incredibly, qualified, practising lawyers agree to act for him. The pretender demands an apology, the journal withdrawn and pulped, a super-injunction to stop the press reporting his unconscionable legal action, lots and lots and lots of money by way of damages on top of his legal costs because, after all, lawyers like that don't come cheap. Unbelievably, the action is not laughed out of court by the judge. Welcome to censorship, libel-style.[45]

So to answer the question, why is the public so much more sceptical about science than scientists? Because we are misinformed, deceived and intentionally confused.

When experts disagree, it's usually over extent or probability rather than whether a phenomenon occurs at all. We, like they, must wait for the results of ever more precise experiments or calculation to settle the science more accurately. However, it remains a fallacy to dismiss the broad consensus of scientific thinking because it's not unanimous, finely tuned or precisely aligned.

Reductio ad absurdum

Reduction to absurdity is a popular technique and is as old as the hills. It's a way of attacking an opponent's case by belittling the reasoning it uses.

A reductio ad absurdum argument tries to show a statement is true, because denying it leads logically to a ridiculous conclusion, or indeed that it's false, because accepting it would end up with an absurd outcome.

"Yes, yes, your gods are mighty and immortal. But so were the gods of ancient Rome. What are they doing now? Updating their profiles on LinkedIn? Working in a zero-hours warehouse? Management consultancy?"

---

[45] All characters appearing in this paragraph are fictitious. Any resemblance to real persons, living or dead, is purely coincidental. But it does happen. See *British Chiropractic Association v Singh* as an example, which led to a change in UK law.

"Of course flying is the safest form of transport. If it weren't, there'd be convoys of boats sailing across the Atlantic. We'd see long chains of low-cost kayaks dodging crashing planes, with paddlers being asked to pay to watch a film projected onto the side of an iceberg. There'd be Polar Bears flogging duty-free stuff."

"No, partying till dawn is not the best way to revise for an exam. If it were, the exam paper rubric would say: "Have a nap then answer whatever you want. Help yourself to the fridge.""

Politicians, parents and comedians all enjoy skewering their opponents' position, suggesting that something false and ridiculous will ensue if we follow their argument.

"My nephew Cuthbert said he wanted to learn the tuba because his friend Tarquin was going to. His father asked if Tarquin jumped off a cliff, would Cuthbert do the same?"

Suppose, for instance, you were debating with an advocate of unfettered bonuses for business bosses:

"Of course they have to pay eight-figure bonuses to themselves! Otherwise they wouldn't bother coming into work. Then the boardrooms of Britain would be full of poor people, carving their initials into the wood panelling and drying their washing on portraits of the founders. And some of those portraits are worth a lot of money. Certainly more than the average employee earns. This argument isn't about rat-gagging greed, it's all about the portraits. How else do we look after the portraits?"

To argue that it's wrong to pay stupid amounts of money to people, we simply take the opposite stance and follow the thinking until we reach an absurdity to mock. Or we can caricature it as the opponent's position. (See *strawman argument.*)

It's different to an appeal to ridicule, in which an opponent's argument is dismissed by mockery. With reductio ad absurdum we pursue the logical consequences of a position.

Some say the only way to protect UK citizens from terrorists is to give GCHQ more powers to monitor everyone's online activity and read our emails. But the government has to sell the idea to the public. With greater access to our information, GCHQ will be able to offer a Remind-You-Of-Your-Password service. You forget your Netflix password, click a button, your phone rings and a voice tells you: "It's 1h34rtH4rryP0tt3r and your tea's getting cold." But not terrorists. By making them figure out their own passwords, they won't have time to plant bombs. That's how it will work: more surveillance, fewer bombs. Also they'll know who the terrorists are because they'll be the ones trying to order explosives on Amazon Prime.

It goes without saying that this type of argument only works if the position you argue against does indeed have some reasoning to exploit. If it doesn't, just ignore it.

Persuasive definitions

This is an enjoyable way of spiking an opponent's argument. It introduces a certain bite, painting your own case in colours of virtue and wiping your opponent's in smears of grime. It's also poor reasoning, so enjoy it, but don't rely on it to win over anyone who disagrees with you. It's sometimes referred to as a definist fallacy.

It takes the form of stipulating a *true* or *normal meaning* of terms but actually providing a loaded definition:

"An atheist is a sinner who wishes God didn't exist in order to live an immoral life."

"Socialism isn't a love for the working class; it's hatred and resentment of the middle class, which it denigrates as bourgeois."

"Progressive politics means persecuting straight, white males."

"Conservatives' defence of free speech means giving fascists and racists a platform to spread hate."

Persuasive definitions are designed to pack an argument with a favourable or pejorative payload, disguised as an honest portrayal. They frequently appear in speeches, debates and opinion columns where emotional appeals are de rigeur, and they are intended to sway opinion rather than explain or accurately define. They are most often deployed in front of a sympathetic audience by someone playing to the gallery.

You can play persuasive definitions with family and friends whenever you're watching the news. Note the language used by interviewees. Spokespeople are trained to use a vocabulary that redefines the issue in hand:

Abortion – induced termination of pregnancy, or murder of unwanted, pre-term baby.

Marijuana – gateway drug, illegal narcotic, causes mental problems, or mild plant extract, less harmful than alcohol, effective for chronic pain.

Government investment – taxpayers' money spent on things I like.

Taxpayers' money – government money wasted on things I dislike.

Agency staff – zero-hour workers at our beck and call.

The gig economy – millions of zero-hour workers.

Pro-Europe – anti-fascist, enlightened, intelligent, progressive.

Anti-EU – regressive, backward-looking, anti-immigration, racist.

Pre-rapist – male university student. [I kid you not!]

These definitions are only persuasive to like-minded people, and reinforce the prejudices they already hold. As the saying goes, prejudice is the reasoning of fools. In work meetings you will come across persuasive definitions shaping and reinforcing corporate orthodoxy:

"Let's not forget, good customer service means fast delivery."

"In this organisation, being effective means we follow procedures every step of the way."

"In this company, our employees are *human capital*."

When managers at work keep repeating certain persuasive definitions, it usually indicates they're getting some form of resistance from other members of staff. The aim is to embed the ideology they embrace into other employees. In everyday conversation, persuasive definitions are routinely deployed to carry a payload of opinion:

"Punk music is just rock with the musicianship removed."

"Vouchers are the gift-of-choice for those with no imagination."

"A husband is just a life-support machine for a wallet."

A persuasive definition purports to be a commonly accepted meaning of a term, but as with coin-flip term like freedom fighter / rebel, it carries a point of view. In the USA, the names given to federal legislation are often persuasive definitions, setting out the lawmakers' fond hope for the effect of the new laws, and making it more awkward to vote against:

> No Child Left Behind Act; Help America Vote Act; Prison Rape Elimination Act; Respect For America's Fallen Heroes Act; Healthy, Hunger-Free Kids Act; Unlocking Consumer Choice And Wireless Competition Act; Every Student Succeeds Act.

There may be a bit of wishful thinking in those titles, too.

Judgemental language / prejudicial language

Following neatly after persuasive definitions, judgemental language is a generic phrase encompassing the many situations in which people choose pejorative or critical statements to sway a listener.

In May 2016, a headline on Drudge Report:

> "Murdered gorilla seen 'protecting' child"

A child had fallen into a gorilla enclosure, so keepers shot the animal to protect it. The word *murdered*, rather than a more neutral *shot* or *killed* conveys the editorial opinion. It leads readers toward the view that the gorilla's killing was criminally wrong.

Judgemental language is not a fallacy in itself, but it does beef up arguments and lend vividness to anecdotes that are fallacious, as well as distract people from the main argument. When it's obvious, it's unsubtle. Referring to *shyster* lawyers, *quack* homeopaths, *fraudster* bankers or *kiddie-fiddler* priests is no better than name-calling, however satisfying. But judgemental language clothes itself in seemingly reasonable vocabulary.

> "In business, the only people to trust are family, not the long-term unemployed losers the welfare people send along."

This suggests that unemployed people are untrustworthy, with the added slur that they may have been unemployed for a long time with good reason.

> "Calling in favours from friends is fine but, in the long run, you'll save time and money using professional session musicians for

recording your demos."

Here the implication is that whoever you're friends with, they're not going to be as professional in their abilities or approach as seasoned pros.

"I don't even own a tick-tock watch. Everything's on my phone."

You can detect a certain snootiness towards the mechanical delights of a wearable chronometer.[46]

If prejudicial language is done properly, you'll scarcely notice it sliding in under your radar. It's this cloaking device of reasonableness that makes it effective. Which brings us to politically correct (PC) language.

At best, PC language tries to cut offensive slurs from the vocabulary of acceptable discourse. At worst, it hides uncomfortable truths and sidesteps legitimate judgement or fair comment. We no longer refer to people as *fat*, *stupid* or *lazy*. They *have an eating disorder*, are *academically challenged* or *motivationally dispossessed*.

Laudably, PC language tries to describe at what people can do, not what they can't. *Physically challenged* and *differently abled* are ungainly phrases, but don't dismiss people they way *disabled* and *crippled* seem to. But it takes away some of the natural pathos when a homeless person is described as *residentially flexible*.

Take it too far, and PC language becomes a rich source of comedy. That management cliché *brain-storming* is now *thought showering*. A person who is *parentally challenged* is *a bit of a bastard*. *Criticism* is *non-traditional praise*. A *prisoner* is a *client of the correctional system*.

But there's a darker side to political correctness. In an online debate, it was persuasively defined to give it a light, cleansing ring:

"Political correctness merely means not generalizing entire groups of people based on their skin color, religion or ethnic group."

---

[46] Actually, I rather like "tick-tock" as an adjective for something that's old-fashioned and rudimentary: *"Mate, you're still playing cassette tapes in your car? That's a bit tick-tock."*

Oh, political correctness means so much more than that! It's not "mere" and its reach is much more pernicious than that noble aim. Language shapes expression and thought.

The fictional government in Orwell's 1984 devised *Newspeak*, a vocabulary that got rid of words it didn't want people to have available to them, preventing them from thinking unacceptable ideas, or *thoughtcrime*. *Goodthink* was a noun and verb describing opinions approved by The Party; the opposite was *crimethink*. Written decades before politically-correct language emerged as a social trend in the West, Orwell's novel is remarkably prescient.

Political correctness also applies to policies and measures designed to avoid the appearance of offence or criticism of protected groups.

> In 2012, eight Pakistani men and one Afghan were convicted of running a child sex exploitation ring in Rochdale, UK. The 47 victims identified were mainly white British girls. Ensuing reviews suggested social services and police had failed to investigate properly because of fears of being labelled racist. In 2015 Greater Manchester Police apologised for not investigating the allegations more thoroughly between 2008 and 2010.

Some organisations are better than others at achieving a clear and reasoned neutrality in their language. The BBC's editorial policy[47] is to avoid words like *terrorist* when *attacker, gunman, bomber* or *kidnapper* are more accurate. The BBC also seeks to avoid inconsistency that might smack of partiality. It reports a *terrorist attack* rather than a *suicide bombing*, and uses *assassinate* rather than *murder* to avoid seeming to use judgemental language. Its policy on *refugee, migrant* and *asylum seeker*:

> The BBC uses the term migrant to refer to all people on the move who have yet to complete the legal process of claiming asylum. This group includes people fleeing war-torn countries such as Syria, who are likely to be granted refugee status, as well as people who are seeking jobs and better lives, who [sic]

---

[47] The BBC has a reputation for objectivity that is worth protecting. Some other broadcast news channels are so slanted they make North Korean rhetoric sound like an apology from Beatrix Potter.

governments are likely to rule are economic migrants.[48]

You may believe the workplace is a bastion of calm, rational communication. And it's true that extreme and frank language will secure you a meeting with HR. But business uses judgemental and prejudicial code words and phrases about you, mostly behind your back. The language itself may be bland, but the phrases can be deadly:

What you do, for example:	Business vernacular:
Disagree with a decision	"He's not a team player."
Decline to work late or over the weekend	"She lacks commitment."
Criticise a colleague / situation	"He has a negative approach."
Do something your own way	"She's unmanageable."

Good luck with that annual appraisal.

Emotive language

In business, presentations prove but speeches persuade. A well rendered speech will lift the heart, strengthen the arm and have fists punching the air. The rhetoric of a speech is crafted to make listeners believe in you, more than simply agree with your point of view.

The vital ingredient is emotive language, which is where rhetoric and reasoning diverge. Reasoning demands facts and evidence, while rhetoric can dispense with them.

A Churchill speech to parliament:

"You ask, what is our policy? I say it is to wage war by land, sea, and air. War with all our might and with all the strength God has given us, and to wage war against a monstrous tyranny never surpassed in the dark and lamentable catalogue of human crime. That is our policy."

---

[48] Source: bbc.co.uk © 2015 BBC.

The fallacy of presentism might insist that a more felicitous, modern phrase than *monstrous tyranny never surpassed* might be *our European partner*. But with Germany's blitzkrieg (lightning war) sweeping across Europe, Churchill declined to list the rational facts and figures, such as numbers of enemy soldiers and their proximity to the UK (his audience was all too aware of the salient details), instead aiming for a rallying call to arms. Stirring stuff: it worked.

The problem arises if an argument relies on emotive language to manipulate or browbeat listeners into agreement. Red-top newspapers have a specific vocabulary of emotive terms that excite readers more than plain English. People (usually celebrities) don't criticise, they *slam*. A disagreement is a *rift*. The protagonists are *warring*. Any response in the negative is a *denial*. Its positive equivalent is a *confession*. Highly-paid managers are *fat cats*. Adulterers are *love rats*, and pursue their *romantic trysts* in *love nests*. The same applies with marginally greater subtlety to tabloid TV news. They are both in the business of selling access to readers' or viewers' eyeballs to advertisers. The more sensational the headlines, the more advertising money rolls in.

Emotive language has been used to control behaviour since the year dot. Religious leaders use the word *faith* to describe their own religion, and *cult* or *sect* to depict someone else's. Criticism of the faith is *blasphemy*, walking away from it is *apostasy*. Disagreeing with doctrine is termed *turning your back on the gods*; *weakening to Satan's entreaties*, and so on.

> In modern times, a prime minister seeking MPs' support for a Middle-East bombing campaign suggested that those who planned to vote against him were *terrorist sympathisers*, as if being a fellow-traveller of murderers were the only reason not to give full-throated support to a remote military adventure.

Emotive language is also a feature of that other great power see-saw – parent and child:

What a child calls it	What a parent calls it
My friends	That crowd of worthless idiots
Skipping classes	On the road to prison like Uncle Billy

Going to a party with friends	Wasting money on drink and drugs
Music	Your grandfather fought a war so you can listen to that tuneless trash?
What I plan to wear	You look like a tramp

While not fallacious on its own, emotive language may be a sign of an ad hominem attack such as poisoning the well, or an argument from outrage. In argument, emotive language carries no more persuasive weight than plain speaking.

Empty truth

An empty truth is a statement that is technically true, but only because the situation it describes doesn't exist.

> "I never let my girlfriend drive my Ferrari for two reasons: I don't own a Ferrari and I don't have a girlfriend."

The empty or vacuous truth is a much-loved technique among spokespeople who need to deny outright that the nice folks they speak for have been up to some hanky-panky.

> "No terror suspects have been tortured in this country."

There's an outside chance that a plain reading of the statement may be factually true. More likely, given the precise phrasing, the statement is accurate because suspects are tortured elsewhere.[49] So the statement can be clinically true and utterly meaningless. Empty truths abound:

> "We have no knowledge of any transgressions committed by anyone in this corporation." [We never checked.]

> "We have no record of any accusations made against ministers

---

[49] It's called "extraordinary rendition" – seizing a suspect abroad, and dragging them off to a compliant third country for chit-chats in interrogation centres where the guest rooms have no mini-bar or Xbox. Not only does the practice allow security services and their political masters to appear to have clean hands, it prevents house prices being affected by nuisance levels of screaming.

and senior politicians in the 1980s." [Not since that unfortunate shredding accident yesterday.]

"No pupil in this school failed GCSE Latin." [No-one sat the exam.]

"Sadly, I never had a number one single." [I never recorded a song.]

The empty truth is a premise which is both true or false because there's nothing to validate or falsify. And it crops up when you have a conditional statement based on a false premise.

"If that's justice, I'm a banana."

"If Rome were the capital of France, it would be in France."

Other examples are the weasely non-apologies used by figures whose sole regret is getting caught:

"If I have anything to apologise for [I don't], that is a matter of regret."

"It was never my intention for people to take offence." [Who are these losers?]

"If people are offended, I'm sorry." [If people take offence, that's their choice.]

"If there has been any wrongdoing, we will investigate thoroughly and bring to book anyone who has broken the rules." [This matter is at an end.]

These standard forms of non-apology go through the motions of contrition but make it clear they think the complaints are trivial and contrived.

As an argument or supporting statement, an empty truth is as close to a misrepresentation as it's possible to get.

Reductio ad Hitlerum

This colourful fallacy is one where someone compares an argument – one that is blameless in every way – with something Hitler, the Nazis or the Third Reich would have approved, and is therefore wrong.

140

It's both a form of ad hominem and a specific instance of guilt by association, except the alleged connection with Nazism is spurious. In using it, the intention is to sidetrack a discussion, not to illuminate it. Hence it's a red herring fallacy.

> "Naturally, he loves watercolour painting, Hitler's preferred medium."

> "The new deputy head's regime makes assembly totally silent. Today St Winifred's Primary, tomorrow Nuremburg."

> "I never liked that pop group. Hitler called his dog Blondi."

> "Of course the chairman likes Wagner, the Nazis' composer of choice."

> "The new corporate policy is bound to find some support, even if it's only among the HR Director's brown shirts."

> "Stop correcting my English, you grammar Nazi."

The phrase reductio ad Hitlerum was first used by Professor Leo Strauss in 1951. There's also a parallel reductio ad Stalinum fallacy, which paints opponents and their works and pomps in the extreme left-wing colours of another tyrant.

A modern take on this fallacy is Godwin's Law of the internet. This observation states that the longer an online discussion continues, the more likely someone will compare a participant to Hitler or the Nazis. But anyone who needs to play the Nazi card is resorting to an ad hominem attack. They have already lost the argument. Think of it as a white flag of surrender.

Loaded question – complex question fallacy

You have to love online discussion boards:

> "Are the Apollo moon landings still taught as historical fact in schools?"

Some questions come scattering broken glass. They have a big, disparaging assumption built into them, which can't be answered without appearing defensive, or seeming to validate the assumption. The sceptic's implied assertion is that the Moon landings are contentious, a view at least as valid as saying they were real achievements, and that raising the question is a level-headed enquiry. Trying to equate an overwhelming consensus with crackpot conjecture is a false equivalence fallacy.

The standard example of a loaded question is:

"Have you stopped beating your wife yet?"

Here we have an emotive, derogatory assumption tied to a false dichotomy. Loaded questions are handy rhetorical devices, often exploited in the political arena.

"Have you found it hard to sleep at night because innocent civilians are being killed in this war?"

"Does it bother you that the poorest people in society are losing their welfare safety net and turn to suicide?"

"When the votes are counted, do you think throwing the gates open to waves of immigrants will be the policy that lost you the election?"

These are complex questions. They presuppose facts that have not been proven independently or been agreed by the parties involved. In the examples: civilian casualties; welfare loss leading to suicides; open gates and immigration waves. These unconfirmed premises prompting the questions are bare assertions of fact. Accordingly, they make unsound arguments.

Complex questions need not be fallacious per se. If the question assumes something that is broadly accepted as proven, or which the respondent would readily agree to, it's legitimate. For instance:

"Which is the fastest breed of dog?"

This (not altogether probing) question presupposes there are different breeds, and that bookies have managed to figure out which make of mutt needs the shortest odds. Both presumptions are true, and no-one would have any hesitation accepting them. However:

"Minister, shouldn't leprechauns pay a windfall tax on their rainbow gold?"

... is a complex question. It makes an assumption that leprechauns do exist; that there is gold at the end of a rainbow; and that you can overcome their magical defences long enough to force them to fill in a tax return. That's two *falses* and one *probably-not*. Any sensible respondent would ignore the question, and suggest you cut back on the recreational drugs.

Journalists love loaded and complex questions, because they're tricky to deal with without appearing devious, or inadvertently owning up to some embarrassing flaw. Put simply, it's a trap. Even when fairly and effectively dealt with, there's always a good chance the interviewer will follow up with:

"You're dodging the question"

... and keep hammering away.

Faced with a loaded question, reject the premise of the question. Point out the inherent flaws in it and re-phrase it into something that is at least germane to the debate. Better still, turn the tables, and engage full strawman and false dichotomy modes:

"Have you found it hard to sleep at night because innocent civilians are being killed in this war?"

"Every target was carefully evaluated for its military value and our people take every possible step to minimise injury to civilians. To suggest that our men and women, the bravest of the brave, who put their own lives at risk every day far from the safety of your television studio, would go out of their way to murder innocent people is an atrocious, outrageous lie. They aren't here to defend their courage and honour but I am. You should apologise immediately. Do you apologise, yes or no? Yes or no? No answer? Then I choose our men and women in uniform and I'm finished with you."

"Does it bother you that the poorest people in society are losing their welfare safety net and turn to suicide?"

"Every suicide is a tragedy, and I don't think you should sully the memories of loving families with cruel and naïve smears about their state of mind. They aren't here [etc.]"

"When the votes are counted, do you think throwing the gates open to waves of immigrants will be the policy that lost you the election?"

"The only waves of immigrants I know of are the poor wretches cast adrift in leaking boats, abandoned to their fate on the open seas. Women and children exploited by traffickers. You would prefer to see them drown? I can't agree with you on that. All lives are precious to me and my party. They aren't here [etc.]"

But they don't answer the question, you say. It doesn't matter. Loaded questions aren't asked to get answers. They are designed to ambush and embarrass. While two wrongs don't make a right (see *tu quoque*), it's satisfying to turn tables on lazy and slanted questioning.

False analogy, false equivalence

An analogy is comparing two things, usually with the aim of explaining or clarifying one of them. Here's a clunky analogy about the real qualities we look for in love being on the inside:

> "Finding true love is like metal-detecting for buried treasure. You can't see what you want by looking on the surface."

An argument by analogy takes the form of linking things A and B that seem to share a common property. You extend this to imply that, because A has some further quality, B must share that same quality – in this example, the amount of training needed:

> "Airline pilots are like taxi drivers. They both take people from one place to another. There's no difference between them. Why do pilots need so much expensive training?"

Analogy stumbles if the two things have only a superficial resemblance and are otherwise completely different; or the differences are irrelevant to the conclusion; or only happen rarely. In these cases, the argument feels strained. Take this simile of the EU juggernaut as a humble bike:

> Former president of the European Commission Jacques Delors said, "Europe is like a bicycle. Stop moving forward and you fall."

It's a contrivance which suits the argument that the EU must press ahead and evolve. But Europe is nothing like that simple and harmless mode of transport. An opponent might easily counter the nonsensical analogy with:

> "Europe is like an aircraft sailing the blue skies of political imagination. Sooner or later it has to come back down to Earth, or crash killing everyone on board."

Argument by analogy can be pithy, catchy and witty. But when we liken two things that are vastly different in importance or relevance, we are far short of being convincing. It's called false equivalence.

> "A book about reasoning is like making a do-and-don't list. There were only ten commandments, but this book has a hundred fallacies. So it must be ten times more important than Moses' effort."

> 'Cousin Vera accidentally switched off Great Aunt Ruby's freezer and £200 of food was spoiled. Cousin Bernard criticised her, but Vera reminded him of the time he left the lid off a tin of paint and it went hard. "It's hardly the same," he said.'

People use analogies in everyday speech. Any shared quality will do to link generally dissimilar things:

> "The Russian Tsars and Uncle Billy both liked a nice bit of Fabergé, except Uncle Billy stole his."

> "You're hunting UFOs. Cousin Vera's searching for the perfect recipe for syllabub. You guys have so much in common."

> "Hawks and helicopters both hover in the air. It would save money if we could run helicopters on dead mice."

The more obscure and fanciful, the more entertaining and memorable the comment. Accordingly, you find opinion pieces in the media that are positively starlit with false analogy and equivalence because the media (sweeping generalisation) are primarily concerned with audience figures not factual depth. They often reveal themselves in lurid similes and colourful metaphors:

> "Cyclists, like sneak-thieves and pilferers, choose on the spot which road laws to obey or ignore. They are the opportunist burglars of the transport world."

> "The town council, re-igniting the suffering of tens of thousands of Roma in Nazi concentration camps, evicted the travellers from the railway station car-park."

> "The coalition party leaders, like two diseases battling for control over the host body, haggled over cabinet posts."

In the smoking, fox-hole-strewn battlefield of online debate, the air is radioactive with false analogy. Any sense of proportion goes into the recycle bin. Forums are littered with vernacular equating anyone with a different point of view to some extreme description:

Grammar Nazi! Attention whore! Klan apologist!

In the USA, a civic registrar who refused to issue a marriage licence to gay couples was called an *American Taliban*, which is a reductio ad hitlerum type of argument. Now that print media have online versions with comments sections, false equivalence reasoning abounds:

"What's wrong with calling people queer? I don't mind being called straight."

"If cops kill kids on the streets, we might as well arm the school kids."

"Social services should have prevented that child being murdered. They should prosecute the social worker for manslaughter."

"I'm not excusing terrorist murders, but those French cartoons were provocative."

While false equivalence may be good entertainment, it does nothing for superior argument. Often it tells us more about the speaker than their reasoning. Alas, university campuses, once ground-zero for contentious opinions and mighty thinking, have become intellectual shopping malls using false equivalence as currency:

"The university should provide safe spaces for survivors of micro-aggression and harmful opinions."

Survival is getting past a threat to life, not a state of discomfort or irritation. Unwelcome opinions (real and imaginary) are being likened to deadly encounters. It escalates the level of perceived aggression from a contrary point of view to a physical attempt on life. *Survivor of* is loaded language in the extreme. Moreover, exaggerating tiny or non-existent offenses to hideous proportions using overblown vocabulary is a false equivalence. It's like comparing your headache to someone else's cancer. I put it to you that that is a fair analogy.

Equivocation

Comedians rejoice! Words and phrases can have two or more meanings. Plays on words are a rich source of comedy. But if you switch between meanings to complete an argument, you've wandered into the fallacy of equivocation.

First the comedy:

> 'The judge said, "Life!" I thought, that's a short sentence.'

> '"Don't strike me off," pleaded the doctor. "I need my practice." "You certainly do," said the medical council.'

> "My doctor told me to drink a bottle of wine after a hot bath, but I couldn't even finish the bath water."

> "The circus clown may be clever but he's out of work. He's nobody's fool."

Ho ho. When you use a word in more than one sense, your argument becomes misleading or surreal. For instance:

> Outside the weather's bright

> If something's bright, it can't be stupid

> Therefore, the weather can't be stupid.

Guffaws all round? Perhaps not.

> Nothing is better than true love

> Lager is better than nothing

> Therefore, lager is better than true love.

Hashtag pantomime, lol, etc. In both cases, the middle term switches to another meaning of the word or phrase. *Bright* has two senses and *nothing is better* has a different meaning to *better than nothing*.

Used in arguments, equivocation looks like this:

> "A priest is a man of God, so women can't be priests."

> "There's a man-eating tiger on the loose. So women will be safe fetching water."

A common and deliberate use of equivocation lies in confusing the everyday meaning of theory and its scientific meaning:

> "The theory of evolution is just that, a theory. Guesswork."

In common usage, theory means: an unsubstantiated hypothesis, a speculative (especially fanciful) view.[50] But that's not the meaning of a scientific theory, which is:

> "a system of ideas or statements explaining something, esp. one based on general principles independent of the things to be explained; a hypothesis that has been confirmed or establish by observation or experiment and is accepted as accounting for known facts."[51]

The dictionary goes on to give examples: atomic theory, gauge theory, theory of evolution and theory of relativity. Long story short: scientific theory is not guesswork.

Another word often exploited in equivocation arguments is *faith*:

> "You put your faith in test-tubes and equations; my faith is in God Himself."

They are not the same thing. Like theory, faith has two meanings: confidence in and belief without doubt or evidence. Science most emphatically demands evidence, while religion insists that you suspend that requisite.

Back to deliberate equivocation, which makes these job references possible:

> "No-one would be better in this role than Vera."

> "You'll be very lucky to get Billy to work for you."

> "I'm happy to confirm Bernard is a former employee of ours."

> "Cuthbert's work ethic has had a big influence on the team's overall productivity."

> "Trixie is in a class of her own."

> "The team project was on the threshold of failure, but Billy's contribution pulled us through."

> "There is nothing you can teach Bernard."

---

[50] Shorter Oxford English Dictionary.

[51] Ibid.

Comedy gold, no?

False attribution

False attribution is all over daily conversation like measles. When you invoke a dodgy source to support your argument, that's false attribution. You might be referring to irrelevant, unidentified, unqualified or even fictional sources. Note that false doesn't refer necessarily to the information, but to the source you rely on.

"There's no point voting. That unfunny comedian says so."

"Falstaff tells us that doing things for honour isn't worth it."

"Uncle Billy told me Newcastle United will win the Premier League."

"You have to be careful with injections. Cousin Vera said vaccination causes autism."

Oh, really? And more importantly, what are her medical qualifications? Which studies is she quoting? Here's a fact: non-vaccination allows preventable illnesses to spread – says every doctor.

We seem to put great store by the opinions of celebrities on topics they have no great insight into. (See *appeal to authority*.) Then there's the go-to person for famous quotations:

"As Churchill once said…"

If Churchill had uttered half the things attributed to him, he wouldn't have had time to pursue a war.[52] If not Churchill, try Oscar Wilde, Shakespeare, Confucius, Buddha, George Bernard Shaw, Ghandi or Yogi Berra, all of whom are good for a quote. Most of the sayings attributed to those august thinkers are dubious, but it gives your claim a veneer of authority and scholarship. No matter how famous the speaker is, though, their pronouncements are not necessarily true or accurate or sound.

---

[52] The list of famous and witty things that Churchill never said is endless. Moreover, many that he did say were repetitions from his own favourite authors. He used them a lot, often without flagging them with quotation marks or explicit attribution. He didn't feel the need, since he assumed listeners would recognise them in those better-read days.

False attribution can consist of vague or unspecified sources. Beware assertions introduced with:

"I read somewhere…"

"I saw this programme on TV…"

"I heard that…"

"You know what they say…"

"It said in the paper that…"

These are oblique appeals to common knowledge or bandwagon arguments.

Quoting out of context

Poetry time:

If you can bear to hear the truth you've spoken

Twisted by knaves to make a trap for fools[53]

Quoting out of context is a form of false attribution. It's an informal fallacy, and is as popular today as ever. Taking an opponent's words out of context in order to beat them up is standard practice among politicians. You try to make your opponent look extreme or silly, both for its own sake and to make it easier to demolish their case. Misrepresenting an opponent's position is a strawman argument.

Another common scenario is to selectively hijack a well-known person's utterances to support your argument, which is an appeal to authority. Some of the best (that is, worst) examples are book, DVD, cinema and theatre notices, known as blurb. PR practitioners – no strangers to the sleight of hand that is enticement – extract with surgical precision the exact words that make their dud production sound like the second coming.

In these kinds of review, the phrases underlined would appear on the promotional posters:

"If puerile smut is your thing, you'll love this."

"The original version was a tour-de-force. This is utter drivel."

---

[53] *If* by Rudyard Kipling. often voted Britain's favourite poem.

"It's a peculiar film of no great merit other than its brevity."

Look for the ellipses, which tell you that inconvenient wording has been cut out:

"...You'll love this "

"Original... a tour-de-force "

"A... film of... great merit "

The plot of many a murder mystery hangs on the accused being recorded saying something innocuous. Their words are edited by the killer (into what the industry calls a *Frankenbite*) and used to frame the innocent person.

Obviously, there's a funny side to quoting out of context. It works well visually:

> A politician photographed in front of a sign for the place Mordon, where his head obscures the letter D.
>
> The Scottish politician snapped alongside the slogan, Flying Scotsman, covering up the letter F.
>
> A youthful-looking candidate running for office in Virginia, obscuring the letters: IA.

Puffing out promo material for entertainment is relatively harmless, all things considered. Much worse is the habit in pseudo-scientific writing of "quote-mining" broadly-accepted scientific publications to stitch together a dissenting argument with apparent authority. It's a form of cherry picking and false authority.

Quote-mining takes time and effort. It's not a momentary oversight, or a casual lapse, like a cut-and-paste accident, or predictive text on a phone. It's a calculated manoeuvre to hoodwink people. If you have to stoop to that level of intellectual fraud, it may be time to re-evaluate the truth of your cause.

If-by-whiskey fallacy

This, surely, has to be the politicians' very own fallacy and has the best name of all. The if-by-whiskey argument uses emotive language to seemingly support both sides of a contentious issue, depending on the view of the listener. Does that sound like a politician or what?

The fallacy takes its name from a real event. The politician in question was the fabulously named Noah S. "Soggy" Sweat Jr. in 1952 answering a question about whether he would legalise liquor in the state of Mississippi. He answered:

> "If when you say whiskey you mean the devil's brew, the poison scourge, the bloody monster, that defiles innocence, dethrones reason, destroys the home, creates misery and poverty, yea, literally takes the bread from the mouths of little children; if you mean the evil drink that topples the Christian man and woman from the pinnacle of righteous, gracious living into the bottomless pit of degradation, and despair, and shame and helplessness, and hopelessness, then certainly I am against it.

> "But, if when you say whiskey you mean the oil of conversation, the philosophic wine, the ale that is consumed when good fellows get together, that puts a song in their hearts and laughter on their lips, and the warm glow of contentment in their eyes; if you mean Christmas cheer; if you mean the stimulating drink that puts the spring in the old gentleman's step on a frosty, crispy morning; if you mean the drink which enables a man to magnify his joy, and his happiness, and to forget, if only for a little while, life's great tragedies, and heartaches, and sorrows; if you mean that drink, the sale of which pours into our treasuries untold millions of dollars, which are used to provide tender care for our little crippled children, our blind, our deaf, our dumb, our pitiful aged and infirm; to build highways and hospitals and schools, then certainly I am for it.

> "This is my stand. I will not retreat from it. I will not compromise."

Isn't that magnificent? It remains to this day the staunchest example of political fence-sitting ever. He makes the most passionate, heart-tugging, devious and sincere case in support of both positions. That must be worth a vote.

A modern version of an if-by-whiskey argument might be someone over-eager to please a prospective date:

> "If you like we could go out and have a meal, or a few drinks, see the bright lights, some live music, let our hair down and paint the

town red.[54] That would be great. But if you prefer something quieter, we can stay in, have a nice meal, open a bottle of wine, watch a film, just the two of us. Whichever you prefer, that's what I want to do."

They say you can't please everyone all the time. The if-by-whiskey fallacy is an attempt to do just that.

Incomplete comparison

Step with me into the grubby and misleading world of advertising and promotion, to me as familiar and evocative as the smell of acid to a serial killer.

Advertisers always want to pitch their product as superior to their competitors'. They might want to persuade you their offering is or has:

Better quality, more features, lower price, faster delivery, longer lifespan, wider choice, more relaxing showrooms, less worry, easier comparison, works more quickly, greater familiarity, is bought by posher people, quicker 0 to 60, more authentic, more readily available, more modern, and so on. Whatever you want, we offer better.

But better than what? These comparisons are all incomplete.

If an advertiser presents a complete comparison, it has to be provably true, otherwise the lawyers start sharpening their quills and sending off for yacht catalogues. So they use incomplete comparisons to assert some superior attribute without committing themselves to a side-by-side evaluation. As such, the assertions are meaningless. The technique allows consumers to finish the comparison in their head, making the assessment the most suitable for them. This makes the statements fanciful and speculative. Not only does the consumer not know what's being compared, neither does the advertiser:

A healthier diet for a healthier you.

---

[54] Okay, it's been a while. I have no idea what people do for a lively night out these days. Ice skating? Bell ringing? Brass rubbing?

Healthier than what? A regime consisting solely of pork pies fashioned from pure lard? Healthier than a chain-smoking couch-whale with an aversion to fresh air and personal hygiene?

Incomplete comparison is verbal sleight of hand. It says our product, whatever it is, will make you more like you want to be in your dreams. It preys on people with a poor self-image. All you have to do is give us money and you can immediately feel better about yourself. The misdirection conceals the fact that the product has been manufactured with lots of stuff in it to give it flavour, colour, shelf-life, and so on. I can think of two cases in which *a healthier diet for a healthier you* could literally be true:

> You go outside and dig up a load of vegetables, or
>
> You chase down a wild deer on foot and have a tasty, low-fat venison steak.

Driving to the greengrocer or butcher doesn't count. To sum up, then, incomplete comparison boils down to a slogan that more or less says:

> "Buy our stuff because it's got more of what you imagine it has, and less of what you hope it doesn't."

Persuasive? Not very, which is why honesty is not a cherished quality in advertising. But even outside the marketing department, you'll hear phrases like:

> Sales are up this year – profits are bigger – costs are lower

These corporate blandishments are incomplete comparisons. Precision is missing. What do these woolly statements mean?

Does bigger profits mean more money or bigger percentages? More pound note or dollar bill profits may be made on a larger turnover, which means your percentage margins fell. And if your percentage profits increased, it may be a result of dropping less profitable lines so the sales fell. Costs might be ten per cent lower – which sounds like a good thing. But if sales are 20 per cent lower, it isn't. The question for all casual remarks is compared to what? and in what context? To have any meaning, comparisons need to be complete.

In general, we are pretty bad at comparisons. Every day, we seem to be happy regurgitating glib statements without considering them in the round:

"Supermarket X is cheaper."

"This broadband service is better."

"Electric cars have a better carbon footprint…"

Getting from A to B, yes. But not necessarily when you calculate the energy of mining the elements needed for the battery, and shipping them around the world for manufacture; the fossil fuel power stations generating electricity to re-charge it; and eventually disposing of the knackered unit. The comparison is incomplete.

"Kids today have an easier time of it."

They certainly have more microprocessor-controlled toys and ready access to all the information in the world that's available online. But all that instant and widespread communication through smartphones using social media tends to amplify the anxiety all kids have making friends, fitting in, dealing with peer pressure, handling the hormones, and so on. Again, easier is incomplete.

"It's cheaper by train."

I think you'll find walking's free. Wait, you mean over a distance? Try hitch-hiking. When making comparisons, it's important to know what's being compared, and having all the relevant information needed to make the comparison reasonable. Lacking a complete picture, an argument that relies on unfinished slogans is weak.

Inconsistent comparison

This fallacious type of argument can be summed up as comparing apples and oranges. Again, it's a feature of advertising. First, let me boast about my new wheels:

"I have a two-seater that's cheaper to buy than a Ferrari, less expensive to insure than a Porsche, has better fuel consumption than a Mini, and lower exhaust emissions than a Prius. Envious?"

Listing all the famous marques suggests that my new conveyance is in the same league of prestige. (See *juxtaposition*.) Indeed, I'm tacitly suggesting that my recent purchase – all round – is better than those other vehicles in every respect, not just the one attribute I single out for each comparison. I am being deliberately ambiguous, though. The clue is that I haven't used the word car. In fact, I have a tandem bicycle.

Inconsistent comparison has little value because all you're doing is complicating the picture. If I promote a train service as:

"Faster than the bus; cheaper than a plane."

You don't really get much of a feel for the product and its advantages: almost anything can be faster than a bus or cheaper than a fist-class plane ticket. If I said the train was:

"Faster than the bus, but slower than a plane," or

"More comfortable than the bus, but not as luxurious as the plane,"

...the consistent references might help you decide. Advertisers use inconsistent comparison because it works, until they get hauled up for hoodwinking the public:

The makers of a proprietary ibuprofen brand found themselves in trouble for promoting their product as: "Clinically proven to offer faster relief from headaches than ordinary paracetamol."

Which is like saying:

"Our heroin relaxes you more than ordinary raspberry yoghurt."

In general, advertising standards agencies around the world respond promptly to complaints from the public and do a good job of keeping advertisers on their toes.

But it's not all one-sided from those evil advertisers. We shop by comparing dissimilar products, trying to optimise our choice, to get the best option for us. We don't compare a large size, bottle-green, V-neck pullover in 100 per cent wool from Marks & Spencer with an identical product from Matalan. We compare it to a cheaper, navy-blue, roll-neck polyester cotton blend with a cheaper price. Being torn over the shopping trolley[55] is a consequence of inconsistent comparison. For some shoppers, that exquisite dilemma is the bit they enjoy most.

Now, online comparison sites are popular. They (mostly) go to the trouble of listing standard features whereby we can see a side-by-side line-up of price, features, performance, and so on. It's methodical and sensible, if less fun.

---

[55] "Cart" in American.

None of this, however, changes the fact that an argument relying on an inconsistent comparisons is weak.

Kettle logic – alternative pleading

This is another fun fallacy, but with a serious point.

"Cousin Bernard complains to his local council that the dog next door is a nuisance. It barks loudly and wakes him up in the morning. His devious neighbour claims, in the first place, the dog only ever barks in the evening. Even if it does bark in the morning, the dog is kept in the house so its barking would be inaudible outside. Besides, the dog is trained never to bark. Moreover, the dog is a non-barking breed and cannot bark. Anyway, he doesn't own a dog."

The neighbour's statements are comically inconsistent. If any one of those claims is true, none of the others can be. Even Cousin Bernard's worst enemy would have to concede that the neighbour's litany of excuses seems dubious. This is kettle logic or alternative pleading.

The name comes from an example given by Sigmund Freud[56] of someone returning a borrowed kettle which has become damaged. The borrower offers three arguments:

When he gave the kettle back, it wasn't damaged

The kettle was already damaged when he borrowed it

He didn't borrow the kettle to begin with

For any statement to be true, the others must be false. But there's an important role for alternative pleading. In a civil law action, for example, a defendant might well put forward a series of *even if, besides* and *anyway* defences to explain why he's not liable to the claimant. Mutually exclusive defences can be advanced without having to explain how they relate to each other. The judge has to evaluate each on its merits regardless of their collective inconsistency, since any one of them could be successful independently from the others. Faced with seemingly credible defences, the claimant bears the burden of proof of knocking them all down. If he can't, a judge might find room to believe some part of the defendant's story.

---

[56] *The Interpretation of Dreams* – Sigmund Freud (1899).

Outside the legal arena, it's best to avoid kettle logic unless you're aiming for comedy. Most people will just assume you have something to hide, and conclude that if some of the statements must logically be false, they all might as well be.

Moral high ground fallacy

The moral high ground is a misunderstood phrase. These days, it seems to have a pejorative connotation. It's used on people with a superior, holier-than-thou, stuck up, snobbish, aloof, elitist attitude.

But, in fact, if you occupy the moral high ground, you are declining to get involved in activities you don't think are acceptable or legitimate. You conduct yourself in ways that are seen as good and fair. You stand by your principles.

> Although a staunch Irish republican, Frank Carney served in the British army in WWI. After a short political career as a member of De Valera's government, he died at a young age. Among his papers, his family found the many army pension payments that he'd refused to cash on principle.

> "Uncle Billy will not use Barclays Bank on principle because between 2005 and 2009 its staff rigged the Libor[57] bank rate. By *use*, I mean he refused to rob a branch."

The non sequitur lies in assuming any argument that seeks the moral high ground or purports to speak from the moral high ground is necessarily right.

> "Cousin Vera is a vegetarian. She doesn't agree with killing animals. She says the death penalty is wrong."

> "Smokers shouldn't get treatment from the NHS," argues Cousin Bernard, a life-long non-smoker. Bernard is in a position to know.

It's also misleading to claim the moral high ground as way of looking good when it's manifestly untrue. The following slice of rancid hypocrisy comes from the website of a very well-known mobile phone corporation, one notorious for channelling European revenues through

---

[57] London Interbank Offered Rate. It sets the interest rate for many deals between banks. Barclays paid $450m in fines. Other banks colluded too, and were also fined.

a microscopic office in Luxembourg, thus avoiding billions of pounds in UK tax:

> "Working in an ethical way is not a bolt-on, not something fluffy we do after the real business of the day is done – it's at the heart of everything we do, and every decision we take".

It's utter codswallop, of course, and undermines everything else on the website. Abusing the moral high ground is probably what's given the stance such a bad name. But taking the moral high ground can still be a genuine way to live by your principles, doing what you believe is right for its own sake. Go on, make the world a better place.

Moving the goalposts

Most of us have experienced this. In reasoning, moving the goalposts happens when you offer evidence to support your argument, but your opponent demands different or better proof. Your opponent is changing the rules of the debate after you start to win it. This fallacy is sometimes called raising the bar.

> "Okay, so they saw Uncle Billy on CCTV. Yes, they found all the cases of stolen St Emilion in his garage, but where's the DNA evidence?"

> "Cousin Bernard demonstrated that his software did everything the specification asked, but then his boss insisted it had to be optimised for mobile devices before Bernard got the bonus he was promised."

> "I agree the A380 meets the airline's every requirement, but it's not supersonic."

If you're being bullied at work, you'll often find your tasks becoming ever more demanding. It's a depressingly regular feature of harassment, with the aim of belittling, embarrassing or humiliating the victim.

As a logical fallacy, moving the goalposts is a common argument from someone in denial who will not be persuaded, come hell or high water.

> "Fine, so you can prove those fossils are over 6,000 years old. They were made that way to test our faith. You can't prove God didn't do that."

"I accept that nuclear power stations would help combat global warming, but spent fuel isn't compostable."

Mission creep is a fact of everyday life. Athletic records get faster, higher, further every year. Features of high technology products are in constant development. New software versions and updates are so routine, most of us let our computer download and install it automatically. Goalposts move naturally. The fallacy lies in insisting that by changing your standard, you can invalidate a perfectly sound argument. (See *slippery slope fallacy*.)

Verbosity – proof by

If you're a living expert in your field, it can be tedious when some ill-informed amateur challenges your argument or proof. Such lèse-majesté![58] So you deliberately lay out your argument in painstaking, convoluted detail, discouraging any other clever dick in the audience from questioning your authority. In other words, you talk any challenger into silence.

> "I'm not going to give any illustrations of proof by verbosity. You know what's involved, and life is too short. Instead, just picture an example in which my Uncle Billy might explain to a parking warden why he shouldn't get a ticket. Imagine the richness of the language; the detail of the by-laws; the enumeration of facts as he sees them which refute utterly the warden's version of events; the alternative reasoning; the incidental fallacies; all wrapped up in Uncle Billy's compelling narrative style. By the time you lose the will to live, Uncle Billy's just getting into his stride."

Enough. That's 100 words. Verbose enough to make the point. This fallacy also goes by the moniker proof by intimidation, which is a bit clearer about what's happening.

Brow-beating your audience into submission or bamboozling them into dumb acceptance is not a persuasive argument, even if technically your explanation is correct, once unravelled.

A version of argument by verbosity is shotgun argument. A speaker offers a rapid-fire stream of arguments so that opponents can't

---

[58] "Lezz mazhes-tay" Literally, *insult to a monarch*. Figuratively, *presumptuous behaviour* or *disrespect*. You know which dictionary by now.

get a word in edgeways, let alone refute any of them. It was the notorious debating technique of creationist Duane Gish, which became known as the Gish Gallup.

It's a rhetorical technique used by those who for some reason prefer their arguments not to be picked apart. It's akin to bullying, but it plays well to the gallery of supporters. To them, a machine-gun litany of unanswered argument is like watching their favourite scenes from *Friends* on fast forward. In doing so, speakers shield their fans from hearing their point of view challenged. Their manifest lack of debating courtesy means they won't be asked back to speak, which allows supporters to claim opponents are too afraid to argue with their point of view.

But in debating terms, proof by verbosity is like playing a soccer match against a team of none and tying up the referee – you may score a lot of goals, but no-one's impressed.

Repetition – ad nauseam

Ever heard this?

"We've discussed this ad nauseam, let's move on."

Ad nauseam is Latin for *'to the point of sickness'*, and you have to admit the Romans knew a thing or two about tactical vomiting. Some people are a broken record when it comes to a pet hate or hobby-horse. Closing down the argument completely is sometimes the only thing linking you and sanity:

"The conclusion we've reached over many debates stands, unless you have something new to say."

The best way to slap someone down is to explain that the time for debate is over and the ship of deliberation has sailed. Point out that nothing has material has changed in their argument and therefore the conclusion remains the same.

Which takes us neatly to politicians, advertising people and small children. Repeating the same words or phrases without putting forward any supporting argument can at best only nag the listener into submission. Test: match the statement to the politician, advertiser or child:

"I want it. I want it. I want it."

"You want it. You want it. You want it."

"You want me. You want me. You want me."

Advertisers do it to make you remember the utterly forgettable product they're shilling for. Politicians do it to persuade you there is a single, simple solution to your problems, and it only needs an X beside their name. The kid is more honest than that – it just wants what it wants.

Politicians love this proof by repeated assertion fallacy. If you say something often enough, no matter how spurious, people believe it. Political slogans tend to hammer out the points that particular party sees as important. You hear members of the same party consistently singing from the same hymn book across the media landscape. They've been thoroughly briefed with the same talking points by their party's whips.

If persuasion is too ambitious, lawmakers speaking continuously until all the debating time has been used up is a filibuster in the USA, while in the UK we say that a bill has been *'talked out'*.

When someone repeatedly asserts their proposition, despite sufficient contradiction, and uses that repetition as evidence of truth, you're seeing an attempted proof by repetition.

> "We wrote to the military authorities eleven times asking what they were covering up. Each time they denied any cover up. Solid evidence, you'll agree, they have something to hide."

> "The company turned down our repeated requests for an interview. Clearly, we're on the right track, and they're ducking the issue."

> Uncle Billy said to the detective: "I keep telling you. I've never seen that Fabergé Egg before in my life. What more do you want?"

If insanity is doing the same thing over and over again and expecting different results, then arguing by repetition at least deserves some thought about how persuasive your argument is.

11. PAINTING BY NUMBERS

Some people have the gift of numeracy. They have a feel for statistics that gives them an instinct for challenging arguments based on numbers:

> Cousin Bernard read the claim on Facebook: "In the UK 13 million people are living in poverty." Really? he thought. That's about 20 per cent of the population. One citizen in five. Seems like a lot. How do they define poverty? Does it include owning a smartphone and broadband?

In fact, the definition comes from the UK's Child Poverty Act 2010: *'poverty'* is household income below 60 percent of median income. Poverty is being defined relatively, compared to an average. Because median income is a movable feast (okay, a poor choice of words when talking about poverty), and there will always be a distribution of incomes around the median, by definition the poor will always be with us. The definition ensures that somewhere around 20 per cent of people meet the criterion for poverty and would continue to be *'poor'* if the median income figure were to grow.

For the country, then, it's a self-fulfilling condition. It ensures the poverty industry has plenty of ammunition in perpetuity. Unfortunately, the broad definition disguises the smaller number of cases of abject poverty – homeless, no income, reliant on handouts – desperate people who truly need our sympathy and help.

Within the official definition of poverty, we can expect to find families with fair housing, colour TVs, a games console, smart phones and a fashionable sense of victimhood. An absolute definition would identify specific measures of poverty – shelter, sustenance, clothing, literacy. The destitute living on the streets of developing nations would be dazzled by the luxury of poverty in the UK.

It's like defining the standard for an A-grade in a public exam as the top 15 per cent of entrants, regardless of the marks students obtain. A-grades will always be 15 per cent regardless of the changing abilities of one annual cohort to the next. On the plus side, it evens out inconsistent exam difficulty from one year to the next. On the other hand, 15 per cent of a particularly dense cohort is guaranteed to get top grades, as is an outstanding one.

Every day we hear arguments using numbers to reinforce their point. They sound robust and authoritative, but numbers can be deceptive. Often attributed, incorrectly, to Churchill the phrase that sums up the position is:

"There are three kinds of lies: lies, damned lies, and statistics."

Mark Twain claimed it was Disraeli who coined the term. He himself said:

"Figures often beguile me, particularly when I have the arranging of them myself."

Whether we're comfortable juggling numbers or not, we're surrounded by arguments that use them. It's all too easy to baffle ourselves with statistics. For that reason, it's important to be able to spot the main fallacies that stem from a weak grasp of numbers.

Base rate fallacy

As soon as that four-letter word *rate* sneaks into view, the troubling prospect of unfathomable mathematics stirs in most people. Nevertheless, it's important to grasp at least the principles. It's the fallacy by which we may:

- persuade ourselves we might have a serious illness

- get arrested as a terrorist

- get sacked for failing a drugs test at work

The base rate fallacy – sometimes called base-rate neglect – is one where we ignore solid statistical evidence and concentrate on irrelevant, perhaps superficial, things to make a judgement. In other words, we ignore the general, underlying information (the base rate – sometimes called a prior probability), and focus unduly on the instance in front of us.

Let's start slowly:

Under a beach umbrella by the Mediterranean, you see a pale-skinned, red-haired man hiding from the sun. He's reading an English-language newspaper. Is he more likely to be Scottish or American? Is it a simple 50 / 50, yes or no sort of situation?

We think of red hair as a Celtic colouration, reinforced by the many stereotypes of Scottishness from the (historically risible) film *Braveheart* to Groundskeeper Willie in *The Simpsons*. If you know your gingers[59] too, you'll plump for Scottish. Scotland has the highest incidence of red hair in the world, around 13 per cent of the population – some 690,000 people.

With Americans, the incidence is only somewhere between two and five per cent. But the population of the USA is about 316 million. That means there are at least 6.3 million gingers with American accents, perhaps several millions more, and certainly more than the entire population of Scotland.

All things being equal, our pale pal is ten times – an order of magnitude – more likely to be American than Scottish. Plumping for Scotland might have seemed the better bet. But the relevant base rate (prior probability) here is the population size of the USA. In fact, despite the small percentage, its large population means the USA has the biggest number of red-haired citizens in the world.

Another example:

> In 2014, 488 hopeful students applied to Magdalene College, Cambridge. Places were offered to 145. That's almost a 30 per cent success rate. My niece Trixie is easily in the smartest 2 per cent of pupils in her school with a dozen A-star grades at GCSE, so she's a shoo-in.

Ah, if wishing made it so. All things being equal (and fingers crossed the college doesn't uncover young Trixie's criminal record, psychopathic hatred for teachers and recently renewed firearms licence), her chances are no better than 30 per cent. That's the acceptance rate (the base rate) for all-comers.

Trixie may be brainy compared to pupils in her school, but that's irrelevant. She's competing alongside all other applicants who themselves may be the cream of the crop in their own school. If the number of applicants and places available remain consistent, her chances are always going to be 30 per cent. She can't be a dead cert.

---

[59] Lest I be accused of gingerism, let me point out I am the proud possessor of the best possible MC1R gene on chromosome 16.

Now let's look at where the base rate fallacy gets serious. Imagine a bad world where evil types kill innocent people at random. Naturally, governments want to protect their citizens, and to do so they ramp up their surveillance powers.

Suppose a country has a population of 50 million. Assume there are 1,000 terrorists actively plotting murder and mayhem.

The likelihood of a citizen randomly stopped being a terrorist is 1,000 in 50 million, that is 0.002 per cent. Correspondingly, the chance that the person stopped is not a terrorist is 99.998 per cent. Agreed?

To help find the bad guys, the government introduces compulsory identity cards together with CCTV cameras with face-recognition software.[60] Say the system has a failure rate of one per cent[61].

This means that if the system spots a terrorist, it raises an alarm 99 per cent of the time, but fails to alert the security services 1 per cent of the time (a false negative).

When the system sifts through non-terrorists, no alarm will be raised 99 per cent of the time, but on 1 per cent of occasions an alert will be raised (a false positive).

One day, you trigger the alarm. What are the chances you'll be arrested?

If the security operative (with a finger hovering over the big, red, *immediate arrest* button) has a cursory knowledge of the numbers, he thinks one per cent false positive error rate means 99 per cent accuracy. That implies there's a 99 per cent chance that when the alarm goes off, you're a baddie. That 99 per cent is a persuasive figure, so the operator would be derelict in his duty not to push the red button. Clang! You're now under arrest.

---

[60] In 2013 the UK had one CCTV camera for every 11 citizens, many of them under private control.

[61] One per cent is beyond the wildest dreams of spooks everywhere. In fact, surveillance software is being accepted with 5 per cent false positive rates for fingerprints and 20 per cent for facial recognition – although I assume that gets better all the time. Apply the latter figure to our example, and the hit rate of actual terrorists is just under 0.01 per cent per alert. That's a lot of blameless voters and taxpayers being detained for questioning.

The fallacy comes about by muddling the significance of the two failure rates. False positive and false negative do not mean the same thing, even if their occurrence is a similar figure. The false negative rate is only relevant to terrorists – the false negative fails to spot a bad guy. For innocent civilians, it's the false positive we worry about.

The number of alarms per goodie (false positive) and the number of baddies per non-alarm (false negative) are a long way apart, because the two groups are hugely different in size (like the populations of Scotland and the USA, remember?). That means the system generates many more false positives than false negatives. Fasten your seat belt.

> Imagine that, sooner or later, the identity system scans the whole population of 50,000,000 people. Some 990 of the 1,000 baddies will trigger the alarm (huzzah!) – that's a 1 per cent false negative. Ten baddies are left at large to carry on committing mayhem.
>
> Among the 49,999,000 goodies scanned by the system, however, 499,990 will also set off the alarm (boo!) – again, a 1 per cent false positive. In a total of 500,980 alarms, therefore, just 990 will actually be baddies.
>
> So when the alarm goes off, the odds that a person triggering it actually is a terrorist, therefore, is 990 ÷ 500,980, a smidge under 0.2 per cent. That's a vanishingly small hit rate, and far lower than the supposedly intuitive figure of 99 per cent.

When security people think that an alarm means there's a 99 per cent chance you're a terrorist, it goes a long way to explain their disgraceful treatment of innocent travellers at airports in supposedly free countries.

In this example of conveniently round numbers, the huge difference between reality and a wrong base rate inference happens because there are many more loyal citizens than terrorists. Rather like real life, in fact. Society may choose to accept a certain level of terrorist risk if it allows most of its people go about their lives without risk of false accusation. Total eradication of risk has implications for personal freedom. Sensible security, good; disproportionate burden, bad.[62]

---

[62] On 31 January 2015, BBC News reported the UK's Police Federation asking

One day, you may also find yourself working for an employer who believes you ought to take a routine drugs test, in case that during the 128 hours a week you don't work for them, and are not being paid by them, you might amuse yourself in ways they disapprove. Often – not always, but often – tests are standard kits administered and processed en masse by unqualified staff.[63] Drug tests routinely produce false positives at a rate of five per cent to ten per cent (and occasionally much higher) depending on the quality of the lab analysing the tests, while labs claim false positives and negatives of under one per cent. Well, they would.

> After, say, 1,000 employees are tested, you appear among the 50 to 100 completely clean colleagues who show up as false positives (5 to 10 per cent). Your employer wrongly assumes that since false positives are claimed to be under 1 per cent, it's therefore 99 per cent likely that you've been having fun of a kind it doesn't endorse. (See *prosecutor's fallacy*.)
>
> Even so, your employer allows you all to re-take the test, just to make sure the lawyers are happy. Among the 50 to 100 retakes, you end up in the group of 3 to 10 people who yet again show up as a false positive. What are the odds, then, that you're entirely innocent? Well, your employer is mesmerised by the claimed false positive of 1 per cent, and believes it's one in 99 multiplied by one in 99. That is, they think the odds of you innocently failing two drug tests is just one in 9,801, or 0.01 per cent.
>
> Put another way, you're fired, Lebowski, and some folks in the Human Capital team get paid a bonus for weeding out another lying junkie.

---

for all "front-line" police officers to be offered a Taser because of "increased terrorism". Two points: the chances of Tasers ever being used on actual terrorists are roughly nil – see false positives above. Second, in the rock, paper, scissors of personal armament, AK47 beats Taser. Quaking in their boots, terrorists are not. Police should carry Tasers to use on violent drunks and fly-tippers.

[63] By "unqualified" I don't mean untrained. I mean individuals who do not possess a formal medical licence to practise which they can lose if they are sloppy.

The thing that killed your career is trusting the claimed false-positive rate of less than one per cent. That's a dream number, a figure the laboratory sales people used to sell their services to the employer. But if the lab or the employer looked at the second test results, and realised that 90 per cent to 95 per cent of the allegedly positive results from the first test were in fact clean, the company should know that the false-positive rate is running at five to ten per cent. That's high enough to leave between three (actually, 2.5) and ten innocent employees failing two tests.

Another important lesson is for people given bad news after medical tests. They may believe it shows there's a high chance they have a serious illness. And there are certainly cases where a patient is treated for a serious disease when they are not at all affected. Newspapers like the phrase *wrongly diagnosed* because it points the finger of blame more sensationally than *false positive*.

But it's better to give a false positive than a false negative, because you don't want to be given an all-clear when you really do need treatment. So the sensitivity of the diagnostic test may be ramped up to give a false negative of nil. A paradox then arises when the incidence of the illness is actually lower than the rate of false positive readings.

> The test for a disease that affects 1 per cent of the population gives a false negative of nil and false positive of 25 per cent. Your diagnosis comes back positive. You wrongly assume that because there's a 25 per cent false positive rate, the true positive must be 75 per cent. You conclude you have a 75 per cent chance of having the disease.

> In fact, out of a hundred people tested, 25 get the false-positive result, plus the only person who actually has the disease (1 per cent of the population). Since the test gives a false negative of nil, the sufferer is definitely among the 26 people given a positive result. The chances you have the disease is one in 26, around 4 per cent.

Even though the result is unwelcome, a false positive can be much more likely than the illness itself.

Where organisations want us to truly grasp the numbers, they will move heaven and earth to try and communicate what they mean. If it suits their agenda to have the less numerately confident among us simply take their word for it, they'll give us the headline figures. It's always worth digging if the numbers don't feel right. And where the figures look funny, check the definitions being used. One person's *poverty* might be worth walking half-way around the globe for.

Prosecutor's fallacy

Although this is called the prosecutor's fallacy[64], it's an equal opportunity error. Defence teams can make the same mistake, and senior judges in the UK's Court of Appeal, not to mention expert witnesses, can also get it tragically wrong.

The prosecutor's fallacy is a wrongful interpretation of statistics leading you to conclude someone must be guilty because it's too unlikely for him or her to be innocent. To use the jargon, you argue that the probability of a random match (a false positive) is the same as the probability that random person is not a match (false negative). Sounds like a tongue twister. Let's take it slowly:

> All the Scottish police know is that the haggis poacher has red hair. They spot my flame-haired niece Trixie ambling along a glen and arrest her. Although a whopping 13 per cent of the population in Scotland has red hair (about 690,000 people), the constabulary argue that the chances Trixie is not the culprit are 13 per cent. They conclude the chances are 87 per cent that she's the poacher.

That can't be right, can it? The police start from the premise that Trixie is indeed the Moriarty of Hot Haggis. (That's an a priori assumption of guilt.) The only other possible suspects can be the 13 per cent (minus one!) of the Scottish population that also have red hair. Police wrongly think that the chances the red-haired rustler is someone else can only be 13 per cent. Therefore, they conclude, the chances that Trixie is innocent is 13 per cent, so it's 87 per cent likely that they have the right villain.

Police ignore the prior probability that plucking the correct poacher among random gingers on Highland by-ways is a one in 690,000 long-shot. So the actual odds of Trixie, randomly selected, being

---

[64] The legal aspects of this fallacy were described in 1987 by William C. Thompson and Edward Schumann.

the guilty party are one in 690,000, a far cry from the 87 per cent their faulty reading of statistics tells them.

The matching error is the defender's fallacy.

> Police find a fragment of DNA on a stolen Fabergé egg. They compare it to 10 million DNA records on a database. My Uncle Billy is arrested. Police claim the chances of Uncle Billy's innocence are one in a million. If so, his lawyer claims, they should expect to find ten random matches on the database, so the chances that Uncle Billy is the thief are one in ten. There's a 90 per cent chance he is innocent.

If there was no prior evidence pointing to Uncle Billy, his brief would be correct. But suppose Uncle Billy was arrested as one of a number of likely suspects, for example, who were found with the object in their possession – a prior probability. Subsequently the DNA evidence matched. The odds pointing to Uncle Billy's guilt skyrocket from one in ten to around 99.999 per cent, and he really should be looking to cut some sort of deal.

Misreading statistics seems like such an obvious a mistake to make, surely there are experts who make sure nothing goes amiss?

> In 1999, Sally Clark, a UK solicitor, was convicted of murdering her first two children. She lost her first child, it was originally found, to natural causes, probably Sudden Infant Death Syndrome (SIDS). But the second child's death was treated as suspicious. It led experts to re-examine the first death and conclude that this, too, must be suspicious.
>
> Professor Sir Roy Meadow, an expert in child abuse[65], told the trial court that the absence of other risk factors for SIDS (for example, a smoker in the household, a young inexperienced mother, unemployment, etc.) meant the chances of the first child dying from SIDS was 1 in 8,543. The odds of two children dying of SIDS in the same household, he said, was the same number multiplied by itself – one in 73 million.
>
> The court fell for this prosecutor's fallacy – that the chances of two natural deaths were one in 73 million, so the odds against

---

[65] But clearly not an expert in statistics. (See *false authority*.)

Sally being innocent were one in 73 million. The gist of the case against her was: it was too rare an occurrence for Sally to be innocent. Even with no witnesses and no other evidence at all, she was given two life sentences.

Professor Meadow's statistical muddle assumed that the two deaths were unconnected; that there was no common cause linking them. In fact, historical data shows the likelihood of a second SIDS death is significantly higher if a previous child has died in this way. Furthermore, by definition, the specific cause in any case of SIDS is unknown, therefore one cannot presume that the unknown cause is not common to both cases (for example, an inherited, genetic factor).

The prosecutor's fallacy should never have arisen. The burden of proof should have lain with the prosecution to prove beyond doubt that neither death had a medical cause, and that the two deaths were completely independent of each other. In the trial, the relevant question was not: what are the chances against these both being natural deaths? The question should have been: what are the chances that either or both of these deaths are deliberate? In other words, was any crime actually committed? No crime; no case to answer.

At Sally's appeal in 2000, the defence showed that the chances of a double infant murder in the same family were in the region of one in 2.2 billion. If statistics can determine guilt or innocence, the innocent explanation was 30 times more likely than the guilty one. The court of appeal shot down the numbers saying, incredibly, that the figures were a sideshow: "...the point on statistics was of minimal significance and there is no possibility of the jury having been misled so as to reach verdicts that they might not otherwise have reached."

No possibility? The jury wasn't swayed by a professor with a knighthood swearing on oath that the odds against Sally being innocent were 73 million to one? Many clever people in the criminal justice system allowed that statistic to poison Sally Clark's trial and first appeal. Mistakes, amid the glaring publicity of a murder trial, were made by prosecutors, prosecution witnesses, defence counsel, the initial trial judge, the jury and the Court of Appeal judges in Sally's 2000 appeal.

It later emerged that Home Office pathologist and expert witness Dr Alan Williams had failed, unpardonably, to disclose that the second child had died of a bacterial infection. Sally Clark appealed again and was released in 2003. This time, one of the judges described Meadow's statistics as "grossly misleading" and "manifestly wrong".

The prosecutor's fallacy is an elementary induction error, but one that can have profound consequences in legal proceedings. A big number of otherwise smart people in the Sally Clark case failed to grasp the significance of statistics – worse, they repeatedly rejected the correct explanation when it was pointed out to them by expert statisticians.

Whenever people tell you that statistics leave them cold, and they're happy to let others crunch numbers and explain what they mean, remember Sally Clark and the prosecutor's fallacy.

Sally Clark developed profound psychiatric problems. In 2007, she was found dead from acute alcohol poisoning. RIP.

Gambler's fallacy

Caveat: the universe is not here to help you win money.

We're only human. We'd all want to get something for nothing. Beyond that, we search for equilibrium in the world around us. If something happens more often than normal, we feel the event should start to happen less often than normal. It's as if we believe the universe owes us some kind of long-term balance, so it will adjust things to restore stability.

The fallacy reflects a belief in some just-world hypothesis – that karma exists, chickens do come home to roost, and you will reap what you sow. Wanna bet? The universe does what it does: it doesn't owe you or me a thing.

If you flip a coin, and ten times in a row it comes up heads, the temptation is to assume it must come up tails pretty soon. So you raise your stake on the next toss. And it's heads. Again. Yes, the chances of a coin returning heads 11 times in a row are small – one in 2,048, in fact. But for each flip, the probability is always one in two.

The coin doesn't know it's flip number 11, and the universe

doesn't care. When you think about it, the chances of 11 coin tosses coming up heads ten times in a row followed by a tail are still one in 2,048.

Some other examples of the gambler's fallacy:

Shortly after re-building his house after the fire, Uncle Billy cancelled his fire insurance. He said the chances of it happening twice weren't worth buying insurance for. Uncle Billy's using our tent until he can save the deposit for a place to rent.

Immediately after lightning struck the tree she was under, cousin Vera's friend Pandora continued her game of golf because lightning doesn't strike twice. RIP Pandora.

For four winters in a row, Great Aunt Ruby was snowed in. This year she bought a ton of frozen food and waited for the freeze. Unfortunately the mild weather meant her basement flooded, knocked out the power and spoiled all the food.

Dedicated gamblers often believe winning is a matter of skill rather than chance: that people make their own luck. There's a tendency for people to believe that if someone is successful with a random event – sports, for example – they will have a better chance of success in future attempts. This is called the hot-hand fallacy. The player who enjoys a good match or two is expected to continue on a roll – a phenomenon called positive recency. By contrast, where random luck governs the outcome, a gambler expects the winning streak to end next time (and bets against the same result happening) – called negative recency.

12. SAT-NAV REASONING

Some drivers follow their sat-nav instructions faithfully. They obey every order to the letter, yet still end up squashed into a vanishingly thin dirt-track or marooned on a beach. The same happens with thinking.

We try our level best to make accurate statements, use sound arguments, and reach solid conclusions, but still end up on the Goodwin Sands of Reason, with the tide lapping up around our knees.

We think we're listening to the safe and commanding tone of logic in our head. But it turns out that our inner voice's reasoning wasn't as sound or up-to-date as we imagined. So what makes sense to us doesn't always stack up for anyone else. Good intentions; bad reasoning.

Fallacy – argument from

This event is also called, self-referringly, as the fallacy fallacy – so good they named it twice – and argument to logic. It's the kind of mistake you make when you understand a little too much about reasoning. Proof, if you need it, that a little knowledge is dangerous.

It happens when you study an argument, find there's a fallacy, and infer that its conclusion must be false. Confusingly, fallacious arguments can arrive at valid conclusions, just not for the right reasons. It's like tackling a maths problem, making a mess of the calculations, but somehow reaching the correct answer.

Accordingly, when you hear an argument containing some fallacy, you decide its conclusion must be wrong.

> Cousin Vera said everyone going to the wedding was expecting heavy rain, so it would be a good idea to take an umbrella and wellies. Cousin Bernard, ever alive to the bandwagon fallacy, decided to wear a T-shirt and flip-flops. Luckily, Vera brought spare galoshes and a sou'wester for Bernard to borrow.

A similar error is the bad reasons fallacy, where the argument doesn't need to be fallacious, just use poorly evaluated evidence.

> Great Aunt Ruby said the cows were lying down in the field, so it was going to pour down later. Uncle Billy didn't think much of her weather forecasting, so he left the roof of his convertible down.

Uncle Billy now has an attractive water-feature inside his car.

Great Aunt Ruby's chosen weak evidence to reach her conclusion. But rather than dismiss her forecast out of hand, Uncle Billy might have been shrewd to check the weather forecast on TV. Or, you know, buy a sensible car.

It sometimes seems that if you actively reject a poor argument, sod's law says it'll be right. (That's an appeal to probability.)

Masked man fallacy

From its title this really ought to be a fun, quirky fallacy. Alas, it's bit more of a logical puzzler, even though it crops up every day in ordinary discussion. Its other alias – illicit substitution of identicals – is a clue we're not in the ball-pit end of the playground. It's a formal fallacy.

Let's get the masked man out of the way. The title comes from this kind of scenario:

I know who Uncle Billy is

I don't know who the masked man is

Therefore, Uncle Billy is not the masked man. (invalid)

That's clearly an invalid argument, since Uncle Billy is perfectly capable of running a double life. It's possible the person I know and the mysterious stranger are one and the same.

Suppose the two people (or things or expressions) really are the same, and we can have two categorical premises:

Elton John recorded Candle in the Wind

Reginald Dwight is Elton John's real name

Therefore, Reginald Dwight recorded Candle in the Wind (valid)

Swapping the terms Elton John and Reginald Dwight in the conclusion is valid because they are the same person. The second premise tells us categorically that this is the case. So the conclusion contains no more information than we've been given. There are no extra inferences. Swapping the names is a valid substitution of identicals. But suppose the premise was:

DJ John Peel said that Elton John recorded Candle in the Wind.

You couldn't then conclude:

DJ John Peel said that Reginald Dwight recorded Candle in the Wind. (invalid)

That's not what he said. In putting those words in John Peel's mouth, we've made an illicit substitution of identicals. We reached a conclusion by inferring more information than the premise supplied, namely that Elton and Reginald are one and the same.

Furthermore, the information is reported speech ("John Peel said that..."). It's an example of something called intensional context which warns us the information is not a categorical fact, just someone's attitude towards the information. Examples of intensional contexts include:

- Propositional attitudes – know, fear, hope, believe, report, desire (etc.) that

- Modal contexts – necessarily, probably, possibly (etc.)

When you swap supposed identicals within intensional contexts you reach an invalid conclusion. For instance:

Cousin Vera believed the driver was drunk. The driver was Artemis Volestrangler. Therefore Artemis Volestrangler was drunk. (invalid)

The murderer was probably left-handed. Uncle Billy is not left-handed. Therefore, the murderer is not Uncle Billy. (invalid)

The burglar possibly had a moustache; Cousin Bernard has a moustache. Therefore, Cousin Bernard was the burglar. (invalid)

You can see that anyone who has to investigate crime, accidents or other events, and evaluate evidence from witnesses, must navigate through intensional contexts which make *'facts'* much less reliable. In conversation, we tend to summarise the events we're talking about. We slide in and out of attitude and modal phraseology without thinking. We allow our listener to wrongly infer that we've made a factual statement.

Niece Trixie: "Someone washed red socks with my white jumper. I bet it was Cousin Bernard. He's hopeless at that sort of thing."

Cousin Vera: "Bernard should buy you a new jumper."

Trixie: "No, I didn't say Bernard ruined my jumper."

Vera: "Yes, you did."

And so on. Spot the strawman argument that Vera has spun out of Trixie's imprecise supposition. We jump to conclusions for all sorts of reasons because we think the other person made a categorical statement. It's like a grown-up version of the game Chinese Whispers:

Jane to Karen: "I don't know who vandalised my car. It might have been an ex-boyfriend. Possibly John."

Karen to Linda: "Jane said one of her exes vandalised her car. Probably John."

Linda to Maureen: "John vandalised Jane's car."

And people wonder why hearsay evidence is not admissible in court? Gossip, along all its devious byways, exploits our human inability to discern propositional attitudes and modal contexts when we are thrilled by the latest tittle-tattle. We love our confirmation bias.

Why is it important to understand this fallacy? Because at work you have to carefully pick your way through fact, opinion, rumour, belief and so on, in order to make decisions about what is really happening.

Let's examine just one aspect of working life. If your idea of a career means taking charge of people and functions you will spend a fair amount of your time deciphering cryptic office communications and enduring soul-sapping distractions called meetings. These events give rise to the greatest works of fiction in any language – minutes. Minutes are summaries of discussions, decisions and action points. They are (supposedly) contemporaneous notes that are subsequently approved as accurate by the people who attended the meeting.

For instance, the minutes might say:

Marketing reports that the new product range could be delayed by a month at least.

If the new range is something that's timed to launch for a Christmas market or the summer holidays. The delay could cost six months' in-year budgeted revenue. Everyone interested in earning a bonus is awake now. Phone calls are made. The marketing head is invited to have a chat with the CEO. The financial director has already pointed out the cash-flow implications, because accountants are good at bad news and fear. The HR director has dusted down the personal goals for every member of the marketing team to be certain how far up the organisation this catastrophe can be blamed.

Let's see what actually happened. One of the marketing product managers, Nadia, was at a meeting:

Chair: "What's happening with the new product range?"

Nadia: "Everything's on track, apart from a yellow flag on electrical safety testing. The lab has said there might possibly be a delay over the long public holiday weekend."

Chair: "What's the worst case?"

Nadia: "If we have a delay of a couple of days, nothing changes. But if it's a full week, we could miss the scheduled design sign-off, which would delay our production confirmation to the factory in China. They might miss the main sea-container shipping deadline, so we'd probably have to air-freight the launch stock to Europe."

Chair: "That's going to be more expensive. How much later would the launch stock arrive if we shipped it all the way by sea?"

Nadia: "Over a month."

Chair: "Okay, so that's the worst, worst case."

Nadia: "We'll keep an eye on it…"

The minutes were confusingly terse. Nadia may be a representative from marketing, but she isn't the total marketing team or presenting the team's full and considered conclusion. She was riffing on a what-if conjecture. Moreover, most of Nadia's speculation was embedded in the modal context: possibly, if, could, might, probably. The minutes even begin with a propositional attitude ("reports") which should be a flag to readers, but all the other intensional contexts from Nadia at the meeting have been smoothed away, turning what was, at worst, a footnote advisory into a categorical cash-flow disaster.

I'll stick my neck out: a huge amount of unnecessary management conflict arises from misreporting and misinterpreting information arising from the masked man fallacy: inferring information that may not be factually accurate; substituting categorical statements for remarks couched in uncertainty; offering strawman arguments as a substitute for what someone actually said.

> Colleague #1: "We should invest in training."
>
> Colleague #2: "So, you're saying we should cut R&D."
>
> C#1: "No, that's not what I said."
>
> C#2: "If we spend more on training, we'll have to cut something else."
>
> C#1: "Possibly so, but that's a separate conversation. You can't infer I made any statement about R&D."

Double-check who precisely did or said what. Get the actual words used. Pay attention to modal phrasing. You could, of course, actually ask the person involved:

> "Nadia, I may have the wrong end of the stick, but is there going to be any delay launching the new range?"
>
> "No, it's all on track. Why do you ask?"
>
> "Nothing. My mistake."

See? Nothing to worry about. Your bonus is safe. The moral is to make intensional contexts clear, and to give them only the weight they're due. To do that, listen to what people actually say, rather than what you imagine they're telling you. Be scrupulously careful about passing on second-hand, hearsay information. Don't add any more meaning or information that you or others have inferred. If you don't know the facts, say so. Most importantly: don't jump to conclusions. Your confirmation bias will lead you directly to the result you prefer to see, not what is actually happening.

An ability to evaluate information accurately is one of the qualities you need in order to *Be Right*. Organisations are a soup of data, information, rumour, speculation, assumption, conjecture and gossip. If you can't correctly weigh reports, you are part of the problem, not the solution. Please read this section again.

Broken window fallacy

The broken window parable was a 19th century essay on economic theory.[66] The premise was that spending money repairing a broken window might be a good thing. Money circulated from the home owner to the glazier to the supplier to the employee to the baker he owed money to, and so on. Happiness, it was suggested, might be the result. The theory is, the parable admits, absolute piffle.

Fixing the window puts money into the economy – that bit you see. But if you have to spend money repairing a broken window, you've spent twice as much on windows as you need to. The second helping is money you can't spend on something else. Beer, shoes, aeroplane tickets, e-books – all are more fun, I would argue, because they are voluntary purchases, unlike repairs, which are a distress purchase. These are potential expenditures that you don't see – missing, invisible purchases that might have been.

Coming up to date, the fallacy comes from arguing in support of some kind of optimistic, silver-lining mitigation for unfortunate events and overlooking the obvious misery.

> "War in general is a benefit to society. Not only does it stimulate technical advances, and create widespread social cohesion against a common enemy, it also reduces the surplus population."

> Disease in general… (see above)

> "It's just as well the car broke down. It saved us from spending a lot of money at the theme park."

> "Although 200 people perished when the aeroplane crashed in flames, the lessons learned about maintenance procedures would save countless lives in the future."

> "We must encourage motor cyclists to drive like idiots. We need all the transplant organs we can get."

> "Sadly, the little girl died of leukaemia, but her courage was an inspiration to all who came into contact with her."

---

[66] Frédéric Bastiat's 1850 essay *Ce qu'on voit et ce qu'on ne voit pas* (*That Which Is Seen and That Which Is Not Seen*).

The arguments are valid enough, and their conclusion follows fairly from them. But a question hangs over the judgement and the sense of proportion applied to reach it. In this fallacy, people tend to put more value on the upside than on the misery a catastrophe causes. As in many walks of life, people value what's in front of them, rather than what they can't see any more.

In business, people are apt to pat themselves on the back for their achievements. Sometimes it's well deserved. Other times, however, they could have achieved much more of the good stuff (sales, cash flow, efficiency, and so on) but the business cannot see the outcome of investments not made.

> A financial director triumphantly announced the consultancy's marketing budget had been cut by a quarter, yet new business sales were still on target. Bravissimo! The marketing manager pointed out that while marketing investment was indeed designed to generate sales in the short term, it was also spent building the whole consultancy's reputation, leading to bigger and more important assignments, and earning higher fee levels long into the future.

At the time I didn't know the term Broken Window Fallacy.

Two wrongs don't make a right

You've known this proverb since childhood. But people still use the two wrongs fallacy to try to justify reprehensible things they do.

> Someone boasts of taking home some supplies from the coffee shop chain they work at. The thief says the coffee shop deserves it because the chain dodges taxes.

> An animal rights protester damages cars belonging to laboratory staff. He claims his actions were justified because the lab experiments on animals.

> A parent tells a child off for hitting her sister. "She hit me first."

The notion that two wrongs make a right is a fallacy. Just try using that argument in front of a magistrate some day. That said, it also matters – not in reasoning terms, but in realpolitik – who is doing the wrong.

> If you kill, it's murder. If Corporal Smith kills, he gets a medal.

If I stop a ship, it's piracy. If HMS Argyll stops a ship, it's a counter-narcotics operation.

When a criminal kills, some states inflict the death penalty.

If I steal from you, I'll be up before the beak. But many countries have laws that seize the property of convicted criminals who cannot themselves prove they obtained their house, TV, yacht, sports car, bank account, massage parlour through legitimate means. Proceeds of crime legislation allows the state to confiscate personal property, placing the burden of proof on criminals to show payslips and receipts, reversing the usual philosophy that you are innocent until a prosecutor proves you guilty. States call this *restitution*, and indeed it would be if the proceeds made it back to the victims of crime. When it remains in the coffers of the state, we might consider it *expropriation*.

So, arguably, two wrongs can be fine if the party having the final say is responsible for social equilibrium, and is in a position to define its own actions as *not-wrong*. As an argument to justify an individual's actions, though, it's legally and logically fallacious.

A variation on this fallacy crops up when you point out all the other people in the wrong and ask why me?

"Everyone else was talking in class. How come I get detention?"

"I drive over the speed limit every day. Why are you stopping me today?"

"I'm the hardest working person in this branch. Why do I have to lose my job along with all the slackers?"

In short, you're not being picked on for being the worst example. You're in the wrong and got caught. Unlucky. Consider all the other times you got away with misdemeanours.

Continuum fallacy

The continuum fallacy happens where you can't place a hard-and-fast distinction between two situations, a line in the sand if you like. They become indistinguishable, and you conclude they are the same.

The phenomenon also delights in the term the fallacy of the beard and the bald man fallacy. At what point does stubble become a beard; how few hairs can you have before you're officially a cue-ball? The problem sounds like this:

The minimum age to serve as president of the USA is 35. But if a candidate is 34 years and 364 days, in what significant way is s/he too inexperienced to serve? If a day's worth of immaturity doesn't amount to much, then a thousand days is also immaterial. You might as well lower the qualification age to 30, which is the candidacy age for the Senate.

Nice try. In fact, while one day might not make a difference, five years could. Just because there's little discernable difference from one day to the next (in presidential maturity, beardedness and baldness), it doesn't mean those attributes don't mount up to a point where you can say: beard, bald or inexperienced. Sometimes, an arbitrary line is necessary. Consider two arguments:

"We young people are old enough to pay tax and die for our country. Therefore we should be allowed to vote against (or for!) taxes and war, and to drown our sorrows in buckets of booze if we lose the vote."

"It's crazy to say that we're not mature enough to vote. There are plenty of sensible 16- and 17-year-olds and just as many immature 18- and 19-year-olds."

The argument about taxation or military service and representation is reasonable and valid, as it's based on a principle with a clear yes / no qualification – that is, a continuum doesn't apply. But the claim to be mature enough to decide political matters, or to vote free of adult influence, using the continuum argument doesn't work. Who would determine which people are mature enough? The same applies to all age-threshold requirements: the age qualification for members of parliament; to get a driving licence; or to enlist in the military. Sometimes we just have to draw a line in the sand and say: this side, too young; that side, old enough.

Sometimes we're grateful for the arbitrary line in the sand, especially when we're on the correct side of it:

Cousin Bernard had a car accident. Following standard procedures, the police carried out a breath test. He blew 34 micrograms per 100 millilitres, one under the limit. "Sober as a judge!" Bernard exclaimed. "Not really," the officer explained. "Your perceptions, reactions and concentration are still impaired. Two micrograms more and you'd be under arrest."

At work, some large, bureaucratic organisations have rules about staff promotions. Individuals must spend a minimum amount of time in a grade before advancing. If you're ambitious, this will seem irksome and arbitrary. But the continuum fallacy – you gain very little extra experience day by day, so the plea – *why do I have to wait out the full interval before I take over the world?* – won't work. If the rule is applied fairly and consistently, sit it out. If not, it may be that you're not good enough to break the rules for. Sorry.

Texas sharpshooter

When you have a lot of data to sift through and compare, it's tempting to ignore the differences in information and emphasise the similarities. You pick the results that work best for your case and, as likely as not, get the wrong answer.

This false-cause fallacy comes from the gag in which a Texan gunslinger fires some shots into the side of a barn, then paints a target around the best cluster. Basically, you're seeing (or creating) meaning in randomness. The fallacy is also termed the clustering illusion.

It's a different situation if you start with a hypothesis, then gather data to support or refute it. The Texas Sharpshooter fallacy occurs when you obtain a lot of possibly random data, then construct a hypothesis around parts if it.

The so-called prophecies of Nostradamus are usually offered as examples. He published about a thousand quatrains. In the 500 years since, people have lined up particular verses with historical events. The point is that with so many verses and so much history to play with, something's going to appear to marry up. But fans seize upon co-incidences as rock-solid forecasts, and it seems like a shame to spoil their fun. They are codswallop, though. Some other instances:

> Politicians observe that the biggest amounts of illegal narcotics are consumed in the world's richest countries. They conclude that narcotics are good for the economy.

> People interested in alien visits to Earth point to various snippets of disparate 'evidence' – the lines of Nazca in Peru; ancient carvings resembling astronauts and spaceships; the Egyptian pyramids; recently Roswell and Area 51; UFO reports aplenty – as a cohesive body of proof that extra-terrestrials are visiting us, presumably without proper visas and documentation, or vehicle

insurance.

The national lottery top prize is won on two occasions by ticketholders in the same village. People drive for miles to buy their lottery ticket in the village shop with the *'lucky'* lottery machine.

The term Texas Sharpshooter was coined by the epidemiologist Seymour Grufferman. His work looked at how instances of disease manifest themselves in populations. People jump to the conclusion that a cluster of data must be significant and necessarily have a specific cause. It's a non sequitur because a cluster of data can come about by chance with no specific reason. And even if there is a cause, it may have an explanation other than the hypothesis you're trying to support.

So a cluster in your data can't be interpreted as a cause, or used as a basis for some causal connection. It might suggest a hypothesis that you need to go away and test, but correlation is not causation.

Why are people so keen to see clusters in data? Let me see if I can summarise US tort law:

Cluster = cause = blame = lawsuit = class action = riches beyond avarice itself = yacht catalogues

Billions of dollars in spurious compensation claims have been awarded in courts, even when no cause could be proven, because judges and juries chose to believe there can be no smoke without fire.

A study shows that one town has twice the national level of a disease. Lawyers assume there must be a cause, and hunt for the culprit. The only feature of the town distinguishing it from others around it is the presence of a frozen pea factory. Lawyers scoop up a bunch of victims and launch a class action against the frozen pea company. Lawyers cannot prove the factory causes the disease. Indeed, the company demonstrates that towns where its other frozen pea factories are situated show normal or lower incidences of the disease. Even so, the jury finds for the lawyers because the members fell for the Texas Sharpshooter fallacy.

Legal people need to learn about the Texas Sharpshooter fallacy and the clustering illusion. Knowing law is not enough: lawyers must understand the world in all its imperfections and random unfairness.

Where there is no genuine cause, they should tell clients that sometimes bad things just happen. I'm not holding my breath.

Silence – argument from

Silence is the one thing that frustrates seekers of the truth everywhere. Lying, false information, excuses – we have ways of dealing with those, but silence? It is a poor conclusion that uses silence as proof of anything. Lack of information doesn't say anything positive or negative. Consider:

> No news is good news.

> Did Cousin Bernard put petrol in the car? He never said he didn't. Okay, let's drive.

> The police officer gives her evidence. The defence is invited to cross-examine. "No questions, m'lud." Aha, thinks the jury. He admits it!

> "Did you set fire to the curtains, Cuthbert? Cat got your tongue? I'll take that as a yes."

> It is the policy of the security services neither to confirm nor deny any aspect of its operations.

We take silence to confirm what we prefer to believe. But silence implies nothing. You can't you rely on a void of information to infer that anything is true or false. In court that's fine: the burden of proof lies on the prosecution to prove guilt. A defendant can sit in the dock, do crossword puzzles or day-dream about his pet rock. Even on arrest, an English defendant is told:

> "You do not have to say anything, but it may harm your defence if you do not mention when questioned something which you later rely on in court. Anything you do say may be given in evidence."

Silence is absolutely golden; it's the later excuses that'll get you into trouble. In contract law, acceptance of an offer cannot be assumed by silence, except in particular circumstances. So if someone says:

> "If I don't hear from you otherwise, I'll assume you're willing to sell me your car for ten quid."

... they won't have a legal case against you if you ignore them. But in day-to-day discussions we almost always assume that our opponent's silence is an admission of defeat. We always dream up reasons for their silence that are more convincing than the mundane truth. This fallacy is the argument from silence.

History is rich seam of speculation. If you want to cast doubt on a particular fact or event, one way is to point out that certain contemporary commentators are silent on the matter. You infer that some historical figure would or should have known about and mentioned the event, failed to mention it, therefore the event itself is called into question.

> Marco Polo makes no mention of the Great Wall of China. Therefore, he never went to China. Or, if he did, the Great Wall didn't exist.

> There are no contemporaneous accounts of Magna Carta. Therefore, Magna Carta is a myth.

> Pliny the Younger described the eruption of Vesuvius, but didn't mention Pompeii. Therefore, Pompeii didn't exist.

The shaky ground is that what's important today may have been a bit ho-hum back then, not worthy of mention. Magna Carta, for instance, didn't have a huge impact on the country in general. Also, silence can be made to happen: Galileo was famously (but unsuccessfully) gagged by the Catholic Church for promoting the Sun as the centre of the solar system. We have no way of knowing what else has been deliberately removed from history by powerful interests of yore.

At work, if you stumble across a situation where a colleague is unresponsive on some point, and another co-worker concludes:

> He's deliberately holding back. The reason must be X, Y or Z.

...you can open up your big bag of arguments, choose *silence, argument from*, and inform your colleague that they have reached an unsound conclusion. Silence neither confirms facts, nor explains them.

Absence of evidence is not evidence of absence

Following on from the perils of silence, or lack of information, this fallacy delves a little deeper. It says that just because you can't find any evidence of some fact or event, it doesn't prove that fact isn't true or the event never happened. (See also *argument from ignorance*.)

In case the title of this non sequitur gives you a headache, use this translation:

> Absence of evidence = we can't find any
>
> Evidence of absence = they don't exist

Space exploration is a suitable lens for examining this fallacy since it is attributed to Carl Sagan, astronomer and astrophysicist. So let's talk about aliens.

> You find yourself a radio telescope, tune it to a likely frequency, point it out into space and listen for aliens. For many years. Decades. Nothing. Even after you've gone to the trouble of learning Klingon.

If we listen out for aliens and hear nothing, we can't just conclude that aliens aren't out there. Silence is inconclusive. The lack of interstellar chit-chat may mean we should look in different places, or use a better instrument. Silence is not good news, but it's not bad news either.

What we have is absence of evidence. We just can't find any aliens. It proves or disproves nothing. It's not strong evidence that aliens don't exist. We don't have evidence of absence. So it would be erroneous to point to the radio telescope results and conclude that aliens don't exist. Keep looking.

Different situation: suppose you have to look for something and hope you don't find it?

> A doctor – a qualified investigator – looks for cancer in a patient, correctly carries out the correct tests, and doesn't find any trace of malignant cells. As far as cancer is concerned, the doctor has an absence of evidence, which means she can't find any bad stuff. Based on lots of research and experience, and within margins of error, she is sufficiently confident there are no cancer cells: that is, she has good evidence of an absence of cancer. She gives the patient the good news.

But we want to be sure that the doctor couldn't find cancer because the patient really is free from the disease, not that the wrong test was used, or the right test was used wrongly, or that the test itself is ineffective. If any of these things has gone amiss, the patient may be given a false negative result. It has to be a qualified investigation – that is, the best we can do at the time. Even then, in trying to prove non-existence, you can never have absolute certainty. But the doctor is as sure as she can be, and we have to be content with that.

Other situations in which you will be happy to accept less-than-perfect evidence of absence might be:

> You get stopped on suspicion of drink driving, but the breathalyzer light stays green. It couldn't find enough booze.

> After the inevitable school note saying there's an infestation of head lice, you check your kids' hair but can't find any wildlife.

> After an exhaustive driving test, the examiner finds no faults to fail you on. You pass the test.

So the principle can be used for constructive purposes. As ever, it can be abused, too. It's a favourite with people making tendentious claims they can't prove in the cold light of day:

> Cousin Vera claims she has a new wonder cure for re-growing amputated limbs using the healing magic of moonlight and chocolate. After several years of evaluation by health experts, the results show no more limbs re-grew than the statistical expectation (nil). Her cure was declared a complete dud. Cousin Vera claimed that the results of the study were not conclusive proof that the cure couldn't work. They simply hadn't done enough tests.

> A politician invades another country because of reports the country has chemical weapons. After the invasion and an exhaustive search, no chemical weapons are found. The politician claims this is merely absence of evidence – they must be somewhere else; they were moved; they have a cloaking device – not proof they never existed in the first place.

Both uses of the principle are fallacious, smacking as they do of sleight of hand and wishful thinking. In these examples we have pretty good evidence of absence – that is, the wonder cure and the chemical weapons are not real. Cousin Vera and the politician gave it their best shot, but no sign of either. We conclude they don't exist until a better test comes along.

Suppressed correlative – fallacy of

This is something you really must drop into conversation if you want to sound smart. It's nothing to do with smothering a mad aunt in the attic. Imagine an either-or matter.

> Would you like a cup of tea or a cup of coffee?

You pick one. Easy peasy. You have a pair of linked alternatives (correlatives) that are mutually-exclusive. But if you define one option so that it absorbs the other, you make that second option impossible or redundant.

> Would you like a cup of tea or a hot drink?

This is a suppressed correlative. The fallacy's other name, lost contrast, perhaps explains it more clearly. This enchanting example cropped up – where else? – on an internet forum:

> Q – If a man has sex with a male-to-female transsexual, is he straight or gay?

> A – A clitoris is just a tiny penis, so basically we're all gay.

There are layers of delightful wrongness in that exchange. The speaker produces an argument that defines all male sex as homosexual, therefore the option straight becomes impossible. As an argument, the conclusion isn't persuasive, although it certainly roused the homophobes, so to speak. Another example from a US forum:

> Q – Are there statistics that show gun homicides split between legally and illegally obtained guns?

> A – All guns used in a crime were originally obtained legally, only they didn't stay that way.

The answer asserts that all guns start off legal – though they may change hands – therefore homicides all stem from legal sales of guns. As an argument, it removes the contention that only illegally obtained guns are dangerous. Again, it's an unconvincing argument.

In everyday speech we use this fallacy to choose the thing we prefer, often saying that it makes no difference in the long run:

> Aide: We have two choices, Mr President: we can try to rescue the hostages – in which case they may be killed in the process – or we can meet the kidnappers' demands.

191

Mr Prez: We're all dead sooner or later. Storm the building.

There may be other great reasons for not giving in to kidnappers – encouraging more kidnapping being one, or the principle of not rewarding criminal behaviour – but the choice is made redundant by the sweeping, mortal truism. It's not a great argument. The "we all have to die sometime" rationale is possibly the most extreme correlative-suppressing statement of all, as it overwhelms pretty much any other option of any human decision.

If someone ever uses the argument:

Who cares? In the greater scheme of things, the Sun swallows the Earth. The end.

... you know something really bad is about to happen and, worse still, it will be illogical.

Begging the question, circular reasoning

Here's a phrase you hear a lot: *it begs the question*. People use it to mean:

That raises the obvious question, or

That evades the question.

It's a misuse which is fine and dandy for everyday use, but begging the question as a fallacy means something different. Begging the question is circular reasoning, an argument in which the conclusion is the initial premise.

In the book *The Little Prince*[67], the prince meets a drunkard and asks why he drinks. To forget, the drunkard replies. To forget what? That I'm ashamed. Ashamed of what? That I'm a drinker.

Circular reasoning, like climbing mountains because they're there and non-entities who are famous for being famous, can be frustrating:

Cousin Bernard: Who are these talentless nobodies? Why do we have to read about their tiny minds and sensationalised, banal lives? Why are they front page news?

Cousin Vera: Because they're well known celebrities.

---

[67] By *Antoine de Saint-Exupéry, 1943.*

Cousin Bernard: Why are they well known celebrities?

Cousin Vera: Because they're all over the papers. They make the headlines.

That's begging the question for you. To be picky, it's not really a error in reasoning – some people really are celebrities only because they make the headlines. That logic is watertight, if exasperating. But it's a clumsy argument, which doesn't persuade or explain. Bizarrely, the elements of a circular argument can be logically valid. If the premises are true, the conclusion must be true since they are pretty much the same thing. But then the premises need corroboration as much as the conclusion.

A good example of begging the question comes from American comedian, Rich Hall:

Guns make Americans happy. It's important to make Americans happy… because they have guns.

Other examples of begging the question lie in phrases that mean much the same:

You've received this email because you're on our mailing list.

The train didn't run on time because it was late.

An aeroplane stays in the air because it's able to fly.

We ran out of fuel because the tank was empty.

It's illegal because it's against the law.

This drug will calm you down because it's a sedative.

If you get a sense of déjà vu at the end of the argument, the chances are it's begging the question, rather than a glitch in the matrix. If you genuinely want to know what the speaker has in mind – if – you might need some follow-up questions.

Occasionally, a circular argument will be tricky to spot if it's a long and convoluted chain of thinking. But mostly they stand out because they're obvious.

Ludic fallacy

The ludic fallacy is to assume the simple rules of a game apply to a complex system in real life where many more factors may be in play.

Ludus is Latin for sport; ludic means undirected and spontaneously playful.[68]

It's a recently defined[69] fallacy that reflects our attempts to grapple with the complexity of modern life. Often we turn to a model that's too simple for the real-life problem.

For instance, the attempt to predict future events using a model based on estimated historic positions of distant planets and stars is a quintessential ludic fallacy that appears in many of our daily newspapers. Astrology and horoscopes, if you didn't know already, are codswallop.

Clever people put together models to try and predict what will happen in big, unwieldy systems – economies, stock markets, sports, love, war games, and so on. They plug in all the factors that seem relevant, apply weightings that look right, then turn the handle. Results are compared to forecasts, and fed back into the model to refine its predictive abilities.

The problem is that you can only build into your model the variables you know about – so-called known unknowns. The things that never occurred to you – unknown unknowns – can be working away making your model hideously wrong, while you scratch your head puzzling over why it didn't work.

> Some of the most complex models in the world are used for weather forecasting. The processing power needed to calculate all the variables – the known unknowns – is colossal. A simpler (and cheaper) forecasting model might be to copy Cousin Vera who uses wet or dry seaweed to predict the weather. But even she would admit the model's a bit hit-and-miss.

The weather system plainly involves more variables than are available to Cousin Vera's model. Trying to figure out the weather may well be the second-oldest predicting game in the history of humanity.

---

[68] Still the Shorter Oxford English Dictionary.

[69] In *The Black Swan – The Impact of the Highly Improbable,* 2007 by Nassim Nicholas Taleb.

When you try to distil what might make two people compatible, it's easy to be superficial: "What's you star sign?" One TV advertisement for an online dating site claims that its rivals commit the ludic fallacy.

> A man is sitting on a sofa beside a camel. The voiceover says: "Geoff and his companion here are the same age and love long walks on the beach. For some sites this is enough to make them a match."

The ad goes on to say the advertiser's system uses 29 measures of compatibility. I doubt whether 29 comparisons nail down the complete chaos that is personal attraction, but it must be a better model than two or three.

The model you use might be flawless in design as far as you can tell, it's just those unknown unknowns lurking invisibly in the background. The original example of this fallacy was of a coin flipped 99 times in a row and always coming up heads. What's the probability the 100th toss is still heads? We all know it should be 50:50. Hypothetically. But at some point you have to figure that something's wrong with the coin, or the toss mechanism, or gremlins, or Tyche the Greek goddess of luck is playing Candid Camera on us mere mortals. Then you have to adjust what you believe about the fairness of the coin toss, and trot off into the whimsical world of Bayesian probability. But that's a whole new world of complexity.

To sum up the thrust of the Ludic fallacy:

> Don't take a pea-shooter to a gun fight.

Even then, sometimes a colossal, super-sophisticated howitzer isn't enough for the job.

> In the run-up to the UK's 2016 EU referendum, the full consensus of the economic profession, the Bank of England and the UK Government's Treasury insisted that a Leave vote would cripple the UK economy almost immediately, sending the economy to the knacker's yard. Six months after some initial wobbles, the pound was strong, the FTSE at a record high and, according to the IMF, the UK economy in 2016 was the fastest growing among all developed economies.

> The Bank of England's chief economist agreed that forecasts had been wrong. The experts' failure to predict the effects of a Leave vote accurately was blamed on the "deeply irrational"

behaviour of the British people.

The humiliation must be tangible: even non-economists know that if a model fails to reflect or predict reality, the problem lies with the model, not with reality.

Then again, economic forecasting has never been considered an exact science, even by its most feted practitioners:

> "The only function of economic forecasting is to make astrology look respectable." – JK Galbraith.

The ludic fallacy, it seems, has a great future ahead of it.

Division – fallacy of

The fallacy of division is one of the more straightforward problems with reasoning. Here you reason that what works for a whole entity or group must also apply to any of its parts or members.

In ancient Greek philosophy, it was believed that atoms of water would be wet, while atoms of sand would be dry. You can see the thinking: cut off a piece of cheese from a block, and it tastes like cheese; divide a piece of gold into two and each is still gold. The fallacy arises if you assume all things work this way. Some musical examples:

> A choir has singers ranging from bass to soprano. Therefore, every member of the choir can sing bass to soprano parts.

> A standard orchestra features woodwind, brass, percussion and stringed instrument players. Therefore, every member of the orchestra can play all the instruments.

> A six-string guitar in standard tuning has a range of about 3½ octaves, therefore a one-string guitar must have the same range.

The division fallacy is a form of the ecological fallacy. Using statistics, it's common to find out the characteristics of a group, but wrong to infer that those characteristics apply to individuals in the group. For instance:

> Ten percent of Americans claim Irish ancestry, therefore every American is 10 per cent Irish.

> A survey of a school class reveals that 70 per cent of the pupils like to watch Game of Thrones. Therefore, my niece Trixie, a member of the class, will be thrilled to get a box-set for her

birthday.

Not if Trixie happens to be in the 30 per cent that wouldn't watch it if you duct-taped her eyeballs to the screen. Individual members of a group don't necessarily embody all the characteristics of the group.

If you're in a position to draw conclusions about, say, customers or employees, bear the fallacy of division in mind. Or to put it bluntly: despite the generally positive feedback overall, no-one really likes the company Christmas party; no-one enjoys the family day; no-one wants to go on a team-building weekend. Save the money and pay people better.

Composition – fallacy of

Predictably, the fallacy of division has a converse, and it's the fallacy of composition. Here, you infer that some quality about a whole thing is true, based on that quality being present in part of it. For example:

> I hate the company Christmas party, the family day and team-building weekends, therefore no-one in the company wants to attend these functions.

> My favourite football team spent millions signing a top international goalkeeper. We should finish at the top of the league.

> One of the pupils in the class was a savant-level mathematician, so the school should top the science league tables.

> Cells divide to reproduce. Therefore, humans divide to produce babies.

And yet it turns out that human reproduction is more fusion than fission... There are, however, more complex examples of the fallacy. An economic principle shows that if one individual saves money, the total amount of savings increases. But if many people do the same, aggregate savings go down. (It's the paradox of thrift.) Similarly:

> If one trawler takes more fish, its crew makes more money. If every trawler takes more fish, nobody makes any money.

Instances where the whole is greater (or better) than the sum of the parts also highlight the non sequitur.

Carbon molecules individually have certain properties. Bonded together they can form coal or diamonds.

Individuals can help find a missing person by looking and spreading the word. But collectively on social media, the need for help can be propagated almost instantly and exponentially.

Studying the health of large groups is informative about epidemiology, whereas concentrating on a few individuals is less helpful.

The composition fallacy is sometimes confused with hasty generalisation. That's an unjustifiable inference about a group based on one instance. In the composition fallacy, the property you extrapolate is true – it's your reasoning at fault.

In a work context, the danger from this thinking is obvious. If you extrapolate what's true about an individual to, say, customers as a whole, you end up with a lot of unsold stock in your warehouse. Beware managers making decisions about all staff or all customers who begin their explanation with the words: "I think..."

13. MENTAL MUDDLE

Sometimes, we just get it wrong. Like the otherwise intelligent person who for years believed the markings on the car fuel gauge meant:

E – enough

F – fuel needed

...and wondered why the car stopped running one day when the gauge pointed emphatically at enough.[70] We don't know what we don't know, and we don't know that what we do know is wrong until it turns out to be wrong.

This family of fallacies is grouped around the notion all people can be muddle-headed at some point. No matter how smart we may be, sometimes our reasoning fails completely. This section, therefore, looks at the most common brain-fails.

Conjunction fallacy

What better way to start a section on muddled thinking than the conjunction fallacy? A conjunction is just two things joined together.

> My Uncle Billy was a bit of a tearaway, but really has a heart of gold. So which of these is true? a) Uncle Billy spent five years in prison, or b) Uncle Billy spent five years in prison and then started working for a non-profit organisation that helps ex-convicts to re-settle.

It's a tried and tested phenomenon. More people would pick the second statement, even though it's clearly less probable. What proportion of ex-cons go on to work for a charity? I have no idea; it's less than the sum of all ex-lags. So Uncle Billy is much less likely to live up to the second statement than the first.

The conjunction fallacy happens when you assume that some specific conditions linked together are more likely than one broader outcome. In general, like this:

---

[70] I can introduce you the person who was summoned to start the inoperable vehicle, if you don't believe me.

Which do you believe? Statement A, or statement A plus B? I'll take A plus B, please.

It's a bit like betting on a football team, and getting odds of 10/1 against winning the match, but odds of only 2/1 against winning by more than five goals. Winning by a big margin is a subset of just winning, and much less likely than a victory with any winning score. The conjunction of a) a win and b) a big goal difference must be less probable than a simple win. How is it even possible we believe a convoluted set of circumstances is more likely than a simple explanation? But psychologists observe that people just do. As the young say: it's a thing.

Why is it important? Sit on a jury:

> Prosecution: Do you seriously maintain you were randomly driving around to charge up your car battery? A drive that also went past a bank that was subsequently robbed; and for a mile along the precise route the getaway car used; and past the Fat Ox pub where the gang met to plan the robbery; and up to the railway station where later the getaway car was abandoned? Are you telling the jury you went for a random drive and not follow a carefully thought-out journey to prepare a criminal plan?

> Uncle Billy: Well, yes. It's a small town.

The prosecution invites the jury to favour the second, detailed scenario, an elaborate conjunct, over the much simpler explanation. In short, the prosecution wants the jury to buy the conjunction fallacy, despite the fact that a conjunct can never be more probable than the chances of any component part on its own. When an innocent explanation is more probable than a guilty one, that introduces a reasonable doubt.

It's a odd quirk of human thinking that we imagine a complicated arrangement is more likely than the simple situation on its own. We're good at putting two and two together and making a hash of it.

Perhaps, we like conspiracy theories composed of tenuous links. Perhaps we lean towards the level of detail in conjunctions? Perhaps we think they're two distinct alternatives, not one particular set nested inside the more general set of the other? Perhaps we spot the detailed case is less likely, but imagine it's a trick question? Go, as they say, figure.

False authority – celebrity endorsement

Earlier we looked at a fallacy called appeal to authority. Just because an authority figure endorses a product or embraces an opinion, it doesn't make it true. Here we have an even more tenuous reason to trust a statement or argument.

False authority comes about when a person who is knowledgeable about topic A is put forward as an expert in topic B. Celebrities talking about anything other than themselves are unlikely to know the topic as well as an expert. A quick trot through memory lane:

> Dame Judi Dench, Sting and Sir Richard Branson say we should legalise drugs.

> Brian May says bovine TB is not spread by badgers.

> Prince Charles believes alternative medical therapy can be as effective as conventional medicine.

I'd listen to these people on the topics of acting, business, music, astrophysics and being heir to the throne until the cows came home. But fame confers no special insight on social, political or medical matters. People such as these are a weak authority on those extra-mural topics.

Famous faces are paid to sell you things. Every time a footballer wafts a perfume, or an actor drives a fast car, the advertiser hopes you'll transfer your nice warm feelings for the face to the product. It's not a crime. At worst, celebrity endorsement of a product is just a person expressing someone else's opinion while money changes hands.

But if that famous clock turns round and informs you that NASA did not land men on the moon, they are making a statement of fact. Rich musicians, for example, queue up to appear in political programmes and documentaries, talking about the environment, the poor and starving, and social injustice. Because we like them, we should believe them, is the fond hope.

Why is the false authority fallacy so common? Partly because we like it. In the twisted world of celebs, it's the viewer that confers the authority by unconsciously boosting the reliability of celebrities and downgrading qualified experts. Why? Because the general public doesn't understand science, research methods and proof. That stuff is hard. That's why we left school. So we trust the familiar face making bare assertions, and ignore the scientist who's spent a decade begging for research grants to try and investigate the problems of the world.

It's also common because celebrities (or their PR people) do it a lot. Expressing a view on social media keeps the individual in touch with followers and fans. Sometimes deliberately controversial statements are designed to boost traffic. But a big component is the Dunning-Kruger Effect. This holds that low intelligence is often linked to an increase in confidence in opinions, and a reduction in the ability to fairly calibrate ability and expertise compared to others. In a nutshell, some people are too stupid to know they're stupid. So they confidently voice silly ideas as if rock-solid, scientific facts.

That said, we're all susceptible to cognitive bias by which we rate our own opinions as sound. This explains why even intelligent people, given their own newspaper column, are prone to write utter drivel. Being paid to express an opinion gives positive reinforcement to our belief in our own views. It acts as confirmation that we see the world through objective eyes and are qualified to judge it (see *psychologist's fallacy*).

At the same time, we can't dismiss everything a famous person says just because they're famous. They may be experts in a particular field. Classical actor Robert Hardy became an expert on the English longbow, while Danica McKellar, a child star in The Wonder Years, is a recognised mathematics expert. Jeff "Skunk" Baxter, guitarist with the sublime Steely Dan and The Doobie Brothers, has a second career as a defence consultant to Congress and NASA, being a self-taught expert in missile technology. He's most definitely a book you couldn't judge by the cover.

Across the media and in politics, it's common to see references to research and findings of various think-tanks, foundations, policy study groups and *'Centres for...'*. Almost all of these are funded by private interests, personal or commercial, with a mission to push a particular perspective. Propaganda, if you prefer.

These aren't false authorities – these are biased authorities. Under the cloak of reasoned and scientific study, findings are promulgated as if peer-reviewed, balanced and therefore trustworthy. Here's a funny thing: no matter how learned the academics are – the ones paid to carry out research and produce findings – they never, ever produce results that run counter to their sponsor's wishes. Never. That doesn't mean they don't conclude them – only that they don't produce them. The fallacy here is the pretence of objectivity and neutrality. (See *sampling bias*.) It's a wicked world.

Middle ground fallacy – argument from moderation

When you hear an argument in which the positions seem far apart, there's a tendency to seek a solution somewhere in the middle. You hear people summing up judiciously:

We need to find a compromise.

We should explore the middle ground.

There must be concessions on both sides.

Can we meet half-way?

This is a fair approach to resolving a disagreement to which there is no right or wrong, only a stance taken by side A and a deeply held opinion embraced by side B.

I want to sell my gonk collection for £1,000. You want to buy it for £500. You can see where this is heading.

But in the search for factual accuracy, where you have a range of solutions, the right answer can reasonably lie anywhere from one limit to the other, including at the extremes. So it's wrong to assume that the answer to a problem must be found in some middle ground, in a compromise. That's the middle ground fallacy.

Some things only happen in one of two states: light bulbs work or don't; you are pregnant or not; a key fits the lock or not. Facts are true or false. Other things are theoretically capable of compromise, but with unhelpful results:

The goalkeeper argued with the referee. He claimed the ball had not fully crossed the goal line. In a spirit of fairness the referee announced the score was ½ - 0. Then the striker protested, so the referee adjusted the score to ¾ - 0.

Doctors used to cure certain ailments (including blood loss!) by drawing pint after pint of blood from the patient. Modern medicine says that's dangerous, so the answer is to take smaller amounts of blood, say a half-pint at a time.

Planners at Gatwick Airport want to build a second runway, but

> protesters object. So the airport should compromise and build
> half a runway. (Good luck, Biggles)

Blessed are the peacemakers who try to force a compromise. It's fine for uniformly scalable things like money or corn flakes. But it's not necessarily the right decision or fair to both parties. Usually, it's a signal that everyone's had enough with the argument and it's the only way out of a stalemate.

But if your argument has a binary outcome, there is no middle ground. You can't have half a runway or fractions of a goal. In seeking to keep both parties happy, compromise leaves both unhappy, and can lead to absurd consequences, for which, thank the middle ground fallacy. Pick a winner, and know also that a Peacemaker is a type of Colt revolver.

False balance

The moderation fallacy crops up in other guises. False balance in the media is both rife and pernicious. Journalists and commentators feel obliged to present stories showing the range of perspectives, both sides of a debate. That way they avoid accusations of partisanship, bias and ignorance. They seek balance. The problem is they conflate opposing and balance.

Balance means presenting the main views on a topic in an impartial way, showing both or all sides, with equal opportunity given to each to make its point, and making due allowance for the weight of opinion and authority of those who express it.

> A national park is under threat from one the world's
> petrochemical giants putting the case for fracking, coupled with
> an aggregates conglomerate advocating strip-mining. Instead of
> some political cage-fighter or renowned conservationist to argue
> the case against, the producer hauls in a member of a local
> parish council who has misgivings about public rights of way.

When you want to discuss a change in the law, you'd expect the proposal to be challenged in the media by a respected lawyer, not a petty criminal with charges pending. If one side of a debate is put forward by an authoritative figure, with years of study, research and peer-reviewed publications, an enthusiastic, amateur, single-issue campaigner is not balance, because:

> The campaigner may have a perfectly valid point of view, but isn't well enough trained in science to argue in a TV debate. The position she represents doesn't get a fair showing.

> The campaigner may be utterly wrong in fact and argument, but the TV debate presents her crackpot notion and settled science as equally valid views. The position she represents gets a colossal, unmerited publicity boost.

False balance isn't simply a matter of editorial satisfaction, it speaks to the responsibility of broadcast media. People believe what they see on TV and hear on radio because we presume they are fair.

> To support a legal claim against pharmaceutical companies, a lone medical professional claims MMR immunisation causes autism in children. The media present the case for MMR immunisation, supported by almost all qualified medical practitioners, and the contention of the sole dissenter as equally balanced, with arguments for and against immunisation as having equal merit. The lone expert's research is later dismissed by medical authorities as dishonest, while the number of cases of childhood measles soars.

It's easy to see that false balance in the media is a force-multiplier for the effects of muddled thinking. Equally, it happens that legitimate authorities are dismissed as mere players in a broad debate. The BBC website[71] ran a feature on the UK's National Health Service ending funding for homeopathic medicine. It originally explained:

> Homeopathy is based on the concept that diluting a version of a substance that causes illness has healing properties.

> So pollen or grass could be used to create a homeopathic hay-fever remedy.

> One part of the substance is mixed with 99 parts of water or alcohol, and this is repeated six times in a "6c" formulation or 30 times in a "30c" formulation.

---

[71] http://www.bbc.co.uk/news/health-34744858. The report was subsequently changed, replacing the phrase "critics say patients" with "scientific consensus say [sic] patients". Normally, it's considered good practice to note where changes are made to online reporting. Not, alas, in this case.

The end result is combined with a lactose (sugar) tablet.

Homeopaths say the more diluted it is, the greater the effect. Critics say patients are getting nothing but sugar.

Note that "critics" refers to the overwhelming consensus of the scientific and medical community. These are not mere critics. They are the corpus of scientific and medical knowledge, skill, research, wisdom and considered opinion. They represent settled science, and science confidently asserts that homeopathy has no verifiable, repeatable, healing power. Science itself tells us that patients are getting nothing but sugar. By presenting the parties as homeopaths and "critics", the original feature grossly re-centred the weight of argument.

The BBC has fairly sketched out what homeopathic medicine is, so make up your own mind. Take something that might (or might not) have an active ingredient and dilute it 99:1. Then repeat that dilution six times. What percentage of the final brew is the active ingredient? And how much is it after 30 dilutions? Mix it with sugar. What do you have? Pure sugar.

Here's the counterintuitive, dropped-on-its-head-reasoning part: homeopaths claim the 30 times dilution is more powerful than the six times. They claim the more remote the active ingredient, the more effective the solution. Science disagrees. In a 30 times dilution, to be completely sure of having a single molecule of the original active substance (let alone an effective dose), you would need to have a container 30 billion times the size of the Earth.[72] So, pure sugar it is.

Back to false balance – it's not critics saying patients get nothing but sugar, but the laws of science that govern the entire universe.

Comedian Tim Minchin summed it up: You know what they call alternative medicine that's been proved to work? Medicine.

---

[72] Dr Robert Park, author of *Voodoo Science* and executive director of The American Physical Society, calculated that because the least amount of a substance in a solution is one molecule, a 30C solution would have to have at least one molecule of the original substance dissolved in a minimum of 10^{60} molecules of water. This would require a container more than 3×10^9 times the size of planet Earth. Which might be hard to fit in the recycling bin.

In news reporting, beware vague references to critics and supporters, especially when followed by the word *would*:

The government claims the new policy will help many families. Critics would say it damages…

This translates as *"I imagine critics would say this, had I interviewed any."* Which means the same as: *"I think…"* There's a world of difference between *"Critics say it would do this…"* and *"Critics would say it did this…"* The first is a summary of critics' thinking. The second is a wild and unworthy guess.

Job title inflation is as rife in news reporting as everywhere else in business and industry. Reporters are now *correspondents*, *analysts* and *editors*. But what they think or feel is still not news, even if the editor compels them to deliver their report live, knee-deep in flood water, or in a howling gale outside a police station. And even if they are paid to comment on events, and express their view, that doesn't guarantee balance. The analysis provided by the (now-former) reporter is intended to put news events into context. He or she is a proxy for balance. It saves the time and cost of getting a balanced roster of interviewees into a studio.

Printed media can (and do) adopt any editorial slant they want. In the UK, however, TV and radio broadcasters are obliged to present an editorial balance, but sometimes struggle to find sufficient dissent to meet their editorial ambitions. The editorial see-saw goes awry when one of the parties is so extreme, there is no possibility of meaningful balance. If the spokesperson for a terrorist group maintains the random slaughter of innocents is righteous, it seems feeble to have a government minister tell us that killing is very, very naughty. It isn't false balance as such – grotesque imbalance is the unavoidable upshot of extreme positions.

Sometimes an appropriate interviewee isn't available. In that case, in order to explore the topic fairly, it is the job of a professional interviewer to challenge the expert to explain his or her evidence and conclusions. It's lazy journalism simply to wheel in any contrary speaker, then umpire the resulting melee as if the topic is getting a fair crack of the whip.

Conflict sells far better than harmony. Sensational sells better than mundane. A row makes better news than harmony. The media exaggerates the trivial. Off-hand remarks become *stinging attacks*. To offer a mild criticism is to *slam*. An answer in the negative is an *outright denial*. Protagonists probably laugh it off. The fiction that celebrities are in a constant war with each other is designed to sell copies, not report actual news or hold a mirror up to the world. You might call this a form of editorial false imbalance. (See also *inflation of conflict fallacy*.)

Note also that any debate summed up as a for-or-against, yes-or-no discussion, while appearing balanced, is almost certainly a false dichotomy.

Confirmation bias

Everyone has an innate tendency to look for and find information that confirms what we already think or believe. It's an error in inductive reasoning and a form of cognitive bias.

Cognitive bias is the wonky judgement we use to reach conclusions about other people or situations. We find, and prefer, evidence that bears out what we already believe, think or suspect. We overlook facts that run counter to what we feel. Importantly, it changes the things we remember – selective memory is a feature of cognitive bias.

> Great Aunt Ruby reads only the Daily Edwardian and Jingoist Monthly. She likes articles that confirm what she's thought all her life, going back to what she terms "The Good Old Days", and says she's too old to change her mind.

Were it not for cognitive bias, swathes of this book would be redundant. Cognitive bias is responsible for the persistence of super-stitions, for the improbable survival of crackpot medical treatments, and for widely shared prejudices. It makes us susceptible to appeals to emotion and other fallacies of reasoning.

In those his-word-against-mine moments, parties quickly turn to an appeal to confirmation bias:

> Are you going to take the word of a young thug in his souped-up car and no driving experience to speak of? I've been driving for 40 years and never had an accident.

> The old fool just came sailing out. I'm not surprised – he could barely see over the steering wheel. He was probably on medication, not paying attention. Seriously, who are you going to believe, me or the old geezer?

Confirmation bias is unintended – we just seem to be wired that way. But some of the consequences can be weighty.

> The report suggested that an enemy's chemical weapons could be deployed at 40 minutes' notice. "Aha, I knew it'" exclaimed the prime minister and ordered an immediate attack.

> Cousin Vera read an magazine article that said parents should be free to choose whether they gave their children the MMR vaccination. At last, the excuse she needed to ignore the health visitor, her doctor, the school, her friends...

> Cousin Bernard, a lifelong ecologist, invested his pension in ethical projects. Most were worthy endeavours, but were run by enthusiasts rather than avaricious, conscience-free businessmen. He lost most of his money. Cousin Bernard's former investment strategy was described as "wishful thinking" by his new financial advisor.

Even when data is neutral or ambiguous, we interpret it as favouring our existing belief. Confirmation bias makes us more emotional about certain personal issues and more trenchant in defending them – sometimes in the teeth of normally persuasive evidence.

In Voodoo Science, Robert Park wrote:

> "I came to realize that many people choose scientific beliefs the same way they choose to be Methodists, or Democrats, or Chicago Cubs fans. They judge science by how well it agrees with the way they want the world to be."

The best countermeasure is to seek out opinions we disagree with and test facts that inconveniently upset our argument. The system we call Scientific Method has developed expressly to offset human fallibility in reasoning, and to ensure objectivity of scientific thought and discovery.

Now the big *however*. Science itself is proving tricky to, well, prove. A recent study[73] found that a large proportion of medical research findings published must be false or wrong. Since then researchers in a range of fields have found it impossible to reproduce the

---

[73] *Why Most Published Research Findings Are False*; John P. A. Ioannidis, 2005.

results – the touchstone of scientific method – of between 51 per cent and 89 per cent of published papers. Psychology has emerged as a significant problem field. It's not boffins trying to hoodwink us. The fact is there are several aspects of academic publishing that reward unintended bias.

Academics are under huge pressure to publish papers, and journals like strong results with headline-making findings. They prefer sparkly things like innovation and confirmation of hypotheses over dull method and falsifiability. This creates a publication bias which sees impressive, positive results favoured over down-beat but worthy studies.

That said, researchers themselves are susceptible to confirmation bias. Where there is a great deal of random data, they are apt to find correlations that fit their hypothesis (see *Texas Sharpshooter fallacy*).

It all sounds like bad news, but the alarm bells we hear are the scientific establishment self-correcting back to good practice. The attention on reproducibility of results is itself part of the scientific method. Scientists are right to challenge findings and strive for robust research processes.

Accent fallacy – fallacy of emphasis

The accent fallacy is an ambiguity rather than a full-blown non sequitur. We're talking about accents used in writing, rather than regional speech patterns.

The phenomenon was first described in ancient Greek – a written language that used marks to indicate pronunciation. If you changed the pronunciation of some words, you would change the meaning. Accent fallacy is a type of equivocation.

Modern French words can change their meaning if an accent appears in part of the word:

congres = eels	congrès = conference
ferme = farm	fermé= closed
la = the	là= there
mais = but	maïs = corn

mur = wall	mûr = ripe
ou = or	où = where
pécheur = sinner	pêcheur = fisherman
sur = on	sûr = sure

One of the admirable traits of English is that it got rid of accents and diacritical marks centuries ago. (It may explain why some spellings and pronunciations are like distant cousins, barely on speaking terms.) Of course, English has words that are written identically (homographs), pronounced differently and have distinct meanings:

Affect, bass, bow, close, desert, discount, intimate, invalid, minute, object, present, row, sewer, subject, tear, wind

In addition, English can change the meaning of sentences by placing the emphasis on different words. This is called sentence or prosodic stress. Spoken emphasis can alter the meaning of the sentence quite profoundly. For instance (as favoured by writers of courtroom dramas):

I am going to kill him [Nobody else is]

I **am** going to kill him [I'm determined to do it]

I am **going** to kill him [I'm setting off to do it]

I am going to **kill** him [I'm planning death not injury]

I am going to kill **him** [Nobody else, specifically him]

Even if spoken emphasis is accurately heard and faithfully recalled, ambiguity can have mortal consequences:

In 1953, 19-year-old Derek Bentley was hanged for the murder of a policeman. Bentley and a friend, Christopher Craig, were attempting to commit a burglary. They were interrupted by police. Craig had a revolver, and shot and killed one of the police officers. In evidence, police said that Bentley used the words, "Let him have it, Chris." Bentley's defence argued about the emphasis used. If he had truly used those words, the literal meaning was, "Give him the gun." Both were convicted of murder. Craig, who fired the weapon, being 16 at the time he killed the policeman, served only ten years in prison.

This fallacy is still relevant. At work, electronic communication means we can all contact colleagues more often and faster. Unfortunately, it's done nothing to improve our communication skills. There's no tone of voice or facial expression to give context and meaning to bare words. Innocent phrasing can be read as hostile, dismissive or presumptive. Flame wars of excoriating emails ensue, copied up the management chain to senior managers. Try talking face-to-face. Failing that, don't make the basic mistake of assuming that someone intended to say what you imagine they did.

Homunculus fallacy

Some people have tried to explain that intelligent life on Earth was spawned by aliens from another planet.[74] Aha! So how did those aliens evolve? Spawned by other aliens from another planet. Aha! So how did those aliens evolve? You get the picture.

Homunculus is Latin for *'small man'*. The title comes from this thought experiment:

> The little man inside the head stemmed from attempts to analyse consciousness and thought. We see the world, but how do we interpret the images that enter our head? Can we understand the work our brain does by describing the process as a little man watching a movie of the world explaining to us what's happening on the screen? If so, how does the little man understand what he sees? Is there another homunculus inside his head too? And so on.

Perhaps the words I'm writing now are being dictated to me by some consciousness inside my head – a little man, for instance. But where does the little man get the words from? Why, from a little man

---

[74] Including ex-cricketer Shane Warne who, on the reality TV programme *I'm a Celebrity Get Me Out Of Here* in February 2016, reportedly explained that humans must have descended from aliens because if humans really evolved from monkeys, why hadn't all other monkeys evolved? He backed up this searing insight with the assertion that the pyramids were too hard to build for humans, and that their presence was evidence of extra-terrestrial stone masons.

inside his head, and so on, infinitely regressing to even smaller men inside heads dictating words.

The homunculus fallacy comes about when you try to explain an event in the same terms that the event is supposed to explain. Then you have to explain that event in the same terms, and so on. Like a recipe for bread that lists bread as one of the ingredients, you end up not explaining anything, instead, you get a version of the nursery rhyme:

Big fleas have little fleas, upon their backs to bite 'em,

And little fleas have lesser fleas, and so, ad infinitum.

Speaking of children, somehow they instinctively home in the homunculus fallacy, which can be frustrating for parent and child alike.

Mummy, where do seeds come from?

They come from plants.

Where do plants come from?

They grow from seeds.

Where do seeds come from?

They come from plants...

The answers may be technically correct, but aren't sufficient to explain plant reproduction. Unless we can find some way to anchor the argument and not rely on further regression, the argument will always be unpersuasive.

Son: Dad, where does rain come from?

Dad (pondering the perpetual cycle of rain, rivers, sea, evaporation, clouds, rain, rivers, ad infinitum): It's God's watering can, son.

Son: Thanks, Dad. That's my homework sorted. Now, where does God come from?

Ho ho. Sometimes we just swap one fallacy for another. As to the claim that life on Earth arrived piggy-backing on asteroids from other planets? Where did life on those other planets come from? Yet more planets? Where did that life evolve? Well, all life in the universe began somewhere. If life evolved in one place, it can evolve in another. It doesn't need to be transferred. Besides, the only place we know there's life is Earth so, in the absence of any other evidence, we're entitled to assume life on Earth began at home.

Mind projection fallacy

Spoiler! In the film The Matrix, reality was an illusion – a software program fed directly into the heads of battery-chicken humans. Philosophers down the ages have argued and disagreed over what reality is. Is there a neutral, objective world which we all perceive differently? Or do we all observe a unique world, and reality is a composite of the bits we mostly agree on?

The mind projection fallacy[75] occurs when you believe how you see the world establishes the way the world really is. You project your subjective interpretation onto things as if they are inherent properties of those things. You may think eating snails nasty, so you project that nastiness as an inherent quality of snails. You picture everyone else who eats them doing so reluctantly, hating every delicious, garlicky mouthful. Of course, in your personal reality, other people see things in the same way as you, so those who don't are wrong or crazy.

Try explaining taste:

> Cousin Bernard went on a blind date. He said his favourite cuisine was Albanian, favourite song was Mouldy Old Dough by Lieutenant Pigeon[76]; place – Turkmenistan; football team – Blyth Spartans; hobby – writing software in Malbolge. Cousin Bernard couldn't understand why she didn't return his calls and texts and emails and social media salutations and letters.

In Cousin Bernard's mind projection, though, his favourite things should be obvious and universal. He also thinks the things he doesn't know about cannot be understood by anyone. He probably explained that to his date when she told him the things she liked.

For most of us, how we see the world squares pretty fairly with how other people do, although sometimes reality seems like one of those irregular verbs:

---

[75] First described in 1989 by Edwin Thompson Jaynes.

[76] In my view, his musical faux pas was not sticking to *French Accordion Classics* by Louis Peguri. Taste. What are you going to do, eh?

I see the world as it really is

You see what's in your head

He or she is hallucinating.

The mind projection fallacy tells us that how we see the world is exactly what the nature of the world is, and that what we don't know or understand is undetermined.

> Mind projection is the premise behind the sci-fi B-movie plot in which an earnest scientist persuades the president that visiting aliens must be civilised explorers and lovers of peace like us. The next scene shows aliens sitting round the Oval Office snacking on the scientist's brain.

Mind projection gives the world the distorted properties that political and religious fanatics imagine to be real, reinforcing the certainty of their dogma or faith, and the righteousness of the actions they take in support of it.

Individuals whose mind projection is radically different to our own stand out as eccentrics. Their world is different to ours. Strange people. We say they're deluded. Perhaps they are, or perhaps it's us. Or, rather, perhaps it's just you. I know I'm fine.

Moralistic fallacy

On the face of it, the moralistic fallacy sounds a bit strange. If it makes things easier, think of it as the reverse of the naturalistic fallacy. (That's still the case even if it doesn't make things easier.)

Put very simply, the moralistic fallacy assumes that stuff which leads to bad social consequences runs counter to the natural order of things, and therefore doesn't or won't happen. By bad social consequences, I'm talking about immoral or politically undesirable results, not pop music of the 1980s and mullet hair styles.

The moralistic fallacy is the assumption that what ought to happen, does happen, the sort of attitude you might find in some grandly naïve Victorian character in a three-volume novel:

Young people abstain from irresponsible sex.

No-one seeks out booze – it's the fault of temptation.

Private diaries are sacrosanct.

No-one is allowed into the park after dark.

No-one cheats on their taxes because it would be immoral to do so.

Taking those fallacious assumptions, it's easy to picture examples that prove how wrong they are:

The boarding school's head teacher, Roger, insists pupils know the dangers of experimenting in sexual activity, so there's no need for separate boys' and girls' dormitories.

Temperance campaigners claimed that alcoholic drink led to poverty and despair. Remove the temptation, and man's natural teetotal state prevails.

Uncle Billy's friend, Digger, believed no-one would ever read anyone else's private diary, so he wrote down where he'd buried "Light-fingered" Lionel.

Cousin Vera, knowing the park closed at dusk, practised her nude yoga on the bowling green. Alas, astronomy evening classes…

Plainly, we can't rely on things not happening because they're not supposed to. Planes would never fall from the sky. Roads would be accident-free. Prisons would be empty, echoing monuments to virtue. But human behaviour is unlikely to follow the strictures of one person's moral code. (See *mind projection fallacy*.)

In business, this leads us to company policy manuals, clunking testaments of wishful thinking and moralistic fallacy. They describe an ideal organisation which is a perfect corporate citizen, paying tax, providing rewarding and fulfilling employment, putting customers first and declaring (fingers crossed): "We're not just saying it, we really mean it!"

If a corporation is challenged to explain why it pays no UK tax and funnels all its profits through low-tax countries like Luxembourg or Ireland, it points to the company policy, exclaiming:

"We're good corporate citizens. We do nothing wrong here. Look, it says so in this policy manual. We wouldn't do any wrong because that would be immoral."

You'll often see the moralistic fallacy elsewhere in organisations. Managers issue trite statements that *"Our customers matter"* to smooth over yet another example of thoughtless indifference to the people who pay them. *"Safety is our number one priority"* as the embers are damped down. *"Your call is important to us"* says the machine endlessly. As if uttering the words makes it so. These are business mantras that have no persuasive quality at all. They are the right thing to say, and no more. As for business slogans and mottoes? See wishful thinking.

Nirvana fallacy – perfect solution syndrome

I don't normally miss the chance to take a cheap dig at grunge music. In this case, the fallacy is that grunge is music. Ho ho.

There's a saying in business that perfect is the enemy of good.[77] It means that trying to reach perfection is costly and time-consuming, meanwhile customers are waving their money at you.

The nirvana fallacy comes in two flavours in which:

There is a perfect answer for a given situation, and

Reasonable proposals are dismissed because they don't measure up to some unrealistic ideal.

In practice, almost any idea, suggestion, proposal, argument can be rejected because it's not a perfect answer. With this fallacy in play, you get a choice between a practical, albeit less-than-perfect option, and a completely unrealistic, unfeasible ideal option, which is in itself a false dichotomy.

You wait to find the ideal candidate for a job instead of picking one of the ten good people in front of you. You yearn for the perfect partner to share your life with, when the person beside you thinks you are theirs. And what could be more ideal than eternal life?

What's the point in trying to cure cancer? We all have to die sooner or later.

---

[77] Actually, the line is Voltaire's: *Le mieux est l'ennemi du bien* – La Bégueule (1772). Best avoid quoting Voltaire in business meetings. Few people will understand and bosses hate anything that makes them look dim.

The implication of this statement is that cancer is necessarily fatal. It isn't, not by a long chalk. And even those who only enjoy a temporary remission often get years of happy life to enjoy. The unrealistic ideal here is eternal life with perfect health.

This statement says: if we can't have an ideal state of affairs, we shouldn't accept a less-than-perfect law.

> Why is 16 the legal age of consent? Kids are going to have sex anyway.

True, where there's a will, there's a way. But the point of the law is to stop young people being exploited, not to abolish hanky-panky behind the bike-sheds. The same – well similar – argument applies to any arbitrary legal limit: drink driving; personal allowances for importing tobacco; minimum age to stand for a legislature, and so on. (See *continuum fallacy*.) Arbitrary thresholds are not ideal for any given instance. They are an attempt at a best fit for all circumstances.

> This new service is okay. You get unlimited access to stream any music or movie you like, but you have to pay for it

Yes, free-of-charge is easily the perfect price. But it's not a business model that allows for the costs of recording and distributing music and films, even if you feel writers and performers don't deserve to earn a living from their work.

Don't bother pointing to other online services and social media that are free. If the product is free, it ain't the product – you are. The site is making money selling your eyeballs to advertisers, and the more details you provide about your life and tastes, the better they can target ads at you, and charge advertisers more for reaching you.

> A land without fear of extremist murders would be a dream come true, wouldn't it? Governments must take every possible step to eradicate the scourge of terrorism.

Reaching that unrealistic, happy state would necessarily involve security measures that place unacceptable restrictions and demands on the overwhelming majority of a population who are not terrorists. Try taking a flight from a big airport these days.

Government measures might also involve removing that other threat to untroubled and uninterrupted government – criticism. In fact, there are already laws against insulting presidents, members of royal families and government officials in such despotic regimes as Austria, Belgium, Denmark, France, Germany, Greece, Italy, Netherlands, Portugal, Romania, Spain and Sweden. Imagine what truly repressive regimes get up to. If the end justifies the means, then the pursuit of ideal security would allow almost anything.

In business, the Nirvana fallacy leads to over-engineered products and gold-plated service. Prices go up, volume sales decline. Competitors race ahead. If your business strategy is to be a luxury brand with hand-made quality, fair enough. Many family businesses are content with the long-term strategy and slow evolution that accompanies such a business model – until the family sells the business.

> Then a new business leader arrives demanding more of those high-value sales because City or Wall Street investors demand bigger returns immediately, and his or her whopping bonus depends on it. Ever-improving financial results are the Nirvana ideal for all investors. Alas, product value and scarcity go hand in hand. When production is pushed up, prices fall, because supply and demand is a law, not a distribution construct. The luxury brand image declines. Grey markets open to shift unsold stock, further slapping the brand reputation. The company claims parallel market stock is fake to bolster its integrity, but manages to cast doubt on all the brand's products. Eventually the local, high-cost operation becomes unprofitable and is shut down. The brand name is bought by a low-cost online retailer who has cheap imitations of formerly luxurious products made in sweatshops in the developing world. And when it's that easy to manufacture '*luxury*' goods, it's also easy to pirate them…

The problem with Nirvana is that everybody wants a piece of it.

Proving too much

With so many fallacies falling short of being persuasive, it's odd that you can go over the top and prove too much. As a fallacy, proving too much comes about when your conclusion infers a larger or wider conclusion that is invalid or absurd. It's a kind of reductio ad absurdum argument. The argument is a fallacy because if the reasoning works, it must also succeed for the absurd conclusion.

> My niece Trixie says modern slavery exists. People are exploited and made to work for no pay. She believes that making people

work for no pay should be a crime.

Certainly, slavery is a crime. But not all unpaid people are enslaved. Family businesses rely on family members to pitch in. Many people give their time to help a charity. Are street collectors and raffle-ticket sellers slaves? What about the many individuals and organisations that work pro-bono[78] for charities and clients of limited means? What about unpaid interns? Trixie undermines her argument about slavery by applying it to every case of no pay. Her case tries too hard, reaching a conclusion that's too broad to be helpful.

> My nephew Cuthbert argued that he was exercising his freedom of expression by playing his music through loudspeakers in the garden at 3 a.m.

Unfortunately his reasoning implies that his freedom of expression includes the right to ride roughshod over the neighbour's right to a good night's sleep, not to mention local by-laws. His rights have no such priority. His argument proves too much.

> Uncle Billy claims he was beaten at school for bad behaviour. To stop corporal punishment at schools, they should close down all the schools.

Only part of the activity of some schools is a bad thing, not their entire existence. Uncle Billy's argument goes to far.

> Cousin Vera argued that motor cars should be banned as they lead to global warming.

Her argument pre-supposes that motor cars are a bad thing in themselves. But they bring incalculable benefits to modern society, which should be set against the pollution. Her argument proves too much.

If I'm labouring the point, it's because this fallacy has a bearing on an important area of reasoning. Arguments about belief and faith often prove too much.

If your local bar-fly challenges you to prove leprechauns don't exist, he's asking you to do something that can't be achieved with complete certainty. (See *argument from ignorance*.) But if you have to

---

[78] Pro bono publico – for the public good. That is, free or unpaid.

admit that Leprechauns might exist (because you can't disprove them), that same logic compels you to admit the possible existence of any and every mythical thing, such as fairies, Yeti, Bigfoot, Father Christmas, the Tooth Fairy, the Easter Bunny, not to mention whole pantheons of deities, past and present. The argument invites you to believe in anything else that can't be, or hasn't been, disproved:

> Cousin Bernard told my nephew Cuthbert he shouldn't be so sceptical about UFOs because no-one can prove UFOs are not visiting Earth. "I can't prove the Loch Ness monster or unicorns are complete fiction either, but I'd be an idiot to believe in them," replied the smarty-pants.

The logic that you should accept fanciful, fictional things because you can't rule them out proves too much. Consequently, using the *"you can't disprove it"* argument is weak.

And sometimes you just have to use a sledgehammer to crack a walnut – it may be messy, but it's fun. The claim that everything happens – earthquakes, tsunamis, disease, famine and so on – as part of some divine plan, proves too much as well:

> Those dead children were all part of the goddess's plan? Really? Okay, right now, She wants you to give me your wallet. Really, She does. How do I know? Because I'm taking it, so it must be part of Her plan for you. Rejoice! Is that all you've got?

As the old adage goes, proving too much proves nothing.

Psychologist's fallacy

The psychologist's fallacy happens when you look at some occurrence or event, and assume your subjective standpoint offers a fair and objective platform to judge matters.

In court, every witness in every case swears an oath that they are telling the truth, and they (usually) completely believe they are. But often other witnesses saw entirely different things happening.

Since its first description[79] the fallacy has broadened from psychoanalysis to encompass other aspects of assumed objectivity. For example, every newspaper column ever scribed is bathed in the author's

---

[79] By William James, an American philosopher and doctor, in the 19th century.

assumption that the opinions they express are fair and sound. More widely, the fallacy crops up whenever you observe someone else's behaviour or capabilities and assume your own personal experience offers an independent yardstick.

> The police report said the fraud victim was naïve, and should have suspected the call supposedly from her bank was bogus.

If you deal with crime every working day, you'd be suspicious of unusual contact supposedly from your bank. Most of the rest of us assume the best in people and take them at face value. That's how confidence tricks work.

Organisations recruit *'people like us'*, individuals who fit the culture, and have a broadly similar outlook beyond the technical skills of the position. Recruiters deny this vehemently – it would suggest they are less than pre-disposed to diversity than their job demands they must be.

In fact, the interview process is riddled with assumptions made by people who use their own experience and capabilities as an objective benchmark for assessing candidates:

> Cousin Bernard applied for a job with a pan-European guttering wholesaler. His credentials impressed the head of IT, but the HR manager preferred a candidate who had written "basic Italian" in her CV. In fact, the interviewers didn't ask Bernard about language skills. They simply assumed he, like them, was monoglot.[80] More's the pity, since Bernard was brought up bilingual by his Italian mother; is fluent in French because of a twenty-year friendship with a pen-pal; and has a fair command of earthy Swedish thanks to Ingrid, the next door neighbour's au pair. Bernard picks up languages like chewing-gum on his shoes. He didn't think to mention spoken languages when he wrote his CV, because in Bernard's mind, languages are for programming.

Every question unasked is answered by an assumption. In a one-hour interview, the scope for unearthing true individuality in candidates is limited. Accordingly, assumptions abound:

> Got a degree? You're smart and can study. Worked for a

---

[80] Understanding one language.

competitor? Same-sector experience. Managed teams? Probably not a psychopath. Member of an Institute? Has professional qualifications. Ad infinitum.

Interview questions confirm the assumptions interviewers have already made from reading your CV or résumé. (See *confirmation bias*.) Gaps get filled subconsciously from the interviewer's own experience and background. It's not necessarily a bad process, and it certainly saves time. But it's colossally more subjective than the interviewers would ever dream of admitting, especially with discrimination laws lurking around.

Many organisations offer rewards to staff to recommend a friend or family member for recruitment. They actually pay money to ensure *'people like us'* join the organisation. While assuming others share our experiences and values is usually a harmless delusion, it can sometimes be a treacherous mistake.

The Cambridge spy ring[81] were upper-crust public-schoolboys who, while at Cambridge University in the 1930s, were recruited to spy for the Soviet Union. They were valuable assets because they were easily accepted by the Establishment as *'sound'* and *'one of us'*, and their background and connections would secure them positions of influence. From sensitive posts in the diplomatic service, MI5 and MI6, they betrayed their country. Without question, those who hired and subsequently managed them, despite many danger signals, assumed the spies shared the recruiters' unalloyed loyalty to the United Kingdom.

On our favourite topics, we assume listeners are on the same page and at least share our interest, if not wild enthusiasm, by not walking away. A friend of mine not always for comedic purposes, would on occasion raise a hand while someone was in mid-flow, and say:

"Let me stop you there. I'm bored already."

Yes, I was often that someone. But if people nod, you plough on, filling in gaps with your own knowledge and background.

---

[81] Kim Philby, Guy Burgess, Donald Maclean, Anthony Blunt, plus (probably) a few others.

In *Being There*[82], the main character, Chance – to use the metaphor of illumination – has the intellect of a birthday candle. At a party, he is seated beside the Soviet Ambassador who begins this exchange:

"Tell me… do you by any chance enjoy Krylov's fables? I ask this because there is something Krylovian about you."

"Do you think so?"

"So you know Krylov!"

The ambassador leans close to Chance, and speaks softly in Russian. Chance, having never heard this language before, raises his eyebrows and laughs with delight.

The ambassador is amazed: "So you know your Krylov in Russian, do you? I must confess I had suspected as much all along."

Chance is a blank page on which the other characters choose to read their own world and experience. The novel *Being There* tracks Chance's rise from obscurity to the highest in the land as a result of the psychologist's fallacy in everyone he meets. (See also *confirmation bias* and *mind projection fallacies*.)

Regression fallacy

One evening, a man and his son stood on the beach throwing pebbles into the sea. As the tide went out, the small boy said, "Look, we're chasing the sea away. It's frightened of us."

Like seasons in a garden, or tides at the shore, a great many things have natural fluctuations and variations, ebbs and flows. Put simply, the regression fallacy credits or blames some false cause, instead of recognising a natural change.

The title comes from the tendency in statistics for variables to regress toward the mean. That is, over time, things return to their average level or state. For instance, in the numerical sport of golf, a

---

[82] *Being There* – 1979. From the novel by Jerzy Kosinski. Screenplay by Jerzy Kosinski and Robert C. Jones.

player's handicap reflects the average number of shots per round over time:

> The week before the golf club's competition, cousin Bernard played a few practice rounds. In all of them, he beat his handicap by several shots. Excited by the possibility of winning his first trophy, Bernard invested in some spiffy, Argyle-patterned socks to play in. Unfortunately, in the competition he only played to his handicap. To Bernard, this illustrated perfectly the importance of sticking with trusted hosiery.

We tend to take action when the variation we are experiencing reaches a peak. Unsurprisingly, a normal regression kicks in at that point, allowing us to credit or blame whatever corrective action we took.

> The osteoarthritis in his knee flared up again, which Uncle Billy treated daily with a few medicinal pints of Guinness. After a few days, the pain subsided. Because the treatment proved so effective, Uncle Billy decided to continue the treatment, as a preventative measure.

Many people say that at some point they've had an ailment so they made an appointment to see their doctor. By the time they're in the surgery, the complaint has disappeared:

> "Typical, just when I get to see a doctor, my body lets me down."

I know one person who insists on an emergency appointment every time she wants to see a doctor, so she can have her symptoms treated 'before they go away'.

The natural self-healing process allows us to credit all manner of whacky cures we've experimented with. Thus, the regression fallacy stimulates the market for all kinds of quack remedies and improbable pick-me-ups, because we're always keen to believe in what we've spent our money on. (See *confirmation bias*, and *post hoc fallacy*.)

Business conditions go through natural cycles of strength and weakness. The standard joke is that whenever the weak cycle comes around, organisations flip their strategy to whatever seemed to work the previous time. And when trading improves naturally in due course, managers can reward themselves handsomely for the effectiveness of their strategic action.

Reification fallacy

Reification means to treat something as if it were real or concrete rather than abstract or an idea, to materialise a concept. The word derives from the Latin *res*, '*a thing*', which gives us words like real, realise and reality. An alternative name for reification is concretism, which sounds like what it means.

Daily discourse is littered with reification in proverbs and clichés, as are books which use metaphors to convey abstract ideas:

> The call of the wild – silence is golden – my heart says yes; my head says no – love laughs at locksmiths – sword of truth – shield of justice...

Poems and lyrics are a rich source:

> Sweet freedom whispered in my ear / You're a butterfly[83]

> Death be not proud, though some have called thee / Mighty and dreadfull[84]

> If you can meet with Triumph and Disaster / And treat those two impostors just the same;[85]

> Some are born great, some achieve greatness, and some have greatness thrust upon them[86]

Smashing stuff. Reification weakens an argument when we rely on it to complete or substantiate an argument. In effect, we infer that concepts or abstract ideas possess qualities from the real world. This delicious bit of creationist sophistry begged for attention:

> "Nature designed beautiful creatures" is an example of the fallacy of reification... God can design creatures because God is a person... Nature is a concept and cannot design anything.

I'm afraid I laughed at the God is a person part. If anything, God is a deity, but I think the writer intended to say God is real or tangible.

---

[83] *Someone Saved My Life Tonight* – Elton John and Bernie Taupin.

[84] *Death Be Not Proud* – John Donne.

[85] *If* – Rudyard Kipling.

[86] *Twelfth Night* – Shakespeare.

Alas, any entity that exists only in faith (and is impossible to see, shake hands, or share a beer with) is by definition abstract, a concept, if not entirely imaginary. So when people speak of a deity as a person (or real or tangible), that's reification.

Moving on, is nature merely a concept? Well, there's a lot of rock-solid nature about and it's very tangible, especially when it tries to kill you. The writer was conflating nature – the real, huge, living, breathing, biochemical factory-complex and geological behemoth wrapped around Planet Earth – and a figurative nature – the phthisic, poetic domain of all non-human stuff. (See *equivocation*.)

Creationists declare that evolution is wrong, that what you see now is what there always was. A common feature is the notion that the universe was instantly brought into existence a few thousand years ago because if you add up all the *'begats'* in the bible, that's roughly when Genesis happened. Every other bit of information that things might be up to fourteen billion years older (such as galaxies, stars, Earth, physics, extinct creatures, and so on) was, some claim, faked by God to test their faith. So, to creationists, every fact we know about the entire universe is wrong because a collection of stories written by a handful of people in the Iron Age didn't spell out an accurate timeframe.

Normally we could simply dismiss creationism as the notion of laughably naïve people. But some creationists want to have what they believe taught in schools alongside maths, physics, chemistry and biology as scientific fact. They seek to elevate their rearrangement of the universe to stand alongside known and settled science as equals. They paint the debate as an equally balanced see-saw of arguments between evolution and creation. (See *false equivalence* and *strawman fallacy*) It isn't.

Evolution – to return to full reification mode – is but a miniscule sip in an overwhelming tsunami of proven, settled science that washes away the sandcastle of creationism. Waste no time on that idiotic cult.

Necessity – fallacy of

The fallacy of necessity is an argument that puts too much emphasis on compulsion in its conclusion. It's a formal fallacy (and links nicely to the next section on deductive reasoning).

Here's an easy one to start with:

> Great Aunt Ruby is a widow
>
> A widow is a woman whose husband has died
>
> Therefore, Great Aunt Ruby's husband had to die. (invalid)

Becoming a widow is an unavoidable consequence of her husband dying, but it wasn't a reason to kill him. Nature takes care of those arrangements, so her husband's demise didn't have to happen, nor did he have to have that smile on his face.

This fallacy arises often when someone gets a bee in their bonnet about a particular conclusion, and tries to justify it by attaching its inevitability to an unavoidable cause and effect. For example:

> Plane crashes happen when planes stop being in the air
>
> Therefore, planes must not take off. (invalid)

Banning take-off would probably improve the casualty figures, but at the expense of journey times. Put technically, the fallacy comes about when we muddle:

> the inevitability of the consequence with
>
> the necessity of the consequent

The inevitability of the consequence is this: if a plane falls from the sky, it must inevitably crash. (Or, you know, experience rapid deceleration when reaching zero separation from terrain.) That's the unavoidable consequence, figuratively and literally.

The consequent is what you do about it. One way to prevent plane crashes would be to forbid aircraft from taking off. But as it's not the only way, it's not inevitable, ineluctable or unavoidable – in short, it's not a necessity. Accordingly, the conclusion is invalid.

Another, real-life example:

> In Australia, a government minister declared that road safety for motorcyclists hadn't improved as much as the statistics for cars. He said: "... we must acknowledge the fact that motorcycles are inherently unsafe, and can never afford the rider the same level of protection as a car. For this reason their use on public roads

must be phased out." (invalid)[87]

Certainly, motorcycles are inherently more dangerous than cars. But a long-term ban is not a necessary consequent. There are other options for reducing accident and fatality statistics, including stronger safety measures and massaging the statistics – one of the main methods authorities use worldwide to demonstrate the effectiveness of their policies. Banning motorbikes is not an inevitable path to aligning road fatality statistics.

Also, since when was it a political or social necessity to align injuries and fatalities of different modes of transport? That would see all road vehicles banished, because air travel is statistically the safest form of transport (see *proving too much*). And if aircraft never left the ground? Chaos for the world, but a super-safe Nirvana for one government minister.

As you've reached the end of this monologue, and stayed the course, you deserve a reward. So I'm going to let you in on a secret. If you plan a career in business, be forewarned that the conclusions of many discussions and meetings in business end with a statement of necessity: Something like:

> Because we're behind sales targets, our profits are inevitably under pressure…
>
> Therefore, we must raise our prices by X per cent
>
> Therefore, we have to cut our human assets by Y[88]
>
> Therefore, it is vital we close our stores in Z locations
>
> Therefore, we have no choice but to squeeze our suppliers, etc.

In the vast majority of cases, these conclusions are bogus. None of the many possible conclusions is in itself inevitable. But the contrived compulsion in the consequent allows the presenter of unwelcome news to wring hands and shrug shoulders, powerless in the face of the overwhelming inevitability of the decision. This fallacy is lubrication for the

---

[87] In 2016, Warren Truss, Australia's Federal Minister for Infrastructure and Regional Development, told parliament that motorcyclists were 20 times more likely to be killed than car users, so motorcycles must be banned.

[88] Please, at least have the candour to say: "We're going to sack some people."

delivery of bad tidings. If it were a fragrance, it would be called *Reluctance.*

Worse, managers can persuade themselves that the decision they've reached really is inevitable. In some cases it may be a lesser of many possible evils; in most, though, it's the most expedient for the individuals in the room.

The main force behind all business decisions is money. The enterprise is not making enough of it, not making it quickly enough, or not making it reliably into the foreseeable future. There will be some marketing guff about competition, the trading environment, technology, trends, customers, and so on. These are weather reports. Any business can react in an infinite number of ways. You're smart – you don't need me to enumerate them. (See *appeal to flattery.*)

Moreover, the muscle behind any decision is usually the individual who personally will make more (or lose less) money by implementing the *necessary* conclusion rather than by choosing another course of action. You will hear someone – usually the CEO or most senior person in the meeting – argue doggedly, almost pessimistically, in favour of a so-called necessary course of action to the exclusion of all other options. Some people may have reservations about it, but the chosen path is sold as necessary and decisive.

Decisive is a word leaders love because that's how they see themselves. *Decisive* trumps other people's reservations – of course they are hesitant, they're not leaders. Decisive action is the option that coincidentally will be the best outcome for the leader's bonus. You won't know the bonus details, but you can guess. The decision is couched in a formula of words like this:

> "I see no other choice…"

> "Better to act decisively…"

> "It is with great reluctance that I conclude…"

> "I don't like this any more than you… "

When you find yourself in that lofty position, the actual thoughts running through your mind as you deliver the bad news will be:

> "We're choosing a course of action that's a) best for the people who own the business and b) best for the people who run the business. If you were more important, you'd be in one of those

two groups."

Mastering the fallacy of necessity is an essential tool for being right. Such occasions are moments of truth for leadership. Can you spot when someone is using it to force through a decision? Are they trying – perhaps a little too hard – to be decisive. Can you reel off several further business options that would satisfactorily deal with the problem, but without the bad consequences of the option that's being promoted?

In many descriptions of the fallacy of necessity, you find this example:

> John is a bachelor. A bachelor is unmarried. Therefore, John cannot get married. (invalid)

As you ponder the flawed reasoning, you know that whatever conditions, labels, or circumstances have brought him to that point, John can do anything he damn well chooses.

And so it is with business. Your call.

14. DEDUCTIVE REASONING AND FORMAL FALLACIES

WHY BOTHER?

First – getting on that management ladder.

In the big, exciting world of management, employers know that candidates with grand academic qualifications and splendid CVs are not guaranteed to have a lick of sense. They need people who can think and reason, so unsurprisingly they sit job candidates down and chuck a lot of tests at them. Some are psychometric – to find out about management and learning styles, for instance – others test reasoning and comprehension.

If you're looking at management or management consulting positions, you can expect tests that are a little more searching than the usual glorified IQ test. They'll ask you about logical reasoning skills. Commonly, reasoning tests ask you to identify valid arguments for syllogisms, or analyse the logic in a passage of prose. Which leads to a few problems:

Sometimes the 'correct' answers are just wrong. The people administering the tests simply read the answers they're given, or let software do the marking.[89] Often, only the author of the original test understands the answers, and authors make mistakes. Hard to believe, but true. As so much material is copied and re-used, the original author may even be dead. (In Aristotle's case, that's a dead cert.)

Tests don't always make it clear whether they're testing abstract reasoning or practical judgement. Often, questions are deliberately surreal to force you to focus on reasoning that goes against the grain of common sense, for example:

> If some humans are horses and all horses are fish, how many fish are humans? None, some or all?

---

[89] I completed reasoning tests at a management consultancy that contained an incorrect answer. "No-one ever gets that one right," the administrator told me. "In all the tests there's at least one question no-one ever gets right."

Somewhere in there is a perfectly logical argument with an utterly mad answer. Other times, tests use nonsense terms to force you to reason, and not get distracted by meaning. So questions can read like this:

If all Bloots are Chots and some Dips are not Chots, which of the following statements is correct?

a) some Chots are not Dips

b) some Bloots are not Dips

c) some Dips are not Bloots

The vocabulary of reasoning uses a few words in a particular sense. *'Some'* means *'one or more'*, not *'several'*. Two statements linked by *or* can both be true. Unless the test sitter is aware of the special meanings, he or she can only search for answers that sound likely, rather than deduce by logic.

All this being the case, it makes sense to try to understand the small number of valid arguments, and to be aware of the main formal fallacies reasoning is prone to. An understanding of how deductive reasoning works is a distinct advantage to the savvy candidate because most job applicants haven't a clue. When it comes to applying for a job, there's no point dragging yourself down the level of your competitors.

Second, management is big on managing but actually decidedly average at reasoning. When you're climbing the ladder of responsibility, among your colleagues you'll find some good thinkers and, without putting it unkindly, some dunces. They may have buckets of experience in operations or sales or finance, but that gives them no exemption from the deficiencies of reasoning we're all susceptible to.

Can I be blunt? Some managers believe their status itself confers special powers of insight and understanding. If that were so, every organisation would be like an academy; mistakes would be unknown; all decisions would be tip-top; every venture would be a triumph; and every day at work would be like frolicking in the sun-dappled uplands of enlightenment. Alas, most managers use their instinct to make decisions and rationalise their choices afterwards. If pressed to explain the reasoning, the main influence appears to be 'looking decisive'.

Being right will make you stand out from the herd. Your ability to see through the fog of bogus reasoning and half-baked thinking will ensure your opinion is sought and valued. Let others accumulate years of experience learning from their mistakes. Your reasoning skills will let you walk into problems and cut through the competing claims of different opinions. And best of all, you're going to be right.

15. DEDUCTIVE ESSENTIALS

The most sure-footed form of reasoning is deductive. It's the gold standard. Think of it as a formal process wearing a dark suit, sober tie and hand-made shoes. Maybe a cape. Deductive reasoning leads to specific conclusions, incontestable, must-be-true answers. For example:

All humans are mortal (true)

Morris dancers are human (true)

Ergo, morris dancers are mortal (valid)

The conclusion is true, even if it resonates a lot less than "all morris dancers must die", which could easily be mistaken for a slogan or a to-do list.

Mathematics is governed by formal logic, as are philosophy, science generally, programming and other topics that demand a lot of brain meat. Deductive reasoning has an ideal expression, our new friend – the categorical syllogism. Categorical refers a statement of fact – it's not conditional or hypothetical. A syllogism is an argument in which you reach a conclusion from the two premises. This is one of the most common forms:

A = B

C = A

Therefore, C = B

That's it. Nothing scary at all. Here's how it works with flesh on the bones:

All noble gases (A) are (=) stable (B)

Helium (C) is (=) a noble gas (A)

Therefore, helium (C) is (=) stable (B)

Another, this time using an equivalent statement:

Angles less than 90 degrees are acute angles

This angle is 45 degrees

Therefore, this is an acute angle

A syllogism contains three propositions – two premises and a conclusion. It usually opens with a general statement or truth called a major premise. That's followed by a specific instance called the minor premise. The final part is the conclusion. Sometimes the major and minor premises get swapped, but I prefer to be consistent and use the major premise first. It also feels more natural.

Premises	Example
A = B (major premise)	All thieves (A) are (=) criminals (B) (general)
C = A (minor premise)	Uncle Billy (C) is (=) a thief (A) (specific)
Therefore, C = B (conclusion)	Therefore, Uncle Billy (C) is (=) a criminal (B)

Components of a categorical proposition

A categorical proposition is just a sentence. If we break down the sentence, we find two essential common components – a subject and a predicate – plus a quantifier. Let's start with quantifiers.

Quantifiers:

Categorical syllogisms use four quantifiers. Each creates a different type of argument. The four quantifiers are:

All

No

Some

Some Are Not.

Other expressions slot into one of these. For instance, 'every' and 'each' belong in All; 'several' or 'various' go in Some. 'Some' just means 'one or more': it's not a specific amount. It's not 'No' and it's not 'All'.

The four quantifiers produce four types of argument called type **A**, type **E**, type **I**, and type **O**.

Quantifier	Type of argument
All … are	type **A**
No … are	type **E**
Some … are	type **I**
Some are not	type **O**

The quantifiers are used like this:

Type **A** – All public houses sell beer

Type **E** – No sharks hang wallpaper

Type **I** – Some flowers give a scent at night-time

Type **O** – Some pop stars cannot sing in tune

It can help you follow the reasoning if you mentally re-state the premises using the verb to be:

Type **A** – All public houses sell beer = **All** public houses **are** places that sell beer

Type **E** – No sharks hang wallpaper = **No** sharks **are** people who hang wallpaper

Type **I** – Some flowers give a scent at night-time = **Some** flowers **are** flowers that give a scent at night-time

Type **O** – Some pop stars cannot sing in tune = **Some** pop stars **are not** people who can sing in tune

The quantifiers determine the type of argument that follows. Later we'll see how those four types combine to form valid or invalid arguments.

Subject and predicate:

At its simplest, each proposition has two terms. Like normal sentences, propositions divide into subject and predicate. The subject is the noun, pronoun or phrase that governs the verb in the premise. The predicate is the rest of the sentence. All three parts of a syllogism have a subject and predicate.

But when referring to the structure of a syllogism, the terms subject and predicate always refer to those parts in the conclusion. Yes, both major and minor premises grammatically have a subject and predicate, but it's the conclusion that we're interested in. Conclusions of each argument type might look like this:

Therefore, **all** cats (Subject) throw up on the rug (Predicate)

Therefore, **no** cats (Subject) clean up after themselves (Predicate)

Therefore, **some** owners (Subject) use cheap cleaning products (Predicate)

Therefore, **some** cheap cleaning products (Subject) **are not** effective (Predicate)

All conclusions have the sentence order: subject then predicate.

Major term, minor term, middle term:

A quick recap. A categorical syllogism contains two premises and a conclusion. It usually opens with a general statement or truth called a major premise. It's followed by a specific instance called the minor premise. The final part is the conclusion.

Again, the major and minor premises are sometimes swapped around. For consistency, it's best always to put the major premise first. We've already seen major and minor premises, but it doesn't hurt to look again:

A = B (major premise)	All fish live in water
C = A (minor premise)	All sharks are fish
Therefore, C = B (conclusion)	Therefore, all sharks live in water

Within the syllogism are three components, each of which appears twice: a **major term**, **minor term** and a **middle term**.

The major term is the part of the major premise that appears as the predicate in the conclusion – the letter B in the diagram:

A = **B** (major term)	All fish live in water
C = A	All sharks are fish
Therefore, C = **B** (major term)	Therefore, all sharks live in water

The minor term is the is the part of the minor premise that appears as the subject in the conclusion – the letter C in the diagram:

A = B	All fish live in water
C (minor term) = A	All sharks are fish
Therefore, **C** (minor term) = B	Therefore, all sharks live in water

The final term appears both in the major and minor premises, but not the conclusion. This is the middle term. The major and minor premises are linked by the middle term. The link gives logical backbone to the syllogism. In this example, fish links living in water and sharks like a stepping stone between them. This middle term enables us to draw a conclusion about sharks and living in water.

A (middle term) = B	All fish live in water
C = **A** (middle term)	All sharks are fish
Therefore, C = B	Therefore, all sharks live in water

These components are important. In order to reach a deductively true or valid conclusion, we have to be rigorous in setting arguments out accurately. Many of the formal errors in deductive reasoning stem from a misarrangement of the terms.

Four figures of syllogisms

So far, to keep things simple and consistent, I've used the structure of a Figure 1 syllogism to demonstrate the logic of arguments. In fact, there are four arrangements. As long as a syllogism features a middle term in both the major and minor terms, the structure of the argument is solid. The middle term can hop around a bit, appearing in the first or second part of the major and minor terms. The middle term can appear in any one of four configurations called *figures*. This means that syllogisms come in four figures. But only the middle term moves around within the different figures. In each figure:

- the conclusion is always the same: that is, subject then predicate.

- the predicate of the conclusion always appears in the major premise.

- the subject of the conclusion always appears in the minor premise.

- the only change is the position of the middle term in both major and minor premises.

- *subject* and *predicate* refer to how the terms appear in the conclusion.

Here are the four figures of categorical syllogisms indicating the different positions the important terms appear in:

Figure 1 syllogism

Major premise =	**Middle** term	then	Predicate
Minor premise =	Subject	then	**Middle** term
Conclusion =	Subject	then	Predicate

Figure 2 syllogism

Major premise =	Predicate	then	**Middle** term
Minor premise =	Subject	then	**Middle** term
Conclusion =	Subject	then	Predicate

Figure 3 syllogism

Major premise =	**Middle** term	then	Predicate
Minor premise =	**Middle** term	then	Subject
Conclusion =	Subject	then	Predicate

Figure 4 syllogism

Major premise =	Predicate	then	**Middle** term
Minor premise =	**Middle** term	then	Subject
Conclusion =	Subject	then	Predicate

The 'shape' of the arguments in each figure changes. You should recognise figure 1 right away, because that's the figure used in all the examples so far. Again, note the positions of the middle terms, shown in bold and underlined.

Figure 1	Figure 2	Figure 3	Figure 4
A = B	A = **B**	**A** = B	A = **B**
C = **A**	C = **B**	**A** = C	**B** = C
Therefore, C = B	Therefore, C = A	Therefore, C = B	Therefore, C = A

Shorthand for syllogisms

Again, a quick recap to ensure the basics are clear. Every proposition in a categorical syllogism contains a quantifier: **All**, **No**, **Some are** and **Some are not**. These determine the type of argument, which are referred to as **A**, **E**, **I** and **O**.

All =	type **A**
No =	type **E**
Some are =	type **I**
Some are not =	type **O**

In order to keep track of the many possible syllogisms, valid and otherwise, a system of shorthand was devised. A complete categorical syllogism can be summed up by the argument type for each of the three propositions, followed by its figure number.

For example, a syllogism using a **Some**, **All** and a **Some** argument and with middle terms configured as **Figure 4** is described as **I A I – 4**:

Some foods (predicate) are oranges (middle)

All oranges (middle) are fruits (subject)

Therefore, some fruits (subject) are foods (predicate)

Remember the odd example earlier? It's a figure 2 syllogism, with Chots being the middle term.

All Bloots are Chots

Some Dips are not Chots:

Therefore some Dips are not Bloots

The correct answer to the question is c). This syllogism can be expressed as **A O O – 2**. The other surreal example was:

Some humans are horses

All horses are fish

Therefore, some fish are humans

The answer to the question is *some*, and it's an **I A I – 4** syllogism. While it's a logical argument, it's still a perfectly mad answer.

By the way, standard mnemonics have been used to remember the configuration of valid syllogisms. The mnemonics are words whose vowels match the argument types – **A, E, I** and **O** – in the correct order. These mnemonics have been used for centuries, but I'm not convinced they help very much. They sound like minor characters in some obscure Grand Guignol play.

For example, the first, **A A A – 1**, is Barbara. Later comes **E I O – 3**, Ferison. And last of all is **I A I – 4**, Dimatis. In all, there are 24 mnemonics. I include them in the list of valid syllogisms only in case you use another book or website discussing this topic, as a way of cross-referencing different sources.

I don't recommend you begin a discussion in your favourite pub or bar:

"Who else thinks the existential fallacy in a Fesapo syllogism is a nit-picky construct and not really a thing?"

Because welcome to Lonely City. Population: You.

16. VALID ARGUMENTS IN CATEGORICAL SYLLOGISMS

Of the 256 possible combinations, only 24 categorical syllogisms can ever produce a valid argument, so it's easier to list all the possible valid ones than wade through all the duff versions.

Even so, nine of these ostensibly valid cases are questionable – they potentially commit an existential fallacy by referring to an empty category. These are conclusions that are logically valid, but unlikely to have many instances in real life, or to offer strange implications. We'll see examples of what that means as we go along, and the section *Formal Fallacies in Syllogisms* covers existential fallacies in some detail.

That leaves just 15 common, unquestionably valid syllogisms. To make things simple, I've listed all 24 syllogisms, from figures 1 to 4, and in the alphabetical order of their argument types, starting with everyone's favourite, the evergreen, basic **A A A – 1**.

Valid figure 1 syllogisms

Major premise =	**Middle** term	then	Predicate
Minor premise =	Subject	then	**Middle** term
Conclusion =	Subject	then	Predicate

1. A A A – 1 – Barbara

All cats are carnivores

All tigers are cats

Therefore, all tigers are carnivores

2. A A I – 1 – Barbari (possible existential fallacy)

All humans are mortal

All women are humans

Therefore, some women are mortal [some are immortal?]

3. A I I – 1 – Darii

All birds have feathers

Some pets are birds

Therefore, some pets have feathers

4. E A E – 1 – Celarent

No aeroplanes are submarines

All Jumbo Jets are aeroplanes

Therefore, no Jumbo Jets are submarines

5. E A O – 1 – Celaront (possible existential fallacy)

No fish are feathered

All salmon are fish

Therefore, some salmon are not feathered [some are?]

6. E I O – 1 – Ferio

No homework is enjoyable

Some school activity is homework

Therefore, some school activity is not enjoyable

Valid figure 2 syllogisms

Major premise =	Predicate	then	**Middle** term
Minor premise =	Subject	then	**Middle** term
Conclusion =	Subject	then	Predicate

7. A E E – 2 – Camestres

All spaceships are vehicles

No mountains are vehicles

Therefore, no mountains are spaceships

8. A E O – 2 – Camestros (possible existential fallacy)

All clowns wear bright clothes

No funeral directors wear bright clothes

Therefore, some funeral directors are not clowns [some are?]

9. A O O – 2 – Baroco

All taxes are state-run rackets

Some payments are not state-run rackets

Therefore, some payments are not taxes

10. E A E – 2 – Cesare

No walls are entrances

All doors are entrances

Therefore, no doors are walls

11. E A O – 2 – Cesaro (possible existential fallacy)

No rabbits are primates

All monkeys are primates

Therefore, some monkeys are not rabbits [some are?]

12. E I O – 2 – Festino

No websites are magazines

Some TV listings are magazines

Therefore, some TV listings are not websites

Valid figure 3 syllogisms

Major premise =	**Middle** term	then	Predicate
Minor premise =	**Middle** term	then	Subject
Conclusion =	Subject	then	Predicate

13. A A I – 3 – Darapti (possible existential fallacy)

All pubs are licensed premises

All pubs are vendors of beer

Therefore, some vendors of beer are licensed premises [no other kind should exist]

14. A I I – 3 – Datisi

All people are imperfect

Some people are saintly

Therefore, some saintly people are imperfect

15. E A O – 3 – Felapton (possible existential fallacy)

No rap music is tuneful

All rap music is bad language

Therefore, some bad language is not tuneful [some is?]

16. E I O – 3 – Ferison

No dogs are dolphins

Some dogs are strong swimmers

Therefore, some strong swimmers are not dolphins

17. I A I – 3 – Disamis

Some vehicles are fast

All vehicles consume fuel

Therefore, some fuel-consuming things are fast

18. O A O – 3 – Bocardo

Some examples are not correct

All examples are illustrations

Therefore, some illustrations are not correct

Valid figure 4 syllogisms

Major premise =	Predicate	then	**Middle** term
Minor premise =	**Middle** term	then	Subject
Conclusion =	Subject	then	Predicate

19. A A I – 4 – Bramantip (possible existential fallacy)

All landmines are lethal

All lethal things are to be avoided

Therefore, some things to be avoided are landmines [some things not to be avoided are landmines?]

20. A E E – 4 – Calenes

All poisons are harmful

No harmful things are healthy

Therefore, no healthy things are poisons

21. A E O – 4 – Calemos (possible existential fallacy)

All roses are plants

No plants are animals

Therefore, some animals are not roses [some are?]

22. E A O – 4 – Fesapo (possible existential fallacy)

No liquids are solids

All solids are things with mass

Therefore, some things with mass are not liquids

23. E I O – 4 – Fresison

No peninsulas are islands

Some islands are countries

Therefore, some countries are not peninsulas

24. I A I – 4 – Dimatis

Some future leaders are students of logic

All students of logic are intelligent people

Therefore, some intelligent people are future leaders

That's it, folks. The sum total of all possible, valid, deductive arguments.

For the record, there's just one argument that's unquestionably valid in all four figures. It's like O-negative blood, the universal donor of the syllogism world. It's **E I O**: **No**, **Some**, **Some are not**.

In addition, there's one argument that's valid in all four figures, but also subject to a possible existential fallacy in all four figures too. It's **E A O**: **No**, **All**, **Some are not**.

17. Valid syllogism 1—page crib sheet

Here's a one-page summary of all valid syllogisms. Technically, having a copy or a photo of this page in a test would be against the spirit of the exercise. But if it's a recruitment test, they started it (see *two wrongs fallacy*).

1. Identify the three-letter summary of the three propositions in your syllogism. For example, **E A O**.

> All = type **A**   Some are = type **I**
>
> No = type **E**   Some are not = type **O**

2. Identify the figure of the syllogism. Find the common term in the major and minor premises. This is the middle term. Find the middle terms, then see which figure you're dealing with:

Figure	1	2	3	4
Major	**Mid** + Pred	Pred + **Mid**	**Mid** + Pred	Pred + **Mid**
Minor	Sub + **Mid**	Sub + **Mid**	**Mid** + Sub	**Mid** + Sub
Conclusion	Sub + Pred	Sub + Pred	Sub + Pred	Sub + Pred

3. Check the arguments under the correct figure. If your syllogism isn't listed here, it's not valid. Asterisks ** signify a possible existential fallacy.

Figure	1	2	3	4
Valid Arguments	A A A	A E E	A A I **	A A I **
	A A I **	A E O **	A I I	A E E
	A I I	A O O	E A O **	A E O **
	E A E	E A E	E I O	E A O **
	E A O **	E A O **	I A I	E I O
	E I O	E I O	O A O	I A I

248

18. FORMAL FALLACIES IN SYLLOGISMS

If there are 256 syllogism combinations and only 24 can be valid, what happened to the rest? The answer is they suffer from one of the formal fallacies that invalidate the argument. We've looked at all the valid versions, so you don't need to know the formal fallacies in order to work out what's not valid. But knowing the rules will help understand how the mechanics of syllogisms work and why so many were casualties.

Formal fallacies don't consider the sense of an argument, only whether its form is valid. When arguments have a mistake in their logical structure they are invalid, even if the premises sometimes appear to be true and the meaning makes sense:

> Some creatures with wings can fly
>
> All ostriches are creatures with wings
>
> Therefore, some ostriches can fly (invalid)

At first glance, the argument looks promising, but the conclusion is false. In fact, we can see it's an **I A I – 1** syllogism. It doesn't appear in our list of valid Figure 1 syllogisms. That means this form of syllogism can never produce a valid conclusion. What about:

> All creatures that fly have wings
>
> No ostriches can fly
>
> Therefore, no ostriches have wings (invalid)

No, still wrong. The reason ostriches can't fly is not because they lack wings. The problem here is an unstated assumption that all creatures with wings must be able to fly, which is a false premise. This time the structure is **A E E – 1**. Again it doesn't show up in the list of valid syllogisms.

In order to understand why reasoning that looks right turns out to be wrong, we'll look at the different types of fallacy. We saw earlier that some valid arguments can have an existential fallacy. This is a quantification fallacy – it revolves around the quantifiers **All, No, Some, Some are not** – while the others are formal syllogistic fallacies.

Existential fallacy

If there weren't a fallacy called "existential" you'd have to make one up. Existential is the word that makes you sound smart, as if you wander around Lidl quoting Sartre and dissing Spinoza.

In the list of valid syllogisms we came across nine that might have problems with an existential fallacy. We saw that it's possible to construct a syllogism that with resounding logic reaches a conclusion that's complete nonsense. It implies a class of things exists, when we know for sure it doesn't (or shouldn't) – an empty class. Here's an example showing why certain syllogisms can be fallacious. It's an **A A I – 1** argument, which we've already seen is susceptible to an existentialist fallacy.

The explanation involves two new terms: universal propositions and particular statements. An example first:

> All geese are mortal [universal proposition]
>
> All ganders are geese [universal proposition]
>
> Therefore, some ganders are mortal [particular statement – are some immortal?]

The existential fallacy applies here because saying some ganders are mortal implies that some of them (one or more) must not be. That can't be right. So how did we get there?

Sweeping **All** or **No** statements – are called universal propositions since they apply to every member of the class of things they refer to. But they offer no assurance that the things they talk about actually exist. Perhaps they do; perhaps they don't. The premise doesn't care. From the point of view of reasoning, therefore, universal statements – affirmative or negative – do not have what is called *existential import*:

> All leprechauns live in Ireland
>
> No unicorns live in Essex
>
> All Martians like mashed potato

See? Universal statements don't imply their subjects exist, even if they do make you sound like you need stronger medication. Even universal statements that appear as conclusions still carry no existential import.

By contrast, **Some** or **Some are not** conclusions are not universal, it's a particular statement. Only some members of the class have the quality referred to. It's as if someone went through every member of the class and checked to see if each had the quality or not. Those found to have the requisite quality would actually have to exist in order to be matched. Particular statements, therefore, do imply that the thing they talk about exists. In other words, particular statements do have existential import. This is how the four different arguments convey existential import.

Type **A** – **All** A are B   universal affirmative = no existential import

Type **E** – **No** A are B   universal negative = no existential import

Type **I** – **Some** A are B   particular affirmative = existential import

Type **O** – **Some** A **are not** B   particular negative = existential import

A syllogism that suffers from an existential fallacy might look like this. It's an **A A I – 1** format, the first valid one that's listed, but susceptible to an existential fallacy:

> All leprechauns live in Ireland [no existential import]
>
> All people called Zebedee are leprechauns [no existential import]
>
> Therefore, some people called Zebedee live in Ireland [yes, a particular statement]

Here we have a conclusion that some people called Zebedee live in Ireland. Such a conclusion is particular, and it implies the existence of Ireland-based Zebedees. However, it also implies that some people called Zebedee do not live in Ireland, which the major premise doesn't allow for.

When it crops up, an existential fallacy occurs because the conclusion contains more information – the existential import, the promise, if you like, that there truly are some examples of the thing promised – than its premises supply. It is therefore invalid.

In a nutshell, universal premises leading to a particular conclusion suffer from the existential fallacy. As universal and particular premises are determined by their quantifier, the existential fallacy is referred to as a quantification fallacy.

As with many things involving profound cogitation, there are differing opinions among experts. Some argue that affirmative statements (types **A** and **I**) do imply existence, while negative ones (types **E** and **O**) do not. You could also argue that any proposition may or may not imply the existence of something, depending on the individual statement and what it's asserting. In this section, however, I've preferred the version that is, I believe, most widely accepted.

> Rule: A syllogism that has two universal premises (types **A** or **E**) cannot have a particular conclusion (types **I** and **O**). If it does it will encounter an existentialist fallacy.

Four terms – fallacy

A categorical syllogism has to contain three unambiguous terms. Remember this figure 1 structure?

> A = B
>
> C = A
>
> Therefore, C = B

If the syllogism does not have exactly three terms, it's invalid. With fewer than three terms, we couldn't follow a path through the arguments and reach any kind of conclusion.

If there are more than three, the reasoning falls on its nose. There's no room for a "D" in a syllogism.

> All cars (A) have wheels (B)
>
> All tyres (C) have valves (D)
>
> Therefore, … (nothing springs to mind)

So, if you try to shoehorn a fourth term into the argument, the syllogism falls on its face. Sometimes you see an argument that seems to have three terms, but it's an illusion.

> Nothing is better than a loving family
>
> Half a loaf is better than nothing
>
> Therefore, half a loaf is better than a loving family   (invalid)

Ho, ho. There are four terms because "nothing is better" and "better than nothing" mean two different things. The fourth term is caused by equivocation – a word or phrase that has two different meanings. The terms here are:

Nothing is better, loving family, half a loaf, better than nothing

Like trimesters at college, three terms is plenty. We need exactly three terms in three propositions for a valid syllogism.

Rule: A syllogism must have exactly three terms. No more. If you break this rule, you run into the fallacy of four terms.

Undistributed middle – fallacy

This sounds like a diet problem: "Why do I look as if I have everybody else's middle?" It's a formal fallacy that's quite straight-forward once you get behind the jargon.

Remember the basic structure of a syllogism. Both premises contribute one term each to the conclusion, which I have underlined to save wear and tear on your eyeballs in this **A A A – 1** syllogism:

All thieves (middle term) are criminals (major term)

All embezzlers (minor term) are thieves (middle term)

Therefore, all embezzlers (minor term) are criminals (major term)]

The middle term *thieves* links the two premises and provides the logical rigour to the argument. It's the stepping stone between *criminals* and *embezzlers* that allows us to infer something from one about the other. To link the premises firmly, the middle term must be distributed in at least one of the premises.

At this point, let's take a short break to become familiar with distribution in deductive reasoning. It's relevant not just to the middle term, but to the next two sections on illicit majors and minors.

'Distributed' has a particular meaning in reasoning

Distributed means the premises must account for all members of the class of things described by the term. If the syllogism doesn't offer information about the whole class of the middle term, it can't make a robust connection between the major and minor premises. It's like this:

All golfers use golf clubs

Imagine that to make this categorical statement (knowing it to be true), you would have to check the golf bag of every player on the first tee of every course in the world. You'd find at least one suitable smacking-shaped thing on the end of a stick, so the premise would be true. Thus, when you say all golfers do this, you have accounted for every member of the class of golfers. You're in a position to make a categorical statement about golfers' tools which must be true. When a premise says something about all members of a class of things, it is said to be distributed. Here, *golfers* is distributed.

Each type of argument – **All**, **No**, **Some**, **Some are not** – offers a different situation, but the question remains the same:

Have you accounted for them all?

To make a valid argument, the middle term must be distributed in either the major or minor premise. The middle term lies in both premises, and both premises have two parts – a subject and predicate. That means the middle term can be the subject or predicate in any one of the four types of argument. To see if the middle term is distributed, we need to check each argument type, looking at both the subject and predicate of those premises. First, type **A** arguments:

For example: All golfers use golf clubs

To play the game, every golfer needs at least one club, therefore every member of the class of golfers is accounted for.

So the subject *all golfers* **is distributed**.

What about the predicate, the golf clubs? It's fair to assume some are possessed by non-players, shops, museums, gangsters, fairway-side rough, canals and storage lockers as well as golfers. Only some of the world's supply of golf clubs are possessed by golfers. Some is a clue. We have only accounted for the clubs in the possession of actual golfers. The premise doesn't account for all members of the class.

So the predicate *golf clubs* is **not distributed**.

We continue the process with the next type **E**:

For example: No swimmer wears a suit of armour

To be sure our statement is categorically true, we'd have to check every swimmer for a metal exterior. Every member of the class of swimmers would have to be accounted for, as was the case with *all golfers*.

Therefore, the subject *no swimmer* **is distributed**.

For the premise to be true, we must sure all suits of armour were empty of swimmers. We could logically say "all suits of armour are not worn by swimmers". That means all members of the class of suits of armour are accounted for.

Therefore, the predicate *suit of armour* **is distributed**.

The third type of argument is type **I**:

For example: Some chief executives are hideously overpaid

For a **Some** statement to be true, we just have to find one example of overpay and one case of fair pay (to make sure we're not talking about **All** or **No** chief executives). As soon as we have one of each, we can stop looking. Not all chief executives are accounted for – the clue was in the word *some*.

Therefore, the subject *some chief executives* **is not distributed**.

The class of hideously overpaid is not fully accounted for either. We stopped checking overpaid people's job title when we found one non-chief executive, which fulfilled the criterion for *some*. There are other professions and individuals who fall under that description. Only some overpaid people are chief executives.

So, the predicate *hideously overpaid* **is not distributed**.

The final type is type **O**:

For example: Some birthday presents are not Ferraris

Again, the word *some* tells us that not all members of the class of birthday presents are included in the premise. You could imagine checking all the birthday gifts, sifting through the ties and socks until we found at least one Ferrari in a bow (to make sure the situation isn't **All** or **No**).

So, the subject *some birthday presents* **is not distributed**.

Are Ferraris accounted for? Yes, because within the premise all Ferraris are both some birthday presents and not some birthday presents. All members of the class Ferraris are accounted for.

Therefore, the predicate *Ferraris* **is distributed**.

Here's a summary showing whether the subject or predicate of each type of argument is distributed:

Type Argument	Example	Distributed?
Type **A**: All ... are	All golfers use golf clubs	Subject **is** distributed. Predicate **is not** distributed
Type **E**: No ... are	No swimmer wears a suit of armour	Subject **is** distributed Predicate **is** distributed
Type **I**: Some ... are	Some chief executives are hideously overpaid	Subject **is not** distributed Predicate **is not** distributed
Type **O**: Some ... are not	Some birthday presents are not Ferraris	Subject **is not** distributed Predicate **is** distributed

That's it. All you need to know about distribution. It's only a little bit fiddly, but has a huge bearing on making syllogisms valid or not. Where were we?

Undistributed middle – part 2

Okay, back to where we were before our excursion, looking at our earlier example:

All thieves (middle term) are criminals (major term)

All embezzlers (minor term) are thieves (middle term)

Therefore, all embezzlers (minor term) are criminals (major term)

In this **A A A – 1** syllogism, the middle term *thieves* is distributed in the major premise. This means that the syllogism is valid. Fireworks! Streamers!

If we look at an example in which the middle term is not distributed, it suffers from the fallacy of the undistributed middle. This is in the form **A A A – 2** and it's not on the list of valid syllogisms.

All gorillas love sleeping

All students love sleeping

Therefore, all students are gorillas (invalid)

The middle term is *love sleeping*. It's in the **All A are B** type, but as the predicate in both premises, and as the subject in neither. Accordingly, the middle term is not distributed. Put another way, the middle term doesn't link gorillas and students, except for a shared love of sleeping. We can't infer any information from one about the other. The syllogism is therefore invalid, and the conclusion is a non sequitur, despite a certain resonance.

Rule: The middle term must be distributed in the premises at least once. If not, you have the fallacy of the undistributed middle.

Illicit major – fallacy

The fallacy of the illicit major sounds like a yarn by Conan-Doyle. In fact, it's a similar problem to the undistributed middle. It's a formal fallacy that renders an argument invalid.

The fault arises because the major term is not distributed in the major premise. (Now aren't you glad you know all about distribution?) Remember: the major term is the part of the major premise that appears as the predicate in the conclusion:

All interns are unpaid labour

No HR directors are interns

Therefore, no HR directors are unpaid labour (invalid)

Ain't that the truth. It sounds valid enough, because the conclusion makes sense – you never see HR directors trying to get copier toner off business attire[90] and fretting about how to pay for their commute into work.

The major term *unpaid labour* is not distributed in the major premise (**All A are B**). The class of unpaid labour extends beyond interns, so it's not fully accounted for. This example, therefore, suffers from the fallacy of an illicit major. It follows the form **A E E – 1**, which is not one of the valid syllogisms. In other words, no syllogism in this form can be valid.

---

[90] Cold water, not hot.

Rule: The major term must be distributed in the major premise. If it isn't, and is distributed in the conclusion instead, it's an illicit major.

Illicit minor – fallacy

This sounds like a cheeky kid with fake ID trying to get served in a bar. It is, of course, the winsome sibling to the illicit major fallacy. It occurs when the minor term is not distributed in the minor premise.

All trees have leaves

All trees have roots

Therefore, all roots have leaves (invalid)

The minor term *have roots* is not distributed in the minor premise. It leads to a conclusion that makes no sense. It follows the form **A A A – 3**, which is not one of the valid syllogisms.

Rule: The minor term must be distributed in the minor premise. If it isn't and is distributed in the conclusion instead, it's an illicit minor.

Exclusive premises – fallacy

This logical fallacy sounds like a well-appointed pub. If only. Just as we can tie ourselves in knots when we make statements with multiple negatives, so do syllogisms. If we pack negative statements into both major and minor premises, the resulting mess is invalid. This is the fallacy of exclusive premises.

Here's the problem: in reasoning, propositions that are negative exclude one another. So if an argument has two negative premises, it means the middle term (which is supposed to link the two premises, allowing us to draw an inference about one term from the other) is locked out from both the major and minor premise. There's no connection between the two. As a result, it's not possible to reach a logical conclusion.

No cats are dogs

Some dogs are not poodles

Therefore, some poodles are not cats (invalid)

The middle term *dogs* appears correctly in both premises, and it's distributed in the major premise (in the **No A are B** form). It should link them, but the two negative statements exclude each other. The conclusion, such as it is, is not informative about poodles or cats in any sensible way, because *no poodles are cats*. The example follows the form **E O O – 4**. Again, it's not one of the valid syllogisms.

Rule: A syllogism cannot have two negative premises (types **E** or **O**). If it does, it is invalid because of the fallacy of exclusive premises.

Affirmative conclusion from one negative premise

If you look through the list of valid syllogisms, whenever one of the premises is negative – that is, type **E** or **O**, the conclusion is also negative – **E** or **O** – always. An affirmative conclusion – **A** or **I** – following a single negative premise doesn't work. For instance:

> No trucks are ships
>
> Some ships are submarines
>
> Therefore, some submarines are trucks (invalid)

Clearly, something's gone awry here. The format of the argument is **E I I – 4**, which is not a valid syllogism. In fact, no valid syllogism has a negative premise and an affirmative conclusion.

Rule: If a syllogism has one negative premise (type **E** or **O**), the conclusion must be negative. If a conclusion is negative, the syllogism must contain a negative premise.

Negative conclusion from two affirmative premises

This fallacy doesn't need much explanation in the light of the previous section; the title says it all. A valid syllogism cannot produce a negative conclusion if both premises are positive. For example:

> All whales are aquatic creatures
>
> All whales are mammals
>
> Therefore, no mammals are aquatic creatures (invalid)

The conclusion is self-evidently wrong – plenty of mammals are aquatic, including whales. The format of this syllogism, **A A E – 3** is not one of the listed valid arguments. In fact, no valid argument has a negative conclusion (type **E** or **O**) when both premises are affirmative, either **A** or **I**.

Rule: If both premises are affirmative, the conclusion must also be affirmative.

A last look around before we go

Having examined the rules for syllogisms and seen why so many are invalid, let's go back to the beginning. We looked at two examples of invalid reasoning. Simple question – what's wrong with them? Which fallacy is in play?

All creatures that fly have wings

No ostriches can fly

Therefore, no ostriches have wings (invalid)

Some creatures with wings can fly

All ostriches are creatures with wings

Therefore, some ostriches can fly (invalid)

And here we leave syllogisms using quantifiers. Next is the family of deductive reasoning that uses propositions to reach a conclusion: **if... then** statements.

19. HYPOTHETICAL SYLLOGISMS

In this section, we don't need to concern ourselves with quantifiers like **all, no** and **some**. Feel free to loosen your tie or kick off your shoes. The next family of deductive reasoning uses more natural language and arguments are much less grindingly precise. They are hypothetical syllogisms.

Many propositions are compound statements. Inside they contain logical operators that link the different parts. These are words like: **and, or, not, if, only if.**

We're going to concentrate on conditional statements:

If something, then something else.

These are the arguments you will come across most often. In everyday speech, the word *then* is omitted, but the reasoning remains. Here's a hypothetical syllogism:

If I fall off my roof, (then) I will injure myself

If I injure myself, (then) I can't go hiking

Therefore, if I fall off my roof, (then) I can't go hiking (valid)

A hypothetical syllogism is a valid inference. It's sometimes called a *chain argument* because of the way the premises string together.

(As an aside, the ability to think ahead and foresee consequences is a desirable trait in business managers. Some organisations actively test interviewees for their ability to think downstream. They're really testing the candidates' aptitude to make valid inferences.)

For a compound proposition to be true, the components must satisfy the logical connectives. Hypothetical fallacies happen when you infer something that the logical connectors can't guarantee to be correct.

In the format: **If X, then Y**, the **X** phrase is called an *antecedent* because it's the bit that comes first. The **Y** part is a *consequent* because if the antecedent is true, the consequent is the thing that happens. In the example above, we're assuming that the two premises are true.

What we need is a statement which tells us that one of **X** or **Y** is true or not. If it agrees something is true, it **affirms**. If not true, it

denies. Depending on the answer, what can we then infer about **X** from **Y** being true or false, and what can we infer about **Y** if **X** is true or false?

Put together, they form a family of arguments which you will hear every single day of your life, as we juggle to figure out what the consequences of our choices will entail. Often the conclusions will be untrue.

It's important to pay close attention to the premises used in hypothetical arguments. On occasion, people use what sounds like deductive reasoning to add the semblance of rigour to what is really an opinion or assertion, rather than a true statement.

Affirming the consequent

Have you ever driven into a petrol or gas station and wondered which type of fuel you need?

> If I put diesel into my petrol car, then the engine will be damaged [consequent]
>
> The engine of my car is damaged [affirming]
>
> Therefore, I have put diesel in the tank (invalid)

The argument is invalid because putting the wrong fuel in is not the only thing that can damage the engine. The form is:

> If X, then Y
>
> Y is true
>
> Therefore, X is true (invalid)

This is the general form of an affirming the consequent argument. We can only reach a true conclusion if the antecedent is the only condition for the consequent we affirm. So both premises can be true, but the conclusion false, which means the argument must be invalid in all circumstances.

> If a creature is human, then it has two legs
>
> My budgie has two legs
>
> Therefore, my budgie is human (invalid)

Affirming the consequent can be a fertile source of poor excuses. Take illness. The internet lets us diagnose any symptoms we imagine we have, and many people customise their reasoning to reach the conclusion they want.

> If I have flu, then I have a headache

> I do have a headache

> Therefore, I have flu (invalid)

Flu isn't the only sufficient cause of headache – late-night partying might be another. You can picture someone starting with the conclusion they want a day off, and working back to find an excuse.

Note that if the antecedent condition were in the form **if and only if**, then the conclusion would be valid. If having flu were the only condition to cause a headache, then affirming the headache would be proof of flu. But the *only if* condition is a stringent measure.

> If and only if I score 21 with my first two cards do I get a blackjack.

An affirming the consequent argument only provides one logical certainty – a contrapositive. If the consequent is untrue, then the antecedent is also untrue. For example:

> If I have arthritis, then I have a sore joint

> My joint is sore

> Therefore, I have arthritis (invalid)

My painful joint offers no certainty that I have arthritis. My injury could have been caused by a pole-dancing accident. But if I don't have a sore joint, I can conclude that I don't have arthritis. The contrapositive of affirming the consequent is denying the consequent.

This form of argument is a frequent visitor to conversations in which the speaker wants to force a conclusion with the semblance of logic. It's used as a means of sleight of hand, either deliberately, or when someone's just talking bollocks.

Denying the consequent

Denying the consequent is an important argument. Labouring under the formal title *modus tollens*, this is a sort of anti-matter equivalent to affirming the consequent. Denying the consequent arguments are valid. Let's compare the two arguments:

Affirming the consequent:	Denying the consequent:
If X, then Y	If X, then Y
Y is true	Y is not true
Therefore, X is true (invalid)	Therefore, X is not true (valid)

Unlike affirming the consequent, denying the consequent allows you to make a valid inference about the antecedent. If the first two statements are true, the conclusion cannot be false. For instance:

> If it's Thursday today, then it's bin day [consequent]
>
> It's not bin day [denying]
>
> Therefore, it's not Thursday today (valid)

Here, the absence of bin-related activity allows you to infer that it's not that particular day of the week. Another example of denying the consequent providing a valid inference:

> If I hold a UK driving licence, then I must be 17 years or older
>
> I am not 17 years or older
>
> Therefore, I do not hold a UK driving licence (valid)

Based on the structure of the argument, you can seemingly nix any consequent, and thereby invalidate the antecedent. It's a handy format to keep in mind if you have a point to prove.

"If that's justice, then I'm a banana," was the reaction of Ian Hislop, editor of Private Eye magazine, after losing a libel action. The editor is self-evidently not a yellow fruit,[91] and thus invited the world's press to conclude that the verdict was unjust.

Denying the consequent is an important form of reasoning:

> If Uncle Billy is the thief, then the fingerprints on the Fabergé egg are his
>
> The fingerprints are not his
>
> Therefore Uncle Billy is not the thief (valid)

---

[91] Technically, a banana is a herb. Strange, but true.

It's the argument that excludes possibilities, exonerates, and rebuts wild theories:

> If the politician is the child's father, then a DNA test proves it
>
> The DNA test does not prove it
>
> Therefore, the politician is not the child's father (valid)

Denying the consequent is a valid argument provided the premises are sound. Sometimes people use sleight of hand to slide a bare assertion or a false promise into the mix. While the reasoning may be valid, the argument is unsound if the premise is doubtful. How about this conversation?

> "If you have nothing to hide, then you have nothing to be afraid of"
>
> "But I am afraid"
>
> "Therefore, you must have something to hide" (unsound)

Presumably followed by "Gotcha!". Beware of claims presented as truths: they can make for a convincing deceit.

> If my niece Trixie studies hard, then she can pass her exams
>
> Trixie does not pass her exams
>
> Therefore, Trixie did not study hard (unsound)

In fact, there are many reasons why examinees are unsuccessful in their endeavours. Lack of preparation is one of them, but not the only one. And thorough revision isn't guaranteed to lead to success, either. Be alert to glib assertions disguised as an *if... then* premise.

Denying the antecedent

By now you'll have twigged that the names of formal fallacies were not created on the whimsical easel of popular appeal. They come from the dry pens of precise and pedantic people. This cheerful title means no more than saying the hypothetical thing you just mentioned didn't happen or isn't true. It's a formal fallacy, and arguments in this form are invalid.

The form is this:

> If X, then Y

X is not true

Therefore, Y is not true (invalid)

Again, the antecedent is the **if** part of the opening condition. The denying part is the second statement telling us the antecedent isn't true:

If Towser is a St Bernard [antecedent], then he is a dog

Towser is not a St Bernard [denying]

Therefore, Towser is not a dog (invalid)

It's a conclusion that might come as a surprise to Mrs Towser, who is expecting his puppies and a bit of help around the kennel. Towser can be any one (or combination) of hundreds of breeds of hound besides a St Bernard. Here's another, oft-quoted example [92]:

If it is raining, then the grass is wet

It is not raining

Therefore, the grass is not wet (invalid)

This argument overlooks the moisturising power of a sprinkler system. Or dew fall. Or, you know, Towser's continuing incontinence.

At first sight, these kinds of argument can appear valid, especially with abstract ideas. But even where the premises ring true, the conclusion may not necessarily be true as well, which makes it an invalid form of argument.

Affirming the antecedent

The final part of our conditional family deals with affirming the antecedent. It suffers from the Latin moniker *modus ponens,* and it's an extremely common argument that stretches back into philosophical antiquity.

When the second premise affirms that the antecedent is true, the argument concludes that the consequent must be true. Which is what we began with in the first place – a kind of self-fulfilling prophecy. Unlike the previous form, denying the antecedent, this reasoning produces a valid argument.

---

[92] I don't know who first came up with this example. So, props to whomever.

Denying the antecedent	Affirming the antecedent
If X, then Y	If X, then Y
X is not true	X is true
Therefore, Y is not true (invalid)	Therefore, Y is true (valid)

For example:

If today is Monday [antecedent], I must go to work

Today is Monday [affirming]

Therefore, I must go to work (valid)

If the opening premises are true, that is, I have a regular job and today is a normal work day, then the conclusion has to be valid. That being the case, we can say the argument is a valid in form. But the validity of the argument doesn't mean the premises are true. If the premises are unsound, it nullifies any attempt at reasoning:

If it is my wife's birthday, then aliens from Planet Zob must land

It is my wife's birthday

Therefore, aliens…etc. (unsound)

The argument makes no comment on the quality, fairness or morality of the statements, only the reasoning used about them. If you want to give a logical veneer to any personal decision, this is the argument to go for. There's more than a whiff of a *false dichotomy* about many uses of this argument.

If my son's trainers are smelly, then they need to be left outdoors

My son's trainers are smelly

Therefore, they need to be left outdoors (valid)

Affirming the antecedent is a type of argument we encounter day to day – in the disguise of natural language:

If you want fairness for all and prosperity for your family, [then] you should vote for me

After all, isn't that what we all want? [affirming]

[Therefore] You should vote for me!

Okay, it's scarcely Churchillian, but you get the point. Affirming the antecedent allows you to present a seemingly logical conclusion to pretty much any statement. So, thinking of statements that lack a certain objective quality: hello, advertising! Promotional statements are often based on shaky claims at best. The opening premise is often an assertion by the advertiser. Affirming the antecedent arguments (sort of) prove every claim. For instance:

> If I wear New Wolf-Sweat Fragrance for Men, then I am attractive to women
>
> I am wearing New Wolf-Sweat Fragrance for Men
>
> Therefore, I am attractive to women (See *wishful thinking*.)

The argument is risible, but that's the mesmerical world of advertising for you. The other big use of this form of reasoning is to underpin the *fallacy of necessity*, the favourite tool of would-be decisive management. The fallacy of necessity is a formal error in which the inevitability of an outcome of events is applied to the action taken as a result.

> If we need to cut costs, then we must reduce our headcount
>
> We need to cut costs
>
> Therefore, we must sack some employees (unsound)

An affirming the antecedent form of argument seemingly confirms with unerring logic the action you wanted to take in the first place. It applies a varnish of rigour to a business choice. But it's a smokescreen. The opening premise may not be a true statement: the consequent is not the sole or necessary outcome to the antecedent, just the preferred course of action. Be warned.

Also relevant in this section are two further fallacies, *false dichotomy* and the *argument from fallacy*. These have been discussed as informal fallacies, although both are hypothetical fallacies.

20. DISJUNCTIVE SYLLOGISMS

Finally, a proposition that isn't like the others. It doesn't start with a condition, but with what looks like a choice. A disjunctive syllogism is a valid rule of inference.

This argument gives you two apparent options (called disjuncts) linked by an or statement. We learn that one of options is true (or false). We infer the remaining option is false (or true). For instance:

> Either the teacher will mark homework or the teacher will open a bottle of wine [two disjuncts]
>
> The teacher will open a bottle of wine [affirming]
>
> Therefore, the teacher will not mark homework (valid)

The conclusion is valid. The opening statement offers us two disjuncts. The second premise affirms one of them is true. We therefore conclude that the remaining disjunct is not true. This argument is affirming a disjunct. Alternatively, the second premise can deny one of the disjuncts – denying a disjunct – and we conclude the remaining disjunct must be true.

So far, so good. Now the big 'however'. Up to now, we've been presuming that the disjuncts are exclusive. An exclusive-or means **either / or**. Only one statement is true, but not both:

> The plant on my terrace is a clematis or it is a rose
>
> The plant is not a rose   [denying]
>
> Therefore, the plant is a clematis   (valid)

Here, only one disjunct can be true. The plant can't be both a clematis and a rose. If the statement is true – the plant is not a rose – then it must be a clematis. This is an example of exclusive-or, one which we can spot by the situation described. In natural language, or is most often an exclusive situation:

> Let's go and see the new film on Friday or Saturday.
>
> This afternoon I plan to go shopping or dig the garden.
>
> The teacher decided to open a bottle of wine. Red or white, she mused.

Exclusive-or arguments look like this:

X is true [exclusive-] or Y is true	X is true [exclusive-] or Y is true
Y is true [affirming]	Y is false [denying]
Therefore, X is false (valid)	Therefore, X is true (valid)

However, in technical contexts, the exclusive version is sometimes expressed as EOR or XOR to signify an operation that returns the value *true* when either of the disjuncts is true and the other is false, but not when both are not-true and both are not-false.

While in everyday English, *or* usually means exclusive-or, in formal reasoning (say, mathematics, logic, programming, etc.) *or*, the logical conjunction, is inclusive.[93] Inclusive–or means **and / or**. This means that either or both statements can be true:

My neighbour's noisy dog is aggressive or it is badly trained

The dog is badly trained

Therefore, the dog is not an aggressive animal (invalid)

Obviously, my neighbour's noisy pet can be both aggressive and badly trained. In inclusive logical expressions, both disjuncts can be true or just one of them. This means that affirming an inclusive disjunct can lead to an invalid inference that the other disjunct must be false. Conversely, when an argument denies a disjunct, it is a valid inference that the other is true, and this is the case with both exclusive-or and inclusive-or constructions.

X is true [inclusive-] or Y is true	X is true [inclusive-] or Y is true
Y is true [affirming]	Y is false [denying]
Therefore X is false (invalid)	Therefore, X is true (valid)

To conclude: be sure whether the statement you're interpreting is supposed to be informal language or a more formal deduction. Generally, though, if the statement you're questioning is intended to be exclusive, the presence of either / or is a good start. The context should confirm your interpretation:

---

[93] For more examples of *or* as an inclusive term in informal reasoning, see *kettle logic*.

This drink is either beer or wine.

Unless you're quaffing the worst cocktail in the world, that statement is pretty unambiguous. If you intend to convey an inclusive meaning, it might be appropriate (even if inelegant) to make that clear using and / or:

Let's go to the cinema on Friday and / or go for a meal on Saturday.

A word of warning: if you're presented with a hard-and-fast choice between X or Y, be wary of being offered a false dichotomy. (See also *argument from fallacy*)

More logical connectives

For completeness, it's worth making sure we cover the other common logical connectives. If you're a mathematician, or a programmer, you'll know these by heart. But for the rest of us, a reminder won't go amiss. The topic of logical operations is a huge and steep one. It demands a clear mind and a decent run-up to clear the summit. So this list is just a hint of the main meanings you might have to clamber over most often.

A new word: *operands*. Operands are the statements controlled by the connective words. The disjuncts mentioned earlier in this section are operands. In reasoning we try to find a valid argument, while logic identifies statements that are true or false. The way connectives work, however, is much the same:

- And – a conjunction – valid / true if both (or all) operands are true:

    To be an effective cruise liner, a ship must have accommodation for passengers and be able to float.

- Or (inclusive) – true if one or both operands is true:

    For my birthday, I'd be happy to get a book or a DVD.

- Neither... nor – the negation of logical or. When neither operand is true (both are false):

    Because Uncle Billy was in prison at the time, police can neither arrest him nor charge him with robbing the stately home.

- Either... or (exclusive) – true only when operands differ; one is true, one is false:

The two dogs were alone in the house while we were out. Either Towser left us a present on the rug or Mrs Towser did. The goldfish is in the clear.

- If... then – the consequent is true if the antecedent is true:

    If my car passes its annual inspection then I can drive it legally.

- Only if – introducing a material condition that means for the antecedent to be true, the consequent must also be true:

    The astronaut knew she would survive only if her oxygen supply lasted until help arrived.

- If and only if – either both operands are true, or both are false:

    If and only if this is the right key, then we can unlock the door.

- Not both / not and – at least one operand is false:

    Perhaps my lying nephew, Cuthbert, really does have a pet called Joey, but it can not be both a budgie and a kangaroo.

And this, dear reader, finishes the section on disjunctive syllogisms and logical connectives. And it marks the end of our stroll through deductive reasoning.

21. WHATEVER PUFFS UP YOUR LILO

So far, we've looked at categorical syllogisms, together with their hypothetical and disjunctive cousins. These are the main forms of deductive reasoning. There is more to learn about it, if that's your bent. But for the purposes of a good education, you're done. In fact, you now know more than most teachers and academics.

If you're going into business with aspirations of management, you have my permission to feel a little self-satisfied. Apart from a small number of specialists who understand programming logic, or have a background in mathematics or philosophy, you're now the company's go-to person for deductive reasoning. How you choose to advertise the fact is up to you.

But you'll need to be on your toes. Often you'll encounter these formal arguments dressed up in natural language. Management likes to portray itself as decisive and is prone to making categorical statements that demonstrate incisive thinking. As a result you'll hear many affirm or deny antecedent and consequent arguments left, right and centre. Check the truth of *if* and *then* statements, because more often than not one or both will be wrong. Often they will reflect what an individual believes is the case, or wants it to be (see *wishful thinking*). You should also re-read the fallacy of necessity section in this regard. Remember: being decisive is not the same as being right.

That's it. You're done. Relax. Light some scented candles and slip into a warm, soothing bath, or crack open a beer and slam some death metal vinyl on the turntable – whatever puffs up your lilo.

Wear your learning lightly

Congratulations on making it this far. You're now in the one per cent of people[94] who understand deductive and inductive reasoning.

---

[94] That 1 per cent figure is a bare assertion. I have no idea what the true number should be, but it's not a big one. Picture yourself at a sports stadium with 50,000 people. Over the PA, they say there's an emergency, and is there anyone conversant with deductive and inductive reasoning. Will more than 500 people rush to the fore? No, I don't think so either.

You've read explanations and followed examples of over a hundred of the commonest fallacies used in everyday thinking.

At the beginning I said:

> This book is about trying to make sense of the world, and putting a bit more sense back into it.

I hope by now you're in a position to see the world a bit more clearly. If so, you'll know other people see a different world to you. And by now you'll know that most of the time they're wrong. You're seeing poor arguments and reasoning all around you. Well, you were warned.

Now that you know the basics of reasoning, you've passed your driving test, so to speak. You can go out on your own, deal with the changing traffic conditions, the different roads, the wild variety of drivers around you. You only truly learn to drive after you've passed your test. So it is with reasoning.

Make a note of fallacies you come across, even if you can't pin the exact one down immediately. Over time you'll become adept at spotting invalid, weak and unpersuasive arguments, and you'll become more sure of your footing in dealing with them.

Bear in mind that you now have an advantage over other people. Be gracious. Explain and elucidate, where you can. Wear your learning lightly.

From now on, you can expect to be right a lot of the time. Enjoy it.

Appendix 1 — A word on taxonomy

The classification of informal fallacies by academics is excellent for analysing the philosophical texture of the situation: relevance, induction, genetic, questionable cause, and so on. While intellectually rigorous, it's not completely helpful to the people I have in mind. So I've taken a more casual approach.

It's not easy to squeeze all those random and spontaneous arguments and misguided conclusions into any pigeonhole. But I hope the 'family' groupings I've used will help others to see fallacies in meaningful contexts. They have no authority other than they make sense to me.

The family groups I've chosen are:

- The commonest – the fallacies you hear every day. (Some important ones like generalisation and personal attacks have families in their own right)

- Generalisation – the things everybody does, all the time

- Appeals – emotional reasons to ignore what your head tells you

- Personal attacks – ad hominem statements attacking the speaker not the argument

- Not the whole truth – cherry picking and selective evidence

- Time bombs – cause, effect and correlation; old and new; the lens of time

- Denial – refusing to see the obvious or the logical

- Twisted words – deliberate sleight of hand

- Number problems – statistical errors

- Sat-nav reasoning – when we think we're doing a good job at thinking things through, but end up in a mess

- Muddle – when we just don't think about it, and try to muddle through on instinct

You will probably find that some fallacies could easily reside in two or more families. I've plumped for what seemed to me like a fair call. Your mileage may vary.

INDEX